T0339968

Beyond the
Consumption Bubble

Routledge Interpretive Marketing Research

EDITED BY STEPHEN BROWN, *Northern Ireland*

Recent years have witnessed an 'interpretive turn' in marketing and consumer research. Methodologies from the humanities are taking their place alongside those drawn from the traditional social sciences.

Qualitative and literary modes of marketing discourse are growing in popularity. Art and aesthetics are increasingly firing the marketing imagination.

This series brings together the most innovative work in the burgeoning interpretive marketing research tradition. It ranges across the methodological spectrum from grounded theory to personal introspection, covers all aspects of the postmodern marketing 'mix', from advertising to product development, and embraces marketing's principal sub-disciplines.

Beyond the Consumption Bubble

Edited by
Karin M. Ekström and Kay Glans

Routledge
Taylor & Francis Group

LONDON AND NEW YORK

First published 2011
by Routledge
2 Park Square, Milton Park, Abingdon, Oxon OX14 4RN
52 Vanderbilt Avenue, New York, NY 10017

Routledge is an imprint of the Taylor & Francis Group, an informa business

First published in paperback 2012

© 2011 Taylor & Francis

The right of Karin M. Ekström and Kay Glans to be identified as the authors of the editorial material, and of the authors for their individual chapters, has been asserted by them in accordance with sections 77 and 78 of the Copyright, Designs and Patents Act 1988.

Typeset in Sabon by IBT Global.

Library of Congress Cataloging-in-Publication Data

Beyond the consumption bubble / edited by Karin M. Ekström and Kay Glans.
    p. cm. — (Routledge interpretive marketing research ; 13)
    Includes bibliographical references and index.
    1. Consumption (Economics) 2. Consumption (Economics)—Social
aspects. I. Ekström, Karin M. II. Glans, Kay, 1951–
    HC79.C6B49 2011
    339.4'7—dc22
    2010023142

ISBN13:978-0-415-65365-7(pbk)
ISBN13:978-0-415-87849-4(hbk)

Contents

PART IV
The Consumption Bubble and Beyond?

Figures and Tables

FIGURES

TABLES

Part I
Editor's Introduction

Introduction

Karin M. Ekström and Kay Glans

The origin of this book was a roundtable discussion in London in January 2008. It was organized by Glasshouse Forum (http://www.glasshouseforum.org), an international network devoted to a critical scrutiny of capitalism. This gathering was part of the project "A consumed society?", which among other things aims to investigate alternatives to a continuously increasing level of consumption. In the roundtable discussion, the ambiguity of the concept of consumption was highlighted; it has many different meanings and is often elusive. In media and in the general debate, categorical claims about consumption are made that often rest on weak empirical and theoretical foundations. There is a need for more analytical rigour and empirical evidence in the debate.

Research on consumption can shed light on many fundamental questions, such as the character of society, including social and cultural dimensions. These questions generally arouse strong emotions and stereotypical reactions. The intention with this anthology is to move beyond the stereotypes and enrich and sharpen the debate about consumption and changing consumer roles in society. We wish the book to be both informative and provocative. It is an attempt to popularize academic research without simplifying it. State-of-the-art research is presented to an audience which is interested in the subject, but doesn't necessarily have the time to orientate itself in the various academic fields. We hope to find readers in politics and media, corporations, authorities, consumer organizations, researchers and students. The authors are scholars who are experts in the field of consumption. They represent a variety of disciplines such as anthropology, economics, history, marketing, physics, political science and sociology.

THE CONSUMPTION BUBBLE

Before we go on to present the authors and their contributions, we would like to reflect briefly on the consumption bubble we have experienced during the last years. In the autumn of 2008, we witnessed a financial crisis that caused widespread economic turmoil. Stock markets fell dramatically;

large financial institutions collapsed or were bailed out by governments. This challenged the widespread assumed rationality of the market and its capacity to regulate itself. The financial crisis was closely related to the housing bubble, but we believe this was just one of many manifestations of a larger consumption bubble, which has been expanding for quite some time. Its primary dynamic has been overconsumption financed by debt.

Especially in the US, people have for quite some time borrowed money for consumption like never before. State financial institutions have kept the interest rates low to make it easy to borrow money. Consumption is a major factor in making the wheels turn and increasing GDP. As the historian Charles Maier has pointed out, from the 1970s, the US gradually changed from being an Empire of Production to an Empire of Consumption, driving the world economy with its demand (Maier 2006). And household demand has played an extraordinary role in the US economy.

The fact that symbolic consumption has increased in significance has also contributed to the high levels of consumption. Consumption has become an important social marker. Bauman (1998) argues that consumption has replaced the significance of work as a status indicator. We compare ourselves to others and get influenced by others. The paradoxical imperatives of both conforming to group standards and striving to be unique are driving consumption forward. Consumption can be a way to social inclusion, but on the other hand, not being able to consume can lead to exclusion (Ekström and Hjort 2009). Despite the postmodern emphasis on the individual's free choice, we must remember that consumption is restricted by lack of opportunities and different backgrounds. Preference behaviours are often determined by class stratification (Bourdieu 1984).

A strong focus on individual preferences has emerged during the last decades. This position has been reinforced by the dominance of neoclassical economics and its belief in the rationality of the *homo economicus*. Both the rationality of the market and of the individual actor have been questioned as a result of the crisis. We witness an increasing emphasis on the "animal spirits" of the economy, the large role played by emotions (Akerlof and Shiller 2009). This may lay the ground for a new soft paternalism, an ambition to guide the consumer through a world of overwhelming choices (Sunstein and Thaler 2008). Such a project is reinforced by the behavioural sciences, which have documented how difficult it is for the individual to deal with different choices. When discussing choice, it is not sufficient to consider merely individual agency, but to also look at market and societal structures.

It is of course tempting to speculate further how the global crisis will affect consumption and the attitude towards it. American households are busy deleveraging at the moment and there are several attempts to reintroduce thrift as a fundamental virtue, but historically there has not been a very strong connection between recessions and frugality. If the global crisis results in a process of deglobalization, characterized by trade wars, grab for resources and a relative withdrawal from the global economy, it will probably influence patterns of consumption, perhaps making preferences more local, or in fact forcing them to become so. As regards food, self-sufficiency is already seen as an important part of food security after the global food crisis of 2008 (Bello 2009).

For several reasons it seems necessary to consume less in the future. Many people simply cannot afford it. The present level of consumption is detrimental to the environment and a higher level might spell imminent disaster. But are the hyperconsumers able and willing to consume less? Can consumption of services replace consumption of goods? How can sustainable consumption be encouraged? Can we reduce consumption without causing a recession or worse? Several chapters in this book address these central issues from the perspective of different disciplines.

TRENDS IN THE RESEARCH ON CONSUMPTION

Research on consumption developed simultaneously with the progress of consumer culture, in particular during the later half of the twentieth century. Research on consumption today is conducted in many different disciplines, representing different perspectives, theories and methods. Economic theory dominated much of the early work on consumption, in particular during the 1930s and 1940s (e.g., Arndt 1986; Belk 1995; Ekström 2003), but its influence is also noticeable today. Psychology had a great impact on consumer research during the 1950s, 1960s and 1970s and it still has. In the 1980s, anthropology gave vital impulses to consumer research and has continued to do ever since. Also, research on the consumption received increased attention in sociology from the 1980s and onwards. Research on consumer culture and material culture has also expanded during the last decades. Consumer research is today conduced in all disciplines, although sometimes disguised under some other name.

The different disciplines complement each other, but they also have different focus. While earlier studies on consumption often were more applied, today we see more research grounded in theory. The degrees to which consumption studies are expected to solve societal problems differ across cultures and disciplines. Business studies on consumption are more likely to have this tendency. Business studies also generally have a more managerial orientation than a consumer orientation. The realization that the consumer has a lot of power is gradually changing this, and greater stress is laid upon the voice of the consumer.

Even though interdisciplinary research has increased, it is still not very common. A reason for this is that university systems often encourage traditional specialization rather than crossing borders and cooperation across disciplines. In order to achieve a greater understanding of the pluralistic meanings of consumption, this must change. Trying to look ahead, we expect more research on consumption in areas that traditionally have cared less about this, for example, in research on information technology, engineering, design and medicine. Many examples from everyday life show that a consumer orientation often is lacking, for example, when it comes to technologically complex products. Up till now most research on consumption has focused on the private sector, but we also foresee more research on consumption in the public sphere.

Consumption is a concern to many actors in society such as politicians, businesspeople, policymakers, civic associations, etc. Given the central role of consumption, it is quite astonishing that consumer issues often are considered to be the responsibility of a single ministry in governments. The minor importance these issues are ascribed is illustrated by the fact that they are often moved between ministries when governments change. For example, in Sweden, consumer issues at the present sort under the Ministry of Integration and Gender Equality. For instance, the Ministry of Finance, Ministry of Justice and Ministry of Agriculture have handled these issues earlier.

THE STRUCTURE OF THE BOOK

Part II

Part II of the book, "A Changing Society", addresses issues related to the role of consumption in society. It deals with macro perspectives focusing on the structure of society, but also how this impacts the individual.

Deidre Nansen McCloskey discusses in "The Economics and the Anti-Economics of Consumption" what economics and other students of society can learn from each other. She argues that criticism of consumption often is an expression of snobbism, based on a very paternalistic attitude toward the "common" people. Intellectuals, or the "clerisy" as McCloskey prefers to call them, are inclined to view people in general as being manipulated in their choices. It is a way for the clerisy to reaffirm their commitment and preferences. The fear that material wealth and lavish consumption undermines virtues and willingness to act as a citizen can be found already in classical Greece, and has become a major theme at different periods in history. On the other hand, the economist model of consumption lacks a consideration of how taste is acquired and developed as a way of distinguishing oneself from others. Hence, consumption cannot only be studied from an economic perspective.

It may very well be that we are facing a massive commercialization of all spheres of life today, including religion, but this doesn't necessarily mean we are living in a world without values. The French sociologist Gilles Lipovetsky argues in "The Hyperconsumption Society" that we now live in an era of hyperconsumption. Consumption is no longer organized around the household, but around the individual. Class habits, norms and practices that earlier exerted pressure to conformity have lost their capacity. The new style of consumer is described as erratic, nomadic, volatile, unpredictable, fragmented and deregulated. Brand names rather than class habits guide us and have become central to our self-definition. Consumption is more emotional than statutory, having to do more with recreation than prestige. The hyperconsumer is searching for experiences that can vitalize his or her emotions. People are less concerned with pleasure and more concerned with health. However, the hyperconsumption society is not only about the supremacy of the market and pleasure for the individual, but is coupled with the reinforcement of a common core of democratic, humanistic values. Lipovetsky emphasizes that even though hyperconsumption has lots of faults, it has not destroyed morals, altruism or the value of love. Likewise, individualism does not proscribe having values, nor affectionate relationships with others.

Rickard Wilk argues in "Consumption in an Age of Globalization and Localization" that there is not a basic incompatibility between being global and local. The fear of a global monoculture is founded on the belief that globalization is something new and that the world earlier was dominated by local, indigenous cultures. But mass-consumption has been global for hundreds of years without making the world homogeneous. Many of the cultures that to Western observers seemed "timeless" traditional cultures were in fact the product of a long interaction with empires and colonial powers. Rather than focusing on two possibilities, preservation of traditional culture or global monoculture, we need to apply more complex concepts such as resistance, hybridity and appropriation to describe what happens when local culture encounters globalization. Overall, it is very hard to distinguish between good or bad consumption. Why are visits to museums perceived as better than going to amusement parks? Wilk emphasizes that consumer culture is not a single uniform thing, but messy, accidental and contingent, in a constant state of improvisation, collapse and renewal. Principles such as shading and distancing make it impossible to connect the things we consume to their origin and to measure their social and environmental costs. Hence no local cost/benefit equation can address the larger issues of sustainability, according to Wilk. It has to be recognized that benefits in one place have costs in another.

Another dualism that doesn't stand up under closer scrutiny is the classical distinction between individual and society, says Daniel Miller in "Consumption beyond Dualism". The social sciences have positioned the individual in opposition to different kinds of collectives, such as state, society and culture. Miller argues that the study of consumption material culture may be a means to confront and repudiate this dualism. Based on a study of households in South London, he suggests that people are not oriented towards individualism or society. People live within a field of relationships to other persons and also to material things. One is not at the expense of the other. Also, there are few traces of any communal entity such as society or even neighbourhood. People are oriented towards a few core relationships, the people and things that really matter to them. Material objects are viewed as an integral and inseparable aspect of all relationships. This means that the accusation for being "materialistic" in the sense of only caring about things loses much of its relevance. Miller's criticism extends to liberalism, which also conceptualizes the individual as the "other" to society. Most people regard such isolation as a failure. Individualism is most fully equated with loneliness and a lack of relationships.

Consumption is not just about things but also about services, and those are not just private but also public. The public provides many of the services. In "Goods and Service Consumption in the Affluent Welfare State—Issues for the Future", Jan Owen Jansson compares Sweden and the US, often considered to be opposite in the variety of capitalism. It may be somewhat surprising that an alleged welfare state like Sweden spends considerably less on medical care and education than the US. The Swedish welfare state is no longer characterized by a comparatively large share of GDP going into health, education and care of children, elderly and disabled persons, but by the fact that these services are provided basically free of charge. The least expanding part of total consumption in Sweden is tax-financed consumption, but the solution to some fundamental problems ahead of us lies in the expansion of the public consumption, Jansson argues. Manufacturing of goods is increasing the productivity, but will not create more jobs since technology replaces humans. Future employment must to a large extent come from public, tax-financed consumption, and to achieve this goal, the consumption of goods should be frozen at the present level. The reduced consumption of goods would be compensated by better eldercare, education and medical care, and, of course, employment.

Part III

Part III of the book, "Changing Consumer Roles", has a stronger focus on the micro level, social interactions and agency.

How does the development towards hyperconsumption look from the perspective of the individual? The erosion of the traditional constraints surrounding consumption has given the individual greater freedom, but perhaps also a greater responsibility. Many of the functions that earlier belonged to society seem to have been transferred to the individual. In "Selves as Objects of Consumption" the sociologist Zygmunt Bauman contends that today even utopia is privatized. Social engineering has, with the help of bioengineering, been transformed into an individualistic project for improvement, an endless shopping spree for the seemingly perfect mix of personal characteristics. The suggestion is that all problems of existence can be solved or at least well managed by wise shopping. The goal is a kind of effortless enjoyment. Bauman, however, suspects that such a project is inherently impossible, since the effort might be an integral part of the pleasure. Furthermore, this privatized utopias undermine our willingness and ability to act as citizens and work for collective goods and long-term goals. Individualistic self-interest calculating probable gains and losses is often given priority over real care for others.

Choice and consumer empowerment is discussed by Frank Trentmann in "Consumers as Citizens: Tensions and Synergies". He argues that there are two opposite views of choice. The one claims that excess of choice in consumer culture has made consumers sick and depressed, the other that choice is a source of empowerment and democratic renewal manifested in reforms of public services. Both positions are, according to Trentmann, simplified views of consumption and citizenship. Furthermore, it is unjustified to regard the roles of citizen and consumer as mutually exclusive. Citizens do not always act for the public good and people consume for a variety of reasons. The roles often overlap and reinforce each other. Consumption has historically been related to civic activism, for instance, in the organization of boycotts. Examples are given that show that consumption is flexible and modular, offering different social and ideological possibilities for civic engagement. Neither is consumer engagement limited to individual choice, but it can be part of a larger vision of social and international justice. The different forms of political consumption are not antithetical to more conventional political engagement. Rather, they tend to complement each other. One conclusion that follows from this is that one should not view political consumerism as a new political toolkit fit for every occasion. To advance engagement with citizens, any strategy for well-being should recognize the potential as well as the limits of choice.

Franck Cochoy continues the discussion in "Political Consumption Revisited: Should We Resist 'Consumers' Resistance'?" He argues that the methods used in political consumption are not new. They have been used before during periods when the political institutions have been slow to respond with relevant regulations to a new situation. As a strategy for resistance political consumption has several limitations. It has not been successful in mobilizing the masses, and its impact is therefore limited. If political consumerism in the form of, say, fair trade wants to reach larger groups and have some commercial success, it is bound to adapt to the market and use its methods. And the market seems able to absorb this kind of resistance quite well and transform it into—marketing. Therefore, we should think twice before we leave politics to market actors, Cochoy contends. The last surge in political consumerism has been a response to the difficulties in regulating a globalized economy, but in the long run the only viable strategy is to create relevant institutions.

John W. Schouten and Diane M. Martin reach a different conclusion regarding these new forms of activism in "Communities of Purpose". Whether it concerns neighbourhood gardens, cooperatives or cyberspace, consumers engage in so-called communities of purpose to achieve something specific.

These groups are the least known of the consumer organizations, but probably the most important of them all. Their ability to mobilize and leverage resources such as time, money, courage and creativity is impressive. They have the potential to create markets and industries or to bring them down. They are self-organizing communities that form across and largely outside of the boundaries of formal organizations. They tend to flourish through electronic and social media. Their boundaries are highly malleable. They draw from the intellectual, technological and artistic abilities of a very diverse body of people. The rewards for success tend to be non-financial in nature. Schouten and Martin argue that as important it is to understand the nature of communities of purpose, it is equally important to understand the social dynamics that bring them about. How strong this trend is and how unexpected its results can be are shown by the fact that it has influenced a typical brand community like bikers to become a community of purpose, trying to ensure the future of biking by making motorcycles less dangerous to the environment.

Another function that at least partly has been transferred to the consumer is that of the producer. The borderline between consuming and producing has become blurred, and not only when it comes to information technology. Jonathan E. Schroeder shows in "Value Creation and the Visual Consumer" that consumers are no longer the end of the marketing chain, but have a prominent role in value creation, both for themselves and for companies and their brands. This is prominent in visual consumption, which puts the emphasis on looking as the primary consumer experience. The importance of the visual experience can, for instance, be observed in the modern supermarket, where the consumers orient themselves with the help of visual signs. The dependence on visual signs is even greater on the Internet. Schroeder points out that photography surrounds consumption today: it informs, it shows, it communicates, it structures choice, it dazzles and it offers creative ways of thinking about consumer experiences. Many photos are taken by consumers and closely associated with memory and nostalgia. These pictures spread information to other consumers, and are used as unpaid marketing by the companies. Some academics are fascinated by the creative potential of consumer co-creation and consumer empowerment, while others fear that the corporations exploit the consumers. The debate concerns both agency, i.e., how much one person can do in society, and structure, i.e., how society influences and structures individual behaviour, issues that are not easily resolved.

Much of the concern about the dangers of contemporary consumption is focused on children, who are exposed to the market earlier and more massively than before. Some regard children as easy victims of manipulation and hence in need of protection. Others consider children as knowledgeable consumers or claim that they are developing competence and able to handle potential attempts at manipulation. The reality is much more complex than both these positions allow for, says Karin M. Ekström in "'Keeping Up with the Children': Changing Consumer Roles in Families". Children are competent in certain areas but not in others—and the same applies to adults, in fact.

The interaction between the generations is much more complex than it used to be. Until recently parents basically taught their children to be consumers. Today we often witness a reversal of this relationship. Children may be more skilled in using, for instance, new technology and more aware of environmental issues. Therefore, they are able to guide their parents, and even grandparents, both when it comes to what to buy and how to use it.

Part IV

Part IV of the book, "The Consumption Bubble and Beyond?", takes a step into the future, trying to predict what will happen to us as individuals and society if the consumption bubble continues or bursts.

To some extent it depends on what happens with income inequality, if we follow Robert H. Frank in "Relative Deprivation, Inequality and Consumer Spending in the United States". What we perceive as a necessary level of consumption is based on a comparison with other people. Spending decisions are driven not by income alone, but also by the spending of others. Even if you have a very high standard compared to other countries and other times, you can still feel a relative deprivation if people around you are significantly better off. If a small group at the top gets very much wealthier, as in the US during the last decade, it puts a great strain on the rest of the population to consume more, even more than they can afford. This has been the case with the middle class in the US. Its real income has increased very little in recent decades, and it has kept up consumption by ceasing to save and then getting into debt. The median new single-family detached house built in the United States, which stood at sixteen hundred square feet in 1980, reached more than twenty-four hundred square feet by 2007. Consumption is moulded not only by spending patterns in the surrounding community, but also by the consumer's own past experience. Therefore, cutbacks are often difficult and consumption levels change little during recessions.

Both the American household and the state are heavily in debt, and as Maurie J. Cohen points out in "(Un)sustainable Consumption and the New Political Economy of Growth", it seems probable that new rounds of deficit-financed stimulus will be needed to bring unemployment down to politically acceptable levels, increasing the public indebtedness. Even those that have questioned the sustainability of this level of consumption failed to foresee the crisis. The critics have often accommodated to the neoliberal paradigm and tried to formulate strategies that focused on the behaviour of the individual consumer. Cohen argues that by emphasizing consumer rationality and narrow technical tactics, policymakers are marginalizing the essential politics of any meaningful program to elicit fundamental changes in consumption. Commitment to economic growth has dominated all over the political spectrum. To propose strong regulations was considered an extreme position, but the crisis has made a more fundamental questioning of the existing order possible. The attempts to formulate such alternatives are motivated by environmental considerations, but also by the fact that above a certain level economic growth fails to increase well-being. How do we get out of a situation in which companies feel a constant pressure to produce new things, and we as consumers to consume them without feeling any actual pleasure? The suggested solutions advocate among other things a reduced social inequality and a shift in investment priorities from private to public goods. This presupposes a much more active role for the state, modulating both behaviour and preferences. A notable reorientation is occurring away from merely accounting for the impacts of consumption to the formulation of policy programs that connect with more politically robust concerns about public health.

The conviction among economists and many others is that the economy will more or less collapse if people start to consume less. Right now the big question is where the new consumer demand will come from, and many look to the Chinese consumers. However, if the entire world starts to consume like the West does, we will soon face an environmental disaster, Neva Goodwin concludes in "If US Consumption Declines Will the Global Economy Collapse?" As an economist, she is convinced that we are able to change our present excessive consumption patterns without any loss of well-being, but we must learn to think in a different way and change priorities. If the US ceases to be the global engine of demand, it would in fact have several positive consequences. Brain drain would not deprive the rest of the world of the talented people they need. Trade would be more regional and adjust to local demand and, as a consequence, the strain on the environment would lessen. We would consume fewer, more basic goods and more services, rather than accumulation of status goods. More labour would go into such things as production of food, education and care, Goodwin contends. She argues that today there is considerable dissonance between the goals of firms versus the health of society and its members. Furthermore, in response to the common belief that it is essential to leave as much as possible to "the market" because of the superior efficiency of this mode, it is important to realize that efficiency is not a virtue when it is harnessed to the wrong goals, such as short-term profits at the expense of long-term contributions to a healthy society.

It seems likely that a change such as the one proposed by Goodwin would demand a different worldview. Which philosophy could be the foundation of a society that is consuming less? In "Philosophies for Less Consuming Societies" Russell Belk scans some potential candidates. Over the years there has been a number of advocates and practitioners of simple living. It is not a new idea that people would be better off if they consumed less. We find it already in classical antiquity and in the Eastern philosophies. Two streams of philosophical thought concerning living more simply are presented in the chapter. First we have Voluntary Simplicity, which is a freely chosen path to a way of life that is sustainable and uses appropriate technology that adapts to nature rather than high technology that opposes nature. It was predicted to grow in popularity, but encompasses today only a minority of the population. Lately, the vocabulary of Voluntary Simplicity has changed to "downshifting"—working less, eating more locally, driving less and enjoying a moderately different lifestyle with a lesser environmental footprint. It has also embraced movements as "Buy Nothing Day". The second philosophy discussed is Buddhism. Whereas Voluntary Simplicity emphasizes that less is more and that the simpler the life you can lead the better, Buddhism instead advocates the middle way, neither too much nor too little. Buddhism also suggests that we pay too much attention to the problems of poverty and not enough attention to the problems of wealth. There are, however, indications that Buddhists are beginning to embrace wealth as a sign of spiritual blessing. Belk argues that it raises the question of whether the "spiritual materialism" of much contemporary Buddhism threatens to render it less effective in offering a philosophy for simpler consumption. Most Western Buddhists come from upper-middle-class backgrounds, just as voluntary simplifiers, and therefore Belk suggests that being part of a less consuming society is a societal movement rather than an individual lifestyle choice. The support of a sharing, caring community committed to living a life that does not champion the consumption of more and more may be the simplest and best philosophy for achieving moderation in consumption.

Such a change would require that we give priority to those things in life that really are important for our satisfaction. And if you ask people, most respond that most important in life are human relations. John Holmberg and Jonas Nässén point out in "Well-Being the Path Out of the Consumption–Climate Dilemma?" that very few of our most important needs consume very much energy. And the positional consumption of goods that might boost one's social status relative to others, but with little or no benefit for society as a whole, add very little to our happiness. Several studies have shown that shorter work hours are used for activities such as child care, sleep, meals, social contacts and volunteer work, and these types of activities are also more important for subjective well-being than material consumption acquired by increasing income. Holmberg and Nässén argue that radical change is required for climate mitigation. Both reduced energy intensity in society and changing consumption patterns will be required. Holmberg and Nässén wonder why we choose stronger, faster vehicles when the ones we already have are strong enough to pull a reluctant moose or two up a mountain and can go much, much faster than the legal limit. Improvements in energy efficiency may cause so-called rebound effects by increasing energy service demand and economic growth. For example, the cost of driving an extra kilometre is lower in a fuel-efficient car, but may result in driving longer distances. Furthermore, money saved on reduced consumption of fuel can be used for a ticket to a holiday in Thailand. Also, reductions in energy demand by one actor may result in lower fuel prices that may lead to increasing demand by other actors in the economy. They argue that decisions on what should be the long-term goal for climate policy can only partly be supported by science. Ultimately this judgement is an ethical and political issue.

Another idea that has lost a lot of credibility lately is the belief that a developed market economy with a lot of choices for consumers will create a preference for liberal democracy. If you get used to choosing between different sorts of coffee at Starbucks, then you will not be satisfied with only one political party to vote for, as it has been put (Mann 2007). China's development has not confirmed such expectations. The crisis seems to have strengthened China's political and economical position, but also the legitimacy of the political system. As Patricia Thornton points out in "What Is to Be Undone? The Making of the Middle Class in China", the consuming Chinese middle class is to a large extent a creation of the regime. The culture of consumption has been created from above as part of a state-building project and there are as yet few signs that the middle class will take the lead in a struggle for liberal democracy. China's estimated level of poverty is significantly higher than previously imagined, but China has made more progress against poverty than any country in the world since the 1980s. Nevertheless, the future will tell us more about the role of consumption in China and its consequences on the local, regional and global environment considering ecological, economic and social aspects.

REFERENCES

Akerlof, George A., and Robert J. Shiller. 2009. *Animal Spirits. How Human Psychology Drives the Economy, and Why it Matters for Global Capitalism.* Princeton, NJ: Princeton University Press.

Arndt, Johan. 1986. Paradigms in Consumer Research: A Review of Perspectives and Approaches. *European Journal of Marketing* 20 (8): 23–40.

Bauman, Zygmunt. 1998. *Work, Consumerism and the New Poor.* Buckingham: Open University Press.

Belk, Russell W. 1995. Studies in the New Consumer Behavior. In *Acknowledging Consumption: A Review of New Studies*, ed. D. Miller. London: Routledge.

Bello, Walden. 2009. *The Food Wars.* London: Verso.

Bourdieu, Pierre. 1984. *Distinction. A Social Critique of the Judgement of Taste.* London: Routledge.

Ekström, Karin M. 2003. Revisiting the Family Tree; Historical and Future Consumer Behavior Research. *Academy of Marketing Science Review.* www.amsreview.org.

Ekström, Karin M., and Torbjörn Hjort. 2009. Hidden Consumers in Marketing— The Neglect of Consumers with Scarce Recourses in Affluent Societies. *Journal of Marketing Management* 25 (7–8): 697–712.

Maier, Charles S. 2006. *Among Empires: American Ascendancy and Its Predecessors.* Cambridge, MA: Harvard University Press.

Mann, James. 2007. *The China Fantasy: How Our Leaders Explain Away Chinese Repression.* New York: Viking.

Sunstein, Cass, and Richard Thaler. 2008. *Nudge. Improving Decisions about Health, Wealth, and Happiness.* New Haven, CT: Yale University Press.

Part II
A Changing Society

1 The Economics and the Anti-Economics of Consumption

Deirdre Nansen McCloskey[1]

Economists have some ideas about consumption that do not agree with the ideas of other students of society. Sometimes the other students are correct. But sometimes the economists are.

For one thing the economists say—correctly—that the amount of consumption, C, is determined by production, P, down to the last penny. Since the world does not get manna from heaven or an outside Santa Claus, it must get along on what it gets. And there's no way to not consume what we as a world produce, unless we throw it into the sea, or waste it on war. Call the idea "common sense" or "accounting" or the "circular flow", but anyway C equals P.

For another, economists have a vivid statistical knowledge of how very much more the average person in a rich country consumes than her ancestors did—how much more C per person she has. Two centuries ago the world's economy stood at the present level of Chad or Bangladesh or North Korea. In 1800 the average human consumed and expected her children and grandchildren and great-grandchildren to go on consuming a mere US$3 a day, give or take a dollar or two.[2] (The figure is expressed in modern-day, American prices, corrected for the cost of living.) By contrast, if you live nowadays in a thoroughly bourgeois country such as Japan or France you probably spend about US$100 a day. One hundred dollars against three. Such is the magnitude of the modern economic growth that economists can tell non-economists about. The only people much better off than US$3 or so up to 1800 were lords or bishops or a few of the merchants. It had been this way for all of history, and for that matter all of pre-history.

Two centuries later the world supports more than six and a half times more souls. Yet contrary to a pessimistic Malthusian belief that population growth would be the big problem, the average person nowadays consumes almost ten times more goods and services than in 1800. And the real consumption of poor people has recently been doubling every generation. Despite the disturbing pauses during the three dozen or so recessions that have roiled the world's economy since 1800, consumption per person on average worldwide and over the long run has taken to doubling faster and faster. In fifty years, if things go as they have since 1800, the terribly poor will have become adequately nourished, and the ordinarily poor will be bourgeois. It has happened since 1800 in many places, and now is beginning to happen in China and India.

Why? Remember: C equals P. So the larger world C had to be because we are vastly more productive than we once were. And that's the third idea economists possess which other people don't always grasp. In a single country the C can be bigger than the P if the country is stealing from others or getting charity. But in historical fact it didn't happen. Americans and other capitalists (Swedes, for example) have a great mass of goods and services mainly *because they produce a great deal*. Contrary to your grandmother's dictum—"Eat your spinach: think of the starving children in China"— consuming less in America or Sweden would add nothing to the goods available in China or Uganda. Not a grain of rice. Countries are rich or poor, have a great deal to consume or very little, mainly because they work well or badly, not because some outsider is adding to or stealing from a God-given endowment. So being productive and therefore consuming a lot is not immoral, not a result of stealing from the Third World. It is the good luck to be born in America or Sweden.

The next idea is less open-and-shut. It is that economists don't view modern consumption as different in kind from ancient or tribal consumption. The great French anthropologist Marcel Mauss expressed in 1925 the conventional but mistaken wisdom that "it is our Western societies who have recently made man an economic animal. . . . *Homo oeconomicus* is not behind us, but lies ahead. . . . For a very long time man was something different. . . . Happily we are still somewhat removed from this constant, icy, utilitarian calculation".[3] He was wrong to think that there is an advanced form of consumption that is icily utilitarian, since all consumption is of use because people think it is, not because of some useful essence (which is something economists learned in the 1870s, and we have had reinforced subsequently by anthropologists such as Mary Douglas). But he was most wrong to think that earlier people were less economic, less oriented towards prudence. He believed that the modern, allegedly utilitarian consumer is especially greedy. Coleridge and Carlyle and Emerson and Dickens, and behind them Schiller and the German Romantics, accepted the self-glorifying claim of the Utilitarians themselves that prudence was a new virtue, to be set against the splendid irrationalities of the Gothic era. Yet what was actually new in the nineteenth century was the *theory* of prudence, a new admiration for prudence, not its practice. So, especially greedy modern consumers: no.

Many non-economists imagine that anti-virtue, greed in particular, is necessary to keep the wheels of commerce turning, "creating jobs" or "keeping the money circulating". They imagine that people must buy, buy, buy or else capitalism will collapse and all of us will be impoverished. Lenin and Hobson developed a macro version of the idea in their argument around 1900 that imperialism had saved capitalism by providing markets.

Dorothy Sayers, who was more than a writer of mysteries, complained in 1942 as a Christian about "the appalling squirrel-cage . . . in which we have been madly turning for the last three centuries . . . a society in which consumption has to be artificially stimulated in order to keep production going . . . a society founded on trash and waste".[4] In 1942 even some of the economists thought this true. The theory was called "stagnationism".[5] It's a balloon theory of capitalism, that people must keep puff-puffing or the balloon will collapse, one version of the old claim that expenditure on foolish luxuries at least employs workpeople. In line with the usual if erroneous belief that spending on the Second World War had saved the world's economy, the stagnationists predicted that 1946 would see a renewal of the Great Depression. But it didn't. Stagnationism proved false.[6] Instead, world income per head grew faster from 1950 to 1974 than at any time in history, and the liberal countries boomed.

Likewise, a non-economist is inclined to think that Milady consuming a diamond bauble "puts people to work". Non-economists think that economics is about "keeping the money circulating". The vocabulary of generating and making jobs sounds to non-economists tough and prudential and quantitative. It is not. It is silly. The diamond workers would not be idle if "thrown out" of work in the bauble factory. They would in the long run find alternative employment, such as in growing oats for oatmeal or making thatched roofs for peasant houses.

All right. Those are some things that other students of society can learn from economists. What can economists learn about consumption from other students of society?

Take a look, for example, at the writings on "happiness" by the great economist and demographic historian Richard Easterlin. He has argued—against the "freedom-from-want" claims of non-economists like the psychologist Abraham Maslow or the political scientist Ronald Inglehart (who both believed that the hierarchy of needs can in fact be satisfied)—that "economic growth is a carrier of a material culture of its own that ensures that humankind is forever ensnared in the pursuit of more and more economic goods".[7] But wait. Admittedly, we are "ensnared", even "enslaved". Social science in the twentieth century, however, has discovered a reply: *any* level of income is a "carrier of a material culture", US$3 a day as much as US$137 a day. As Easterlin said, "forever". The anthropologists and psychologists point out that any meal-taking or shelter-building or tale-telling "ensnares" its people, the Bushmen of the Kalahari no less than the floor traders of Wall Street.[8] We make ourselves with consumption, as anthropologists have observed. Mary Douglas and Baron Isherwood put it so: "Goods that minister to physical needs—food and drink—are no less carriers of meaning than ballet or poetry. Let us put an end to the widespread and misleading distinction between goods that sustain life and health and others that service the mind and heart—spiritual goods."[9] The classic demonstration is Douglas's own article on the symbolic structure of working-class meals in England, but in a sense all of anthropology is in this business.[10] Goods wander across the border of the sacred and the profane—the anthropologist Richard Chalfen, for example, shows how home snapshots and movies do.[11] Or as the anthropologist Marshall Sahlins puts it in the new preface to his 1972 classic, *Stone Age Economics*: "economic activity . . . [is] the expression, in a material register, of the values and relations of a particular form of life."[12]

Easterlin urges us to resist consumerism and become "masters of growth".[13] One wants to be wary of such urgings that "we" do something, since the "we" is so easily corrupted—for instance, by rabid nationalism, or by the mere snobbery of the "clerisy" (the word is how Samuel Taylor Coleridge and I refer to the intelligentsia and journalists and ministers and professors and the rest of the scribbling tribe). Easterlin would agree. But surely in an ethical sense he is right. "We" need to persuade each other to take advantage of modern freedom from want for something other than watching television and eating more Fritos and strutting about in a world of status-confirming consumption. We are ensnared, admittedly, as our ancestors were. In modern conditions of wide material scope, however, we would hope that the ensnaring would be worthy of the best versions of our humanness, ensnared by Mozart or by the celebration of the mass or by a test match for the Ashes at Lord's on a perfect London day in June. Yet that advice, to be nobly ensnared, has been a commonplace since the invention of religion and literature. It has nothing much to do with the Great (and Liberating) Fact of modern growth—except that thanks to the Fact a vastly larger percentage of humanity is open to the advice. The clerisy thinks that other peoples' spending is just awful—even superb economists like Easterlin or Fred Hirsch or Robert Frank partake in the clerisy's disdain. In 1985 the cultural historian Daniel Horowitz argued persuasively that "at the heart of most versions of modern moralism is a critique, sometimes radical and always adversarial, of the economy. . . . Denouncing other people for their profligacy and lack of Culture is a way of reaffirming one's own commitment."[14]

The clerisy, then, dislikes the consumption of *hoi polloi*. You will get many versions of the distaste in this volume. Especially in the United States, for example, the clerisy has been saying since Veblen that The Many are in the grips of a tiny group of advertisers. So the spending on Coke and gas grills and automobiles is the result of hidden persuasion or, to use a favourite word of the clerisy to describe commercial free speech, "manipulation". The peculiarly American attribution of gigantic power to thirty-second television spots is puzzling to an economist. (I recur for a moment to telling you what other observers can learn about consumption from economists.) If advertising had the powers attributed to it by the clerisy, then unlimited fortunes could be had for the writing. Yet advertising is less than 2 per cent of national product, much of it uncontroversially informative—such as shop signs and entries in the Yellow Pages or ads in trade magazines aimed at highly sophisticated buyers.

Easterlin makes another economist's point: that "how people feel they ought to live . . . rises commensurately with income. The result is that while income growth makes it possible for people better to attain their aspirations, they are not happier because their aspirations, too, have risen".[15] The argument of Fred Hirsch and Robert Frank is similar: standards of consumption are social, and so higher income is spent in an arms race to match other people's consumption, expensive leather furniture in one's *pied à terre* in New York City, say, because that is How We Live Now.[16]

Well, what of it? We are richer, as now China and India are steadily becoming, praise the Lord, or as Japan and Ireland and other once unspeakably poor places have become. We and they consume more, and then aspire for more, and have an expanded idea of how many square metres a livable apartment must have. Still we paint ourselves with our consumption, and have vastly more scope for painting in more comfortable, "richer" ways. Good. The "happiness" literature among economists, you see, is predisposed to find modern levels of consumption vulgar and corrupting, a pointless arms race. The field has become one of the scientific legs of the century-old campaign by the clerisy against the "consumerism" to which the non-clerisy are so wretchedly enslaved, as described in the writings of the economists Hirsch or Frank or Scitovsky, or the sociologist Juliet Schor, or indeed the sociological economist of a century ago, the great Thorstein Veblen.[17] (Such economists do not acknowledge that there have always been such races of aspiration in consumption, leading to the glory of Greece and the riches of England.[18])

In her survey of Catholic and radical thinking on consumption the theologian Christine Firer Hinze worries that in such self-makings in consumption we might lose our virtues, especially our temperance.[19] She recalls Monsignor John A. Ryan's books of economics in the early twentieth century calculating the costs of dignity as against superfluity. Hinze and I agree with the anti-consumption clerisy that it is possible to make oneself badly—she and I are Aristotelians and Aquinians, with an idea of the virtuous life. We are not Utilitarians refusing to judge consumption. The economists can be properly criticized for such a species of amoralism that has corrupted, for example, American schools of business. "Structures of sin" are possible in the sociology of consumption. She and I would urge "a virtue approach to consumer culture", and to much else.[20] But what evidence, really, is there that "the market can neither generate nor guarantee respect for . . . moral foundations"?[21] Doubtless not without ethical effort, yes. But "*cannot*"?

Above all, the economist's model of consumption can be properly criticized for its *thinness*. The main character in the story of conventional economists is someone named "Max U", the unlovely maximizer of utility, *Homo prudens*, the prudent human—never *Homo ludens* (the playful human, whom the economists Schumpeter or Knight emphasized) or *Homo faber* (the making human, Marx's man) or *Homo hierarchus* (the ranking human, which Robert Frank emphasizes) or, as I and most non-economist social scientists would claim, *Homo loquens*, the speaking human. ("Max U", you see, is a man with the last name "U" who has peopled the arguments of economists since Paul Samuelson elevated him to a leading role in the late 1930s. The joke is that the only way that an economist knows how to think about life after Samuelson is to watch Mr. Max U *Max*-imizing a Utility function, $U(X,Y)$. Ha, ha.) The best policy to improve our lives may be artistic and sociological, not economic. Remake our tastes—which are merely "given" in the economist's thin model. Andrew Kashdan and Daniel Klein, who doubt that the "arms race" argument against consumption made by Hirsch and Frank is persuasive, point out that Adam Smith "was critical of luxury and the vanity of the rich, but his approach was to enlighten people by showing them that their self-interest broadly conceived resided in liberal virtues and the market order".[22]

Admittedly, behaviour *is* sometimes best described scientifically as being about the material incentives given to Max U people who have given tastes. But sometimes it is best described as improvisational comedy. The joke then is on the economist. Thus, for example, the "distinction" that Pierre Bourdieu examined in his dissection of the bourgeois and working classes in France is not merely an external constraint.[23] It is a dance. You don't merely get to a higher level of utility if you can name (on a pop quiz set by the sociologist) the composer of "The Well-Tempered Clavier". By doing so you actively distinguish yourself from people with fewer academic qualifications in a qualification-obsessed France. You are playing a social game in which each move has meaning. "Johann Sebastian Bach". "Ah, one of Us. Welcome". Or as Yeats put it, "O bodies swayed to music, o brightening glance:/ How can we know the dancer from the dance?"

But that is what the rest of the volume is about.

NOTES

1. Parts of this chapter are adapted from McCloskey (2006, 2010).
2. Strictly speaking, "1990 international Geary-Khamis dollars". See Angus Maddison in his amazing palace of numbers, *The World Economy* (2006, 642). I used the average of Maddison's world figures for 1700 and 1820. Economic historians agree on a factor of ten or so worldwide since the eighteenth century; for example, Easterlin (1995; 2004, 84).
3. Mauss (1925/1990, 98).
4. Sayers (1942, 1).
5. Hansen (1938, 1941), out of Keynes (1937).
6. Fogel (2005). On the political Left, Baran and Sweezy (1966) kept up the stagnationist argument for some decades after its time.
7. Easterlin (2004, 52).
8. Douglas and Isherwood (1979); Csikszentmihalyi and Rochberg-Halton (1981).

9. Douglas and Isherwood (1979), quoted in van Staveren (1999, 92).
10. Douglas (1972).
11. Chalfen (1987).
12. Sahlins (1974/2004, ix).
13. Easterlin (2004, 53).
14. Horowitz (1985, 166, 168).
15. Easterlin (2003, 349).
16. Hirsch (1976); Frank (1985, 1999, 2004); Frank and Cook (1995).
17. Frank (1985), who is rather more subtle than this characterization suggests; Frank and Cook (1995); Schor (1993, 1998, 2004); Scitovsky (1976); Veblen (1899).
18. Kashdan and Klein make the point against the pointlessness of "positional goods" (2006, 422–424). Today's luxury (argued Friedrich Hayek) is an experiment in consumption. Air-conditioning, once only for the rich, becomes commonplace, on account of the rich's experiment in vulgar, showing-off comfort.
19. Hinze (2004, esp. 179).
20. Hinze (2004, 177).
21. Hinze (2004, 179).
22. Kashdan and Klein (2006, 420).
23. Bourdieu (1979/1984).

REFERENCES

Baran, Paul A., and Paul M. Sweezy. 1966. *Monopoly Capital: An Essay on the American Economic and Social Order.* New York: Monthly Review Press.
Bourdieu, Pierre. 1979/1984. *Distinction: A Social Critique of the Judgment of Taste.* Trans. Richard Nice. London: Routledge and Kegan Paul.
Chalfen, Richard. 1987. *Snapshot: Versions of a Life.* Bowling Green, OH: Bowling Green University Press.
Csikszentmihalyi, Mihali, and Eugene Rochberg-Halton. 1981. *The Meaning of Things: Domestic Symbols and the Self.* Cambridge: Cambridge University Press.
Douglas, Mary. 1972. Deciphering a Meal. In *Implicit Meanings*, ed. M. Douglas, 249–275. London: Routledge and Kegan Paul.
Douglas, Mary, and Baron Isherwood. 1979. *The World of Goods.* New York: Basic Books.
Easterlin, Richard A. 1995. Industrial Revolution and Mortality Revolution: Two of a Kind? *Journal of Evolutionary Economics* 5:393–408.
———, ed. 2002. *Happiness in Economics. An Elgar Reference Collection.* Cheltenham and Northampton: Edward Elgar.
———. 2003. Living Standards. In *Oxford Encyclopedia of Economic History*, ed. Mokyr.
———. 2004. *The Reluctant Economist: Perspectives on Economics, Economic History, and Demography.* Cambridge: Cambridge University Press.
Fogel, Robert W. 2005. Reconsidering Expectations of Economic Growth after World War II from the Perspective of 2004. NBER Working Paper No. W11125.
Frank, Robert H. 1985. *Choosing the Right Pond: Human Behavior and the Quest for Status.* New York: Oxford University Press.
———. 1999. *Luxury Fever.* New York: Free Press.
———. 2004. *What Price the Moral High Ground? Ethical Dilemmas in Competitive Environments.* Princeton, NJ: Princeton University Press.

————. 2005. Motives and Self-Interest. In *The Blackwell Encyclopedia of Management. Vol. II: Business Ethics*, 2nd ed., ed. Patricia Werhane and R. E. Freeman, 369–370. Oxford and Malden, MA: Blackwell.

Frank, Robert H., and Philip J. Cook. 1995. *The Winner-Take-All Society: Why the Few At the Top Get So Much More Than the Rest of Us*. New York: Penguin Books.

Hansen, Alvin H. 1939. Economic Progress and Declining Population Growth. *American Economic Review* 29 (March): 1–7.

————. 1941. *Fiscal Policy and Business Cycles*. New York: W. W. Norton.

Hinze, Christine Firer. 2004. What is Enough? Catholic Social Thought, Consumption, and Material Sufficiency. In *Having: Property and Possession in Religious and Social Life*, ed. William Schweiker and Charles Mathewes, 162–188. Grand Rapids, MI: Eerdmans.

Hirsch, Fred. 1976. *Social Limits to Growth*. Cambridge, MA: Harvard University Press.

Horowitz, Daniel. 1985. *The Morality of Spending: Attitudes toward the Consumer Society in America, 1875–1940*. Baltimore, MD: The Johns Hopkins University Press.

Kashdan, Andrew, and Daniel B. Klein. 2006. Assume the Positional: Comment on Robert Frank. *EconJournalWatch* 3 (3): 412–534.

Keynes, John Maynard. 1937. Some Economic Consequences of a Declining Population. Presented at the Galton Lecture to the Eugenics Society, February.

Maddison, Angus. 2006. *The World Economy. Comprising The World Economy: A Millennial Perspective (2001) and The World Economy: Historical Statistic (2003) Bound as One*. Paris: Organisation for Economic Co-operation and Development.

Mauss, Marcel. 1925/1990. *Essai sur le don*. Oxford: Routledge.

McCloskey, Deirdre N. 2006. *The Bourgeois Virtues: Ethics for an Age of Commerce*. Chicago: University of Chicago Press.

————. 2010. *Bourgeois Dignity: Why Economics Does Not Explain the Modern World*. Chicago: University of Chicago Press.

Sahlins, Marshall. 1974/2004. *Stone Age Economics*. New York: Aldine de Gruyter.

————. 1976. *Culture and Practical Reason*. Chicago: University of Chicago Press.

Sayers, Dorothy L. 1942. Why Work? In *Letters to a Diminished Church*, ed. Dorothy Sayers, 49–72. Nashville, TN: W. Publishing, a division of Thomas Nelson. http://www.stthomas.edu/CathStudies/cst/facdevelop/citseminar/CIT%20 pdf/Sayers%201st%20page.pdf.

Schor, Juliet B. 1993. *The Overworked American: The Unexpected Decline of Leisure*. New York: Basic Books.

————. 1998. *The Overspent American: Upscaling, Downshifting, and the New Consumer*. New York: Basic Books.

————. 2004. *Born to Buy: The Commercialized Child and the New Consumer Culture*. New York: Scribner.

Scitovsky, Tibor. 1976. *The Joyless Economy: An Inquiry into Human Satisfaction and Consumer Dissatisfaction*. New York: Oxford University Press.

Staveren, Irene van. 1999. *Caring for Economics: An Aristotelian Perspective*. Rotterdam: Erasmus Universiteit.

Veblen, Thorstein. 1899. *The Theory of the Leisure Class*. New York: Macmillan.

2 The Hyperconsumption Society

Gilles Lipovetsky

It is widely accepted that we live in a mass-consumption society. However, it has to be pointed out that the type of consumer society created in the 1950s no longer exists. A new consumer society now reigns. I have suggested calling this new stage of consumer capitalism the hyperconsumption society.

If one must talk of hyperconsumption it is because consumption is now expanding at a hyperbolic rate. People consume everywhere: in the hypermarkets and the shopping arcades, in railway stations and airports, in the metro, in museums and on the Internet. There is increasing consumption on Sundays, in the evening, through the night, at all hours and in all places. Religious festivals are changing into spending sprees, a sort of consumption bacchanale, and all previous geographical and time constraints on consumerism are dissolving. We live in a time when the majority of our exchanges have a price tag, and our experiences are bound up in commercial relationships. The empire of brand names and market share extends everywhere, and there is now a quasi integration not only of merchandising goods but also of culture, art, time, communication, life and death. Hyperconsumer capitalism is distinguished by this explosive growth in the marketplace, and by its infiltration into nearly all of life's space-time.

To correctly evaluate the place, influence and idea of the contemporary consumer universe, one must try to place it in the history of modern consumerism—which is already a century old. To this end I will suggest an outline of the evolution of consumer capitalism based on the characteristics of three main phases.

THE THREE AGES OF CONSUMER CAPITALISM

Phase I starts around the 1880s and ends with the Second World War. This phase is primarily the one which sees the appearance of a proliferation of standardized goods sold at low prices, and the mass serial production of goods thanks to new methods and procedures in industrial manufacturing. The first cycle is also the one which saw the invention of mass marketing and the modern consumer. Until 1880, products were anonymous and sold in bulk. This was replaced by the appearance of: (a) the packaging of products, (b) the first major national advertising campaigns and (c) the brand name. It is the era when major brands that are universally recognized were founded in the US (Coca-Cola, Kodak, Campbell's Soup, etcetera). This triple innovation (packaging, advertising and brand name) gives rise to the modern consumer. This is someone who buys a product without an intermediary under an obligation to the trader and someone who is judging the product by its brand name rather than by its texture or seller.

If this phase triggered the democratization of market consumption, then it was obviously only to a limited extent, since most working-class homes did not have the means to acquire the modern goods that would proliferate in the twentieth century: the car, refrigerator, telephone, electric stove, bathroom, etcetera. Therefore, it could be said that phase I created an incomplete mass-consumption: a modern consumer, but predominantly bourgeois or even elitist.

It was around 1950 that a new phase in consumer economy came into being, phase II, which lasted until the end of the 1970s. This second phase is characterized by what is known as the mass-consumption society, synonymous with democratization and the availability of consumer goods to all groups of society. In 1975, 73 per cent of French working households owned a car, 86 per cent a television and 91 per cent a refrigerator. In this context it is no longer only the bourgeois minorities but the majority who have discretionary buying power, in other words, an income exceeding the minimum needed for the bare necessities. This is the start of buying for pleasure—no longer just what is needed. With that, the element of choice, individual motivation and psychological factors will all become increasingly influential. It was during phase II that consumerism entered the age of individualism and mass psychology. Luxuries, fashion, leisure and holidays become legitimate desires and aspirations in nearly all social groups.

At the same time advertising is permanently glorifying pleasure. Images of fun, pleasure, eroticism and holidays are paraded everywhere in the consumer society. Hedonism becomes a universal reference. Universal hedonism combined with the availability of new durable goods (televisions, cars, luxury goods, etcetera) has allowed the privatization of life and the development of individual tastes, behaviour and attitudes. With phase II, consumption has started to be remodelled on a large scale under the banner of the individual, his aspirations and his private happiness.

I put forward the hypothesis that this second cycle has been completed. At the end of the 1970s and the beginning of the 1980s, the third phase of consumer economy was set in motion. We are no longer in the good old consumer society which gently embraced my youth; we are now in what I propose to call a hyperconsumption society.

HYPERINDIVIDUALISM AND HYPERCONSUMPTION

Since the end of the 1970s, technologization of the home has become wide-spread in practically every social group. After that, multi-equipping the home began to develop, with a growing number of households owning several durable goods of the same kind (two cars, several televisions, tele-phones, etcetera). This is the first characteristic of the new society. This aspect is important because until now, a "semi-collective" consumer logic dominated, in other words, one based on equipping the household. This changed with the hyperconsumption society inasmuch as consumerism became more focused on equipping the individuals who make up a house-hold. It could be said, with a wink at Marx: "to each his objects, and to each his time to use them". The consumer society, with its emphasis on holidays, the car and television, has of course favoured individualized behaviour. However, the hyperconsumption society is itself a vehicle for a veritable explosion of individualism, a hyperindividualism; with multi-equipping allowing independent activities; individualized consumerism; personalized use of space, time and goods. In this sense, we have moved into hyperindividualistic consumerism.

EROSION OF CLASS CULTURES AND DEREGULATED CONSUMERISM

Until now consumer behaviour had been very firmly shaped by class habits, norms and practices. A whole set of attitudes and reminders existed to pre-vent the imitation of the behaviour seen in the other classes. These groups exerted various symbolic pressures to construct conformity, and a system-atic class mode of dressing, living, eating and entertaining.

This has changed: the multi-equipping of households, new goods (mobile telephones, laptops, videos, microwaves, etc.) but also the endless differen-tiation of products supplied and growing aspirations for the good life, have all set in motion a huge destabilization of class cultural models. It is a time where constraints and class models are becoming disorganized: consumer-ism has entered a phase of deregulation, deinstitutionalization and hyper-individualism. From now on even the working classes are expressing their taste in fashion, tourism and luxury. And in the upper classes it is no longer scandalous to buy at a low price, and to combine low cost and luxury brands. Just as deregulated and globalized capitalism has become a "turbo-capitalism", so we see the rise of the "turbo-consumer" (Luttwak 1998), a consumer liberated from the weight of convention, ethos and class tradi-tions. From that, the profile of this new style of consumer can be described as erratic, nomadic, volatile, unpredictable, fragmented and deregulated. Because he is increasingly free from the old collective controls, the hyper-consumer is a fickle and uncoordinated buyer.

THE CULT OF THE BRAND

At the same time as class habits are declining, the symbolic power of the brand name is rising. The two phenomena are interrelated. The hyperconsumption society is marked by the omnipresence of, and an obsession with, brand names. Does anything still escape the tidal wave of the brand name? Glasses, pens, watches, leather goods, jewellery, office equipment, telephones, sporting goods, food products, furniture design, everything now is under the rule of the brand name, either national or international: from brands which are constantly working to build up their image and their legitimacy, to develop their reputation and promote themselves, to brands associated with a single product—all are following brand expansion policies in every way imaginable: Mitsubishi makes cars, television sets, lifts; Virgin is a music label, a chain of multimedia shops, vodka, a budget airline company and a mobile phone operator. Armani is now displaying its name on hotels. The power of brand names has been revealed in another way, by the unprecedented increase in the number of imitations available, now on a global scale. In a world constructed of logos and inundated with commercial images, brand names appear as the new great totems in the hyperconsumption society. Today, the buyer wants not so much a product or a completely new style as a brand with its imagery, identity and prestige. A new fascination with brands is growing, which is not confined to the social elites of the Western world, but which touches all nations, all sections of the population and all ages. From now on even the least fortunate recognize and want to acquire top-of-the-range brands. And whilst young people dream less of fashion than of brand names, there are some American parents who are giving their children brand name products (Chanel, Armani, Porsche, L'Oréal). Today young people are infinitely better acquainted with brand names than the names of historical or religious figures. Brands, which are much more than the label on the product, are at the heart of innumerable forums and conversations both real and online. They are objects of consumers' desire; brands make up a culture, they have become part of our daily lives.

Brand power does not only come from marketing drive and investments. It is in fact inseparable from the realignment of class cultures and new aesthetic and consumer anxieties, as these phenomena have caused a kind of hesitation, disorientation and insecurity in the consumer. The brand is exactly what reassures the hyperconsumer who is disorientated and lost in top-quality aesthetics and price. When food scares increase, organic brands are in favour. When class norms of "good taste" become confused and when fashion is multifaceted and Balkanized, without any obvious hierarchy, the brand reassures the buyer who is lost in a vast range offered.

Hence the paradoxical characteristics of the hyperconsumer. On the one hand, consumer disloyalty is growing, as are the hard discount and low costs. On the other hand, brand frenzy is increasing, along with a passion for logos and luxury. If the inevitable decisions of the consumer, constrained by a limited budget, lead him to consider price logic, it certainly does not signify disaffection or disenchantment with brands.

EMOTIONAL CONSUMERISM

To account for the growth in consumerism and its needs, theorists have for a long time favoured the Veblen model, the conspicuous consumption model (Veblen 1899). To briefly summarize, this model holds that we do not consume the goods for themselves or for their usage value, but to gain social esteem, to be conspicuous, admired or recognized as belonging to a group or being distinguishable from inferior groups. This is the outline developed by Bourdieu: one of social distinction (Bourdieu 1979). To my mind, since phase II, this model has already started to show signs of weakness, even if it is still valid: this is the era when Vance Packard wrote a book with the eloquent title: *The Status Seekers* (1959).

It has to be observed, however, that this model is becoming less pertinent as consumer goods become more commonplace and are available to the population at large: refrigerator, television, hi-fi and mobile telephone, none of these have been bought to make the purchaser conspicuous, but rather to satisfy personal, hedonistic, recreational activities. We want consumer goods to be much more than window-dressing to throw in the face of others to be noticed or to stand out.

Consumption for oneself prevails over competitive or conspicuous consumption. This does not imply that caring about others has disappeared. It is still there but wrapped up in a number of other motives which are not dependent on this factor. The era of hyperconsumption coincides with the triumph of a consumption which is more emotional than statutory, has more to do with recreation than prestige. Such is hyperindividualism in consumption: fewer ostensible passions and more the pursuit of sensory, recreational or experimental experiences. Phase III signals the triumph of the acceptability of consumption. From now on, consumption is like a "journey". It stimulates our imagination: what is important is that something new is happening at the core of our daily lives. Somewhat like when going on a journey or on holiday: what counts is not so much the place visited as the journey itself. In our societies, consumption acts as a drug, it is an everyday experience which nevertheless allows us to break up the daily routine a little while intensifying the moment. On this level consumption must be seen less as an alienating force and more as a self-animating force, which explains its emotional power over the individual.

Consumer passion must be interpreted as a more or less successful way to ward off or escape the tedium of everyday life. As for purchasing new goods, the consumer is expressing his refusal to accept objectification of himself and of routine, by wanting to intensify and to reintensify every living moment.

This is perhaps the fundamental desire of the hyperconsumer, to be able to rejuvenate his experience of time, to revive it with novelties which feel like adventures. From now on, it is necessary to think of hyperconsumption as a way to feel youthful, indefinitely rebeginning. The hyperconsumer is no longer obsessed with status but instead wants to rejuvenate his life; he refuses to accept dead time and wants to constantly experience new emotions through new goods. He is the one who dreams of being like an "emotional phoenix" continually rising from the ashes.

THE HYPERCONSUMER AT WORK

Phase II was a triumph of the passive consumer, referring to what Guy Debord called "The Society of the Spectacle" (1967). We witness quite the opposite in the hyperconsumption society: the decline of this model in the face of the incredible development of the self-service concept with the actor-consumer at the forefront carrying out a whole series of tasks which used to be undertaken by the vendor: as counter clerk, advisor, technician and repairman. The hyperconsumer is more and more someone who must work to be able to consume. He is becoming the "prosumer", the co-producer of what he consumes (Dujarier 2008).

The phenomenon started with self-service in wholesale outlets, then in do-it-yourself stores, but it is currently undergoing extraordinary growth through new information and communication technologies. Now it is the consumer himself who installs software on his computer and if the Internet connection does not work it is still up to him to carry out the repairs through the support services. When eating (fast food), in banks, in airports, everywhere, the hyperconsumer contributes to the production of service and has to carry out a whole host of tasks himself. In the supermarkets, he weighs his fruit and vegetables and sticks on the price tags, in the metro he enters his destination into an electronic machine, for his holidays he does his own research on the Internet for information about the hotel, transport timetables and price, he even makes his own reservation, and increasingly, at the end of the process, he will have to sort out his rubbish and put it in the appropriate containers.

Because of the electronic tools and their complexity, the hyperconsumer needs an increasing number of skills and must be formed and "recycled" regularly to accomplish these tasks. It is often said that phase III coincides with consumer and citizen infantilism (Barber 2007): let us not lose sight of the fact that at the same time the consumer is becoming more and more professional.

HEDONISTIC CONSUMERISM AND ANXIETY CULTURE

To characterize this new society some sociologists have talked about the advent of a new neo-Dionysian type of culture built on the one current anxiety and the desire for gratification here and now. Our societies would in that way re-create for themselves what Horace called carpe diem: in other words, living for the day, trying all forms of pleasure and making the most of every moment. I think that these theories are wrong. In reality it is less carpe diem which characterizes the spirit of our times and more anxiety when faced with a future fraught with uncertainty, with risks both occupational and health-related.

Regarding the question at hand here, the principal phenomenon is in fact the fear of unemployment and of uncertainty. It is also the fear of illness, and the obsession with health and longevity. Individualism can now no longer be considered as separate from the obsession with health and longevity. Medical costs, examinations, consultations are all literally exploding. Everywhere, it is all about identifying risk factors and submitting to screening. This is the era of prevention through all sorts of measures that are sport-, nutrition- and health-related (do not eat fat, do not rush and do not smoke). Even everyday conversations are more and more often on the subject of health, nutritional food and fitness. It is less pleasure—as in the 1960s and 1970s—that is the watchword, it is rather health, longevity, prevention and balance.

Consequently, little by little, health has become a point of reference in all areas of commerce: leisure, sport, home, housing, cosmetics and nutrition. All these areas have been more or less invaded, redefined by health concerns, more and more products are sold as hybrids of well being and health (so-called pharmafoods). Consumer interest in medical matters and lifestyles has become one of the big trends in the hyperconsumption society. This again shows to what extent the model of distinction has become obsolete. Obviously this process of increasing medical awareness and obsession with health cannot be accounted for in terms of a symbolic struggle and pursuit of class distinctions.

The second observation is that contemporary validation of immediate gratification, escape and sensual pleasures is in line with the affirmation of a health and prevention culture: in other words, an anxious society diametrically opposed to a Dionysian culture. It is true that our values are hedonistic but our society is neither Dionysian nor dedicated to the delights of carpe diem.

THE OBSESSION WITH A BETTER LIFE

The age of hyperconsumption also sees the construction of a new culture of well-being and comfort. It is as though the level of comfort which was created in the 1950s is no longer adequate. A home is no longer just for sleeping in and protection from the weather: well-being is required at home. There is a real passion for home design which is evidenced by the success of home and garden magazines. People are devoting more and more time, money and love to home improvement, to be able to live in a welcoming, warm and harmonious environment. Modern well-being was technical, quantitative, functional and healthy; hypermodern well-being is qualitative, sensual and emotional, well groomed and individualized.

However, the culture of emotional well-being is not limited to the home and objects: it has acquired a relationship with the body. This can be seen first of all in the area of hygiene, care and beauty. Previously, washing was simply an activity intended to clean the body. Now it is no longer cleanliness which is being sold, but a global sense of multisensory, olfactory, tactile and aesthetic well-being. The growth in sensual well-being is seen in the increase in the number of activities linked to fitness, maintenance of the self and training: work-outs and aquarobics, cardio-fitness, yoga, all of this designed to relax us, banish stress and make us feel better. Added to which is the success of thalassotherapy, massage, saunas, Turkish baths and open-air hot tubs. There is also the tremendous development of board sports geared to sensory pleasure, bodily sensations and emotions linked to contact with nature. A culture of sensual and highly subjective well-being is essential in the hyperconsumption society.

Intimization, autonomization, sensualization: these do not, as such, mean the best of all possible consumer worlds. On the one hand, the hyperconsumer is reflective, he does his research and makes comparisons and he behaves more and more preventively. He favours quality and health. On the other hand, we observe a multitude of phenomena which are synonymous with excess, pathological ill-discipline and "out of control" behaviour. There is no shortage of examples: fashion victims, compulsive buying, drug addicts and addictive practices of all kinds. Anarchy in eating behaviour: bulimia and obesity are well-known examples. Expert commentators have spoken about the advent of an "entrepreneurial consumer", and of an "expert" consumer (Rochefort 1997). This is only half of the story. It is as much an unstructured or anomic consumer as an expert one. The relaxing of collective controls, hedonistic norms, high expectations of quality and liberal education all accompany consumerism and contribute to bringing about an individual detached from common ends and as often unable to resist outside temptation as internal compulsions. This is why one sees a whole host of excessive behaviours and pathological and compulsive consumption. On the one hand, a methodical consumer is developing; on the other hand, there is a chaotic consumer displaying a lack of self-control and subjective impotence.

CONSUMER-WORLD

To arrive at the modern consumer, the individual had to be separated from norms of identity and location; the guilt had to be taken out of the desire to spend; the saving ethic had to be devalued; and home produce had to be belittled in favour of retail goods. In other words, inculcate new lifestyles whilst eliminating any remaining social habits resisting retail consumption. It is by removing these traditional behaviours and tearing down puritanical norms that planet mass-consumption was formed. Credit, department stores and advertising all led to the development of a new moral code and a new psychology. Phase I and II were the training ground for modern mass-consumption.

This context is no longer ours. There are, in fact, no longer norms and attitudes fundamentally opposed to the expansion of monetized needs. All these inhibitions and archaic bastions have been eliminated. All that remains are consumer legitimacy, incentives for instant pleasure, feel-good anthems and self-preservation. The first big cycle of rationalization and modernization has finished. There are no more traditional norms to abolish. Everyone is already trained, socialized and fed by unlimited consumption. The era of hyperconsumption began when old cultural resistance crumbled and with the disappearance of the cultural stops to the taste for novelty and the commercialization of necessities. Finally, hyperconsumption grows when modern consumerism does not unfold on the basis of an antinomian culture. It is no longer cultural resistance to consumption which causes problems but the escape from it, the spiral of consumption no longer coming up against a radically antagonistic model.

In other words, phase III is that state of society where the hedonistic reference point asserts itself as self-evident, where advertising, leisure activities and constant change in the framework of life have become part of everyday life. In reality, there is no longer effective, institutionalized opposition to consumerism. This is why I believe we can talk about hyperconsumption. Engagement in collective combat, revolution, cultural traditions, all of these have stopped being obstacles to the triumph of consumerism.

Even religion no longer constitutes a counter-force to the reign of what I call the consumer-world, a restructuring of existence by the spirit of consumerism. The church no longer emphasizes the idea of mortal sin and no longer really glorifies sacrifice and renouncing the joys of worldly pleasure. Christianity has come round to the ideal of happiness on earth. At the same time, on the basis that large religious institutions have weak organizational abilities, the massive trend is towards individualizing belief and action accordingly, and to affect and relativize religious beliefs. In this sense, even spirituality is so to speak "self-service" when expressing emotions and feelings, and in the quests spurred on by the desire for a better life. It is increasingly the subject's quest for psychological realization that is as much at the centre of the experiences of actual believers as new religions without God. Of course, believing is not consuming. The spirit of faith is not to be confused with the pragmatic and changing spirit of consumerism. All the same, contemporary reaffirmation of spirituality by believers is marked by the same traits that define the turbo-consumer experience: temporary participation, à la carte behaviour and the primacy of subjective well-being and emotional experience. From this point of view it could be said that the contemporary religious individual appears more as a continuation of the hyperconsumer by other means than a negation. Once again, it is clearly not about assimilating spirituality with consumerism, but simply about seeing the principles of hyperconsumption penetrate into the very heart of the religious soul.

The dynamics of the consumer-world do not stop there. All major social institutions have been reformed, reviewed and revised by turbo-consumerism. The list is long.

Take the couple, for example. They are becoming deinstitutionalized. They are becoming more insular and more unstable, as witnessed by the decline in the number of marriages, the increase in divorce rates and the precariousness of relationships. The family no longer completely escapes the culture of consumption, the temporary, individualized and contractual strategies of the consumer subject. This is even more obvious in the political arena. The electorate is becoming more volatile, with a large number of citizens displaying a floating allegiance to political parties. They change camps according to the nature of and the stakes in the election, and they make their voting decision at the last minute—so great is their indecision. Finally, the strategic vote from the consumer tends to replace the class vote of former times. Relationships with trade unions express the same logic. Here again it is a temporary and distanced relationship which wins through: the member has become simply a subscriber. A utilitarian style of relationship has replaced the sense of identity which until a short while ago used to prevail in the trade union world.

The issue is to know where the frontiers of the consumer world need to be set at a time when the spirit of consumerism is invading nearly all areas of life: family, religion, politics, Europe; but also sexuality, procreation, school. The principles of self-service: mobility, tenuous relationships, utilitarian exploitation by institutions and cost and benefit calculations by the individual are now in one way or another essential in nearly all areas of life. That is to say that the market has become, second to economic transactions of course, the model and the vision which governs all—or nearly all—social relationships.

Everywhere the market arena has extended into areas which were previously off-bounds. Everywhere the logic of personal options is becoming widespread—temporary and contractual relationships, the client perspective, search for the best mix of quality and price and the maximization of advantages. Phase III can thereby be defined as the society in which the ethos of consumerism restructures more and more arenas, including those outside monetary transactions.

A WORLD WITHOUT VALUE?

It is well known that with the triumph of the market society, new anxieties and new questions arise. With what some call market totalitarianism, is there not a big risk that we will see sociability, social confidence and finally all the nobler values and even feelings which define humanity waste away?

I do not share this pessimism, because, it is worth stressing, the growth of techno-commercial dynamism is not absolute. Moral decadence, so much talked about, is a myth. A strong and broad consensus supports liberal modernity on ethical and political foundations. Protests and ethical commitments are increasing, even in consumption: it is particularly noticeable with fair trade and solidarity products. Partnerships and ethical commitments are also increasing; networks of solidarity and donations to victims (the last tsunami is proof) have never been so great; and human rights groups are seeing unprecedented membership. All values, all reference points for the senses (justice, truth, love, friendship), all of these have not disappeared. The hyperconsumption society is not only about supremacy of the market and pleasure for the individual. It is coupled with the reinforcement of a common core of democratic, humanist values. For this reason we can be relatively optimistic about the future: whatever the current impasses, there is still a self-critical and self-correcting voice in our democracies. The age of hyperconsumption is not closed, it is not locked away and it is not devoted to exponential nihilism.

We need to stop demonizing the world of hyperconsumption. It has lots of faults but it has not destroyed morals, altruism, resentment or the value of love. In films, songs, novels, the press, advertising, indeed everywhere, love is presented as an ideal, the quintessence of life and the most emblematic image of happiness. The couple has never been based on this sentiment. What is of higher priority or more imperative to us than our children and the love we have for our children? We not only "consume" love in the media, we believe in it: it is recognized as a pre-eminent value. That is the good news: not everything has been taken over by exchange value and commercial consumption. The hyperconsumption society is not integral nihilism, nor does individualism proscribe having values or affectionate relationships with others.

THE FUTURE OF HYPERCONSUMPTION

However intense the criticism against it, the hyperconsumption society is only at its beginning. The most probable scenario in an era which offers no credible alternative is its growth on a planetary scale. Of course, the degradation of the ecosphere, our limited natural resources and climate change necessitates the introduction of production methods and consumerism which are less aggressive and damaging to nature. However, the process needed for a more frugal economy does not mean the end of the hyperconsumption society, that is, a society dominated by unbounded commercialization to satisfy needs. In the longer term, an alternative future is possible, which would be marked, on the one hand, by a decrease in the consumption of fossil fuels, and on the other hand, by an increase in renewable and clean energy. This change should be accelerated by the triple impetus of technological progress, social conscience and state regulation. This is a process to enable reconciling economic development with environmental protection. Under these conditions, the energy and ecological deficits which we are facing could enable sustainable development in the hyperconsumption society rather than be the cause of its destruction. This evolution is equally viable because of the demand for consumer services (in some countries they already account for half of household expenditure) which is a type of consumption that is more sparing with energy and uses less natural resources.

Consumer passions and the general commercialization of lifestyles are gradually spreading everywhere: health, fertility, leisure, games, transport, culture, education, communication, information and the protection of nature: they are all needs which will tomorrow be annexed by marketing logic, and which will begin phase III worldwide. Neither the protests of ecologists nor newer, more frugal modes of consumption nor "alternative consumers" will be able to stop the approaching omni-merchandising of lifestyles. Tomorrow, inevitably, all the countries on the planet will be bundled into the era of world consumerism.

REFERENCES

Barber, Benjamin R. 2007. *Consumed. How Markets Corrupt Children, Infantilize Adults and Swallow Citizens Whole*. New York: W. W. Norton.
Bourdieu, Pierre. 1979. *La distinction*. Paris: Editions de Minuit.
Debord, Guy. 1967. *La Sociéte du spectacle*. Paris: Buchet/Castel.
Dujarier, Marie-Anne. 2008. *Le travail du consommateur*. Paris: La Découverte.
Luttwak, Edward. 1998. *Turbo-capitalism*. London: Weidenfeld and Nicolson.
Rochefort, Robert. 1997. *Le consommateur entrepreneur*. Paris: Odile Jacob.
Veblen, Thorstein. 1899. *The Theory of the Leisure Class*. New York: Macmillan.

3 Consumption in an Age of Globalization and Localization

Richard Wilk

I am lucky enough to live in a beautiful patch of woods in southern Indiana and one of my great pleasures is to watch the wildlife and forest outside my office window. The weather can change quickly here—native Hoosiers say that if you don't like the weather now, just wait an hour or two. I can also watch the regular cycle of seasons, which vary a bit in timing from year to year. But having lived in the same house for twenty years, I can also see a third kind of change—winters are getting warmer, there is less snow and summer is coming earlier, symptoms of global climate change. Systems theorists have names for these three kinds of change. Weather is relatively random noise, produced by a chaotic atmosphere. Seasons are cyclic fluctuations around a mean, driven by positive and negative feedback. And global warming is a secular change, a transformation of the underlying forces which drive the whole system.

The economy has exactly the same three levels. Markets fluctuate all the time in unpredictable ways, following a longer-term cycle of recession and recovery, growth driven by rising profits, more employment and greater investment and then contraction. But what about the equivalent of climate change? This would have to be our expectation that the long-term trend of the economy is always going to be growth, that whatever happens in the short term, the next generation is going to see a bigger economy, higher incomes and more consumption.

Markets—even the most complex—are fundamentally products of our beliefs, like our confidence in the soundness of money, our trust in the honesty and solidity of institutions and our expectations for the future. This is why past recessions, and even the Great Depression, have always been followed by recovery and new periods of growth and abundance. Recession creates fertile ground for recovery because people defer their expectations, expecting that the economy will recover. Consumers feel that they deserve to increase their standard of living after they have had to tighten their belts or even sell off assets during a long recession. This belief in progress and long-term growth is so basic and fundamental to the way we think about our world that we rarely question it. Every aspect of consumer capitalism is premised on the prospect of continuing growth, higher rates of consumption, so we perceive any period of "slowdown" or contraction as an exception, a stutter in what is otherwise a continuing trend.

What we need is a secular change in direction, the economic equivalent of climate change. The past two generations have been raised with a more global consciousness, an understanding that the world has limits, and that growth cannot go on forever without consequences. Everything people see and hear in the news about global warming and peak oil just confirms that things cannot keep growing indefinitely, and when peoples' beliefs change, this could have a concrete affect on the economy. About 88 per cent of my freshman anthropology students last year believed that "protecting the environment is going to require us to make major changes in the way we live". Study after study show declining numbers of Americans believing that their children will be more prosperous and live in a better world. So can this recession be different, signaling not just another cycle, but a real change in direction?

THE GLOBAL REACH OF CONSUMER CULTURE

One of the images I often use in teaching my students about globalization and consumer culture is the logo of a large US paint company called Sherwin-Williams. It shows the planet Earth, and above it a tipping can of red paint. The paint is pouring out of the can onto the top of the Earth and is coating the planet, before dripping off into space below. This simple graphic provokes us to think about how and why consumer culture has become a global phenomenon. Is it really an unstoppable and natural force, like gravity pulling paint down as it spills? And is the spreading consumer culture really like a coat of uniform paint, a single colour which is flooding the vast diversity of the earth's cultures and places, replacing them with shiny uniformity? If this is so, the prospect of stopping the environmental catastrophes of climate change, driven by the rapid pace in increasing levels of consumption, seem slim.

It is common to think of consumerism as a kind of communicable disease, and globalization as an epidemic. These metaphors break down, however, when we ask more pointed questions. Exactly what do we mean by "consumer culture"? And how have modern high-material and energy-intensive forms of consumption spread around the planet? The answers to these questions show that consumer culture is not uniform, and that it has a long and complicated history. Far from spreading like paint, it has moved according to human design and social principles we are just beginning to comprehend. It is not a force of nature, but the product of human decisions and behaviour, and that means that it can be changed and influenced by human action—even at the global scale.

If the "Sherwin-Williams" theory really is wrong, it cannot give us any help in thinking about alternatives, because we need to really understand a phenomenon in order to change it. With a better understanding of what consumer globalization really is, and how it works, we can return to the problem of epidemiology—how it spreads, what symptoms it causes and how we might think about changing, or at least channeling, that spread into more beneficial directions, for individuals, cultures, nations and the planet as a whole. Though these issues and problems are vast and complex, they are also supremely important, because the growth of consumer culture, its spread and intensification in so many places around the world is the basic impetus which is driving the unsustainable use of energy and materials, and the pollution which is the cause of global climate change.

CAUSES

Philosophers have pondered the reasons why people in one culture might want to buy things from afar instead of their native local products. Even in classical antiquity, schools like the Stoics argued that people would be much happier if they led simple lives and were satisfied with the natural products of their own land. The following quotes illustrate the main positions in the debate about why people so rarely follow the Stoics' advice:

> Human desires are insatiable . . . this gives rise to constant discontent in the human mind and a weariness of the things they possess; and it is this which makes them decry the present, praise the past, and desire the future. (Machiavelli, as quoted in Burnham 1968)

> In most nations, foreign trade has preceded any refinement of home manufactures and given birth to domestic luxury. The temptation is stronger to make use of foreign commodities which are ready for use and which are entirely new to us, than to make improvements on any domestic commodity, which always advance by slow degrees, and never affect us by their novelty. (Hume 1752, discussed in Wilks 1979, 7)

> The bourgeoisie, by the rapid improvement of all instruments of production, by the immensely facilitated means of communication, draws all, even the most barbarian, nations into civilization. The cheap prices of its commodities are the heavy artillery with which it batters down all Chinese walls, with which it forces the barbarians' intensely obdurate hatred of foreigners to capitulate. (Marx and Engels 1848/1955, 53)

> As native subsistence systems undergo pressure because of sedentation and encroachment, people respond by intensifying subsistence production and adopting different technologies in order to do so. . . . The availability of steel axes, knives and machetes, and firearms is especially important. These are more efficient and durable than their handmade

counterparts . . . "luxury" items . . . may be a way of conserving capital because such items as radios, wristwatches and handguns hold their value better than cash . . . Thus, we think that while industrial goods may have an intrinsic allure to native peoples, practical requirement brought about by sedentation, encroachment, colonization, and subsistence intensification are of greater importance. (Gross et al. 1979, 1048–1049)

These basic arguments, and variations on them, are founded in different definitions of human nature and world history. Machiavelli tells us that the desire for consumer goods flows from the inherent acquisitiveness of all human beings. Quickly bored by what they have, they are always on the lookout for a new luxury or product which will raise their status. Hume believed that people are novelty-seekers, always thinking that foreign goods are better than their own. Marx and Engels thought that capitalists used cheap goods to undercut and destroy rival systems of production, and their followers have elaborated ideas about the ways advertising and marketing seduce people into giving up their own freedom in order to get cheap imports (Adorno 1991). Gross and his co-authors say that people want "better" goods—more convenient, cheaper, more durable and technologically advanced, in other words, the products of more advanced civilizations.

Machiavelli and Hume were writing before we knew very much about human history and the wide variety of different cultures in the world, so it made a lot of sense to them to attribute the consumer cultures they saw in Europe to a universal human nature. By the time Marx and Engels were writing, it was clear that in many human cultures, over long periods of history and pre-history, people were not insatiable and had no great appetite for imported goods, so the cause could not be a universal natural urge. People began to ask instead why European consumer goods were so widely attractive, so that they became the cutting edge of the English, French, Portuguese, Dutch and Spanish colonial empires as they spread around the world. Were they a part of a system of coercion and subversion, or a blessing which brought health, convenience and well-being? These very same questions and issues continue to dominate debates about global consumer culture today.

SYMBOLS

The late twentieth century saw an unprecedented economic interdependence among nations. Local self-sufficiency and economic autonomy seem to be extinct in most of the world. Whole nations have become dependent on imported foods, imported clothes, imported experts, foreign television programs—even imported religions and educational systems. Countries like Nigeria, which used to produce their own food and export a surplus, now depend on imported wheat, since bread has become a national staple. They pay for wheat with petrodollars, while Nigerian farmers, now unemployed, flee to crowded and impoverished cities (Andrae and Beckman 1985).

Countries that want to exclude foreign culture and develop autonomously are dwindling in number—who is left besides pathetic cripples like Myanmar and North Korea? The world is littered with failed attempts to exclude consumer culture. Under socialism, bedraggled Albanians hauled their last sheep across the border into Greece to trade for Korean TV sets and stereos. Cubans express deep pride in their urban gardens and other attempts at self-sufficiency, while driving ancient vehicles around decaying cities, watching their children plot to escape to Miami. It does indeed look like global consumer culture is an unstoppable force.

The most prominent symbols of globalization today are probably the golden arches of McDonald's and the Coca-Cola logo. The *Economist* has even created a "McDonald's index", which compares the cost of living around the world by looking at the local price of a Big Mac, which became a kind of universal currency. Most people see this spread of consumer culture as something recent, superficial and destructive to "authentic" local, national and folk culture. After all, consumer culture represents uniformity, the spread of Western goods, and therefore a loss of the rich diversity of local tradition. The prospect of global "monoculture" has led many to think that the greatest problem of globalization is finding a way to preserve cultural diversity, saving and protecting traditions, communities and ways of life from the onslaught of mass culture and Westernization (Friedman 1990, 1992).

Others who accept the inevitability of globalization have sought ways to compromise and reduce its impact, building movements to adapt and maintain local and ethnic traditions of food, music, dance and language. The appreciation of cultural diversity runs very deep in Western culture, a legacy, perhaps, of the nineteenth-century German Romantic tradition that was so important in the founding of the social sciences in great universities. The idea that advertising and uncontrolled capitalism destroys peoples' culture and "seduces" them into buying things they do not need also goes very deep into liberal political thinking in the West (Baran 1957).

The alarm over the global spread of a uniform culture is no longer confined to the West. In most countries around the world people on both the Left and the Right are afraid that their traditional and local ways of life are under assault, being polluted or displaced by consumer goods and cultural values that come from the West, and particularly from the United States. On the other side, authors like the conservative Samuel Huntington (1996) favour the spread of American culture and values, and see it as the only viable alternative to a world of fundamentalism and the chaotic clashes between traditional cultures. On the Right, the spread of consumption is usually seen as a sign of the success of capitalism in improving everyone's way of life, bringing the cornucopia of prosperity to people whose "traditional culture" created poverty and ignorance.

HISTORY

All of these ideas about the spread of consumer culture are founded on the assumption that globalization is something new. They imply that until recently, the world was composed of isolated islands of local culture, now threatened by an onrushing wall of multinational corporations, fast food, high technology, tourism and credit cards. History should give us pause before we accept this idea.

New research tells us that mass-consumption has been "global" for hundreds of years. The invention of steamships, railroads, telegraphs and telephones have each engendered an industry of pundits ready to tell the public that the world is becoming a global village, connected with unprecedented ease and speed. Now we are told that the Internet changes everything, just as our ancestors were warned that the speed of travel on steam railroads was shrinking the world and transforming the experience of space and time.

Archaeologists and historians now find that there were many long-distance movements and exchanges of ideas, objects, languages and people during the last five thousand years. Periods of isolation and stability are exceptional, harder to explain than normal periods of change. Small, isolated static cultures are comparatively rare. Anthropologists have had to admit that many of the "timeless" traditional cultures they used to write about were not isolated at all (Wolf 1982). Actually some of the most "traditional"-looking places had hundreds of years of history of contact and commerce with great empires and colonial governments.

This discovery has a profound effect on our understanding of globalization. It suggests that there may not be a basic incompatibility between being global and being local. In the past, even when conquered, colonized, forcibly resettled, taken as slaves and caught up in terrible epidemics and invasions, people have found ways to create and maintain distinctive local cultures, languages, traditions and beliefs. Whatever the homogenizing forces, new local languages and forms of expression grow again and again, suggesting that whatever the global milieu, we are happiest when we are embedded in communities we know well.

Of course, we also know of hundreds of cultures that have been totally destroyed and crushed, that have disappeared entirely either by accident or design. Thousands of cultures are known only from scattered historical records and through archaeology, while their languages and customs are gone forever. If we have any concern for the maintenance of cultural diversity today, we really need to know what has enabled some cultures to survive earlier waves of globalization. How does a culture adapt and persist? If consumer culture has already spread (like the red paint) over the world, how can we measure and understand its changing nature, its intensity and diversity?

THEORY

The idea that there are only two possibilities—either preservation of "traditional" culture or global monoculture, has given way during the last few decades to more complex concepts like *resistance, hybridity* and *appropriation*. Each has various shadings, but they build on three basic concepts about what happens when local culture encounters globalization. Resistance means rejection, either through direct action like burning down a McDonald's restaurant, or indirectly by limiting the amount of foreign programming shown on television, or arresting women who wear "Western" dress. While most people in North America and Europe think that in the long run, when it comes to consumer culture, "resistance is futile", there are millions, perhaps billions, of people who have not given up the fight, for whom globalization is a great evil. Of course fighting globalization usually means adopting the tools and technologies of mass media and the Internet, which can end up causing the very corruption they were meant to stop.

Instead of a grey world of cultural uniformity, Ulf Hannerz (1987) sees a process of "creolization" that constantly throws out creative new mixtures of local cultures. Hybrid cultures emerge at the margins and among mobile cosmopolitans, and a world where migration is common leads people to move between and among cultures (Pieterse 2003). This is a world where reggae emerges from the slums of Kingston and mixes with hundreds of other local musical styles in a creative ferment. Chinese entrepreneurs in Guangdong take the McDonald's fast-food concept and blend several Chinese regional cuisines to create a successful chain like the California Beef Noodle King, which is now expanding into Europe. Hannerz's idea of creolization allows people to move through a global marketplace without losing their cultural identities; they just have to keep up the creative acts that, says Hannerz, lie at the core of all cultures, even ones that seem highly traditional. Instead of nostalgia for the past, we should welcome all kinds of new traditions.

While creolization is a free process of mixture, appropriation is really a reversal of the direction of globalization. Instead of Western culture absorbing and destroying local cultures, through appropriation a local culture absorbs and then neutralizes the invader by transforming it into something familiar. Many scholars, for example, have argued that Japanese culture has been able, for thousands of years, to take in food, dance, religion and a host of other cultural elements from abroad without losing its continuity and identity. Baseball did not turn the Japanese into Americans, but instead baseball became Japanese (Whiting 1977). Similarly, Americans have adopted and appropriated sushi without becoming culturally more Japanese. For some people, this argument comes down to an issue of power; only the dominant cultures in the global arena are capable of choosing and appropriating whatever they want from the cultures of the world. Other people inevitably suffer cultural imperialism, since they do not have the economic or cultural power to resist the flow of foreign products and culture.

My own discipline of anthropology has a long tradition of studying cultural appropriation, celebrating the power of all cultures to take the foreign and make it local. Ralph Linton's classic essay "One Hundred Percent American" makes the point that everything that is now considered typically American, from apple pie to pajamas, came from some other place (Linton 1936). They became "American" by appropriation and domestication into existing rituals and cultural practices. More recently, James Watson's collection *Golden Arches East* demonstrates how the McDonald's restaurant has been changed and transformed as it has been adapted by consumers in East Asia (Watson 1997). While Korean and Taiwanese culture have been changed by the arrival of McDonald's, they have also changed McDonald's in ways that make it more appropriate and local. In the business world, this process of local adaptation of global consumer goods is now called "glocalization", and has been adopted as a market strategy by many multinational corporations.

THE PERSISTENCE OF THE LOCAL

In 1985 an American English teacher named Will Baker took twenty high school students on a tour of urban areas of twelve countries around the world in search of the "Global Teenager" (Baker 1989). They expected to find that teenagers were becoming more alike—attuned to the rhythms of MTV, more materialistic, interested in fashion, sex and global media, and alienated from their families and nations. In their interviews and surveys Baker's students did find that teenagers were knowledgeable and sophisticated about music, global brands and consumer culture. But Baker's students were surprised to find that everywhere teenagers put their family and country first. They were patriotic and religious and showed no sign of giving up their own cultures and languages at the same time that they wanted more consumer goods and a higher standard of living.

When Baker completed his study, global religious fundamentalism was already a rising force, and many of his respondents expressed the idea that community and especially religious values were more important than wealth or owning consumer goods. Fundamentalist leaders have a vested interest in portraying a world in which spiritual values and material desires are completely opposed and incompatible, and evangelists of "modernity" in the US and Europe have been equally strident in asserting that people will have to give up their parochial local culture if they want to enjoy the economic bounty of global capitalism and democracy.

Instead, as I suggested earlier, a long-term analysis shows us that there is nothing incompatible between having local culture and being involved in global commerce. It is too easy to portray the world's people as simple victims of an all-powerful mass media which is forcing consumer culture on them. Advertising does have huge power and influence, and consumption can lead people into endless cycles of debt and unhappy forms of materialism, where the pursuit of wealth substitutes for social life, spiritual growth and other forms of pleasure. But in practice it is very hard to separate "good" consumption from "bad"; why should visiting museums to view fine art be inherently better than going to amusement parks? Is a collection of old master paintings less materialistic than a box of comics or a garage full of motorcycles? Why should a fast-food hamburger be censured, while a plate of fresh foie gras in a gourmet restaurant is praised? Recent studies show that eating centrally prepared and highly processed food is much more energy-efficient than making home-cooked meals from fresh ingredients purchased individually in a variety of stores. What yardstick do we use to measure the negative aspects of consumption—energy saving, purity, justice, local flavour, organic?

Real people are caught somewhere in between the extremes of the local and global. They are influenced by what they see in mass media, but they also value their traditions and communities. They are subject to powerful and often oppressive institutions, corporations, employers and governments that want to manipulate them, but they also resist and scheme and find ways to exercise freedom and autonomy. Consumer culture is not a single uniform thing, a coherent force with a specific group of agents behind it. It is instead messy, accidental and contingent, in a constant state of improvisation, collapse and renewal. It is also a growth machine, ever on the search for cheaper labour, new products and services and new markets.

Over and over again in world history, we have seen how the engine of consumer capitalism takes societies and turns them inside out, making them into consumer cultures. Sugar, tobacco and alcohol are usually the first "treats" offered by traders and travelers, and then once the local ecology and productive system has become thoroughly dependent on these addictive products, people are exposed to more (Jankowiak and Bradburd 2007). Cajoled by doctors who tell them they need to buy soap and medicines, their children educated by foreigners, people slowly lose their economic autonomy and the sense that their own culture provides all the values they need to survive and prosper. By the time they are aware of the true cost of what they are buying—everything from rotting teeth and drug abuse to collapsing families—it is too late because they have lost control of their land, water and other vital resources.

These billions of people move onward, deeper into consumer culture, with the goal and promise of prosperity before them. As I argued earlier, their ideals and visions of the future are not uniform. People continue to want very different things, but they also seek what they consider to be basic requirements; food security, owning a dwelling, having some means of transportation, health care and education for children, electricity and running water, household furnishings and a group of basic appliances usually including a stove, lighting, a television and refrigeration.

Unfortunately, we have also found that when you add advertising and social competition to these relatively simple desires, the process of growth in peoples' wants rarely stops. It is one of the great failures of social science in the last fifty years that we still do not know why some people seem to be happy with a stable level of consumer culture and others get on an endless cycle where wants become needs, and every new acquisition or activity just requires more consumption, in an endless upward spiral (Schor 1998; Shove 2003; Sanne 1995).

This might all be of academic interest, a story about events taking place among exotic people in far-off places, if not for the forces of economic globalization which have drawn us all into a single global marketplace, while also making us aware of the limits of the global environment. This raises the urgent problems of the limits of our knowledge about how consumer culture connects people with each other across the earth. Once we can envision a single global consumer culture, then we can think about the issue of equality, about how that consumer culture can and will be distributed among the ten billion souls who will soon share it.

MAKING CONNECTIONS

Recent figures say that the average item of food (out of the thirty thousand in the average North American supermarket) has traveled fifteen hundred to two thousand miles to reach your plate. This exhausting physical journey is nothing compared to the social and cultural distances crossed by all the different parts of complex machines like computers, air conditioners and automobiles. The global commodity chains that lead from the farms and factories to millions of shops and then billions of homes are the largest and most complex artifact ever constructed by human beings. Given their size and complexity, it is no wonder that nobody can really perceive or understand more than tiny bits and pieces, single threads in a huge bundle of cloth that covers a whole planet.

Because the consumer cannot see the machinery, the bounty of the world appears almost as an act of magic. It takes real detective work to discover the origins of even the most mundane products, a can of soda or a pair of shoes (see Ryan and Durning 1997; Cook et al. 2004). In many cases the task is impossible, because companies do not keep records, there are too many sources or the sources are actively concealed. Months of research may be required to find the pedigree of a single jar of pickles.

A global perspective on trade and the sources of goods raises many concerns. The length and complexity of modern consumer supply chains make it particularly hard to trace the environmental costs of making things, carrying them around the world and then disposing of them, over even more distances. Thomas Princen (2002) has recently developed two concepts, *shading* and *distancing*, which point to the important role of corporations and advertisers in blocking or altering the information about goods which reaches the buyer. Princen's goal is to show how trade can sever the feedback connections between consumption and production, so that signals about environmental or social damage caused by production are blocked from consumers and do not figure into the market price of things we buy.

Princen uses the term *shading* to refer to the process of slanting or highlighting certain kinds of information, particularly those which shift attention away from externalized costs. Shading highlights benefits and minimizes costs, sometimes by shifting the costs onto another party, or measuring them only in the short term. For example, Chiquita's plantation-produced bananas are cheap and they contribute export earnings to Honduras, Ecuador and other Latin American countries which desperately need the foreign exchange. On the other hand, the cheapness of these bananas is driving thousands of small farmers in eastern Caribbean islands like Dominica out of business, and local government agencies or international donors will have to pay the costs of helping those farmers find new occupations, aiding the devastated economies of the islands. And in the long term, island bananas are sustainably produced using rainfall, hand labour, few chemical inputs and long-term soil conservation methods. The low price of plantation bananas is based on subsidized cheap fuels and chemicals, starvation-level wages for non-unionized workers and short-term agricultural practices based on limited genetic diversity and intensive use of soils, which leads to crop disease and clearing new areas of rainforest.

Shading conceals the illegal or semi-legal shady practices of adulteration, dumping and evasion of quality regulations by highlighting prominent and visible advantages. So, for example, Wal-Mart is shading when it trumpets low prices and latest styles, while the real costs of cheap or attractive products are never totaled up. By subcontracting out production, the large firm evades any responsibility for the illegal activities involved in making what they sell. When they do not pay for health insurance for their workers, they force local and federal governments to cover the costs of emergency care when those workers finally end up in the hospital. The farmworkers who picked the green beans may have been illegally exposed to pesticides and penalized for taking bathroom breaks, but the vendor has a legal shield.

Shading also obscures the "true" costs of goods under the guise of normal business practices, technological efficiency, quality standards and fair commercial competition, which often promote unsustainable practices. According to Princen, many forms of competition in the marketplace which favour short-term profits over long-term stability, or domination of markets by a single large company, inevitably lead to long-term environmental damage and reduce sustainability.

Distancing is simply the separation of consumers from producers—when people buy products from a local farmer or factory, they may well know some of the workers or the managers. If there are pollution issues in a nearby river, it will be reported in the news and widely discussed. A bad smell hovering over a building will raise obvious questions. This kind of information is completely lost when you buy anonymous products from distant sources in a hypermarket or mall.

Distance also conceals aggregated effects. One jar of salmon caviar from the shelf does little damage to the huge spawning runs of the Pacific coastal rivers of Russia, but thousands of individual purchases together can entirely wipe out a whole species. Because the purchases are spread out over a wide area, no individual sees overconsumption taking place. At a distance it is easy to think that just one small portion of an expensive spice could hardly do any harm to the forest where it was gathered.

Imbalances in bargaining power are a more subtle form of distancing. For example, a manufacturer of exotic fruit-flavoured sodas can buy pine-apple concentrate from many companies in countries as diverse as Thailand, Costa Rica and the Philippines. This is why buyers often seek out and promote new areas of production, driving producers to compete with each other. To reduce their costs they might hire child workers or clear thousands of acres of mangrove forest or switch to a cheaper and more toxic insecticide. This in turn pushes the social and environmental costs of production even further away from the consumer, so they are even less likely to be seen or counted.

According to Princen, the more producers there are, and the more they are dispersed and separated from one another, the less accountability there will be. Each time a good changes hands, information is lost and account-ability is reduced. By the time a product has been processed, blended and packaged, its origins may have been completely lost. The industrial food-processing business demonstrates how all of these sequential distancing effects can wash products of their origins and turn them into anonymous and interchangeable substances, no more than industrial feedstocks. When I tried to trace the origins of the ingredients in a bottle of a fruit drink, the manufacturer confessed that they did not know the source of the "crystalline fructose sweetener" in any particular batch of bottles; they had several sup-pliers, none of whom could trace the source of the corn they started with.

Advertising, marketing and labeling are the final and often completely opaque barrier to consumers learning about the origins of products. A bottle of mineral water has a beautiful snow-capped mountain against a blue sky on the label, not an industrial well and reverse-osmosis plant. The gasoline that comes out of the pump at your local filling station has a major oil company brand, which tells you nothing of the dispossessed fishing families, polluted rainforests and other "externalized costs" of oil production. Green labels and fair trade products are a beginning, but why should it be up to consumers to try to penetrate the veil of misinforma-tion which keeps the whole chain of production, trade and disposal out of view (Hudson and Hudson 2003)? So far the international groups which are supposed to regulate trade, like the World Trade Organization, have been more concerned with promoting trade at any cost, and have made few efforts to measure and account for those costs. Very few organizations are tracking the way trade moves the costs and benefits of consumption around the world, much less helping protect environments and people so they do not become a "cost".

CONCLUSION—UNSPEAKABLE TRUTHS

The present global recession has put a damper on the growth of consumer culture in rich countries, though many large economies like China and Brazil continue to grow rapidly. The slowdown presents an opportunity to think about the role of growth in the economy and the importance of growth as a fundamental ideology of modern capitalist culture. I have discussed some of the reasons why, short of an economic collapse of unprecedented scale, the intensification of global consumer culture will continue, though in a diverse set of directions in many parts of the world. And because of various forms of distancing and shading, it is practically impossible to connect all the things we consume to their origins, to understand the full measure of their social and environmental costs. Because of the way global trade easily moves costs and benefits around the globe, no local cost-benefit equation can address the larger issues of sustainability. The price we pay for something online or in a shop does not really reflect its cost. So we cannot count on "market mechanisms" to solve our problems through the laws of supply and demand. Rising prices alone are not going to stop us from consuming the future; more fundamentally, the tools of neoclassical economics have proven to be more of a problem than a solution in approaching these systemic problems. The complications of this global economy also show us how that issues of equity, justice and sustainability are closely intertwined. National and local systems of law and government cannot deal with causes and effects which exist far away (Lofdahl 2002). International regimes which can really address these problems are still relatively ineffective (Diehl 2001).

Most environmental scientists say that we have already exceeded the carrying capacity of the world, that we are already causing significant and permanent damage that cannot be undone (Redclift 1996). Yet billions of people still hold onto the prospect that they will someday be able to buy a motorcycle or car, own a home, a TV set, a computer and some of the luxuries which have become "needs" in rich countries. Even with continuing technological progress, new sources of energy, more effective use of materials and more productive farming, the gap between what people want and expect and what the world can provide is growing, not closing. The distance between rich and poor is also growing on a global scale. The poorest billion are still living in total poverty, lacking property and possessions and living from day to day on scraps, tiny wages or unproductive land. There are enough resources on the planet for all of us to live at a very modest level of comfort, but only if resources are magically redistributed, an event which is hard to see happening.

Our political leaders would have us believe that we can "grow" our way out of these problems, and that prosperity will continue to spread indefinitely. The comparatively rich billion people who enjoy the comforts of consumer culture have been told that they do not have to make substantial sacrifices. By increasing efficiency, inventing cleaner technologies, making better use of energy and buying green products, the wolf can be kept from the door. But the mathematics don't really add up—even if we grow renewable energy production by 10 per cent per year, we will only be keeping up with rising demand, rather than reducing overall emissions (United States Energy Information Administration 2009). We now face the problem the failure of "win-win" solutions promising business as usual, that we can actually have a sustainable consumer culture which continues to give people the freedom to buy anything they can afford, to import and use goods that cause damage elsewhere (see Jackson 2009).

Instead in the next years the task will be to open public debate about truths which are more than *inconvenient*—they are presently *unspeakable*. A global economy within limits has to be built on a recognition that benefits in one place have costs in another. A truly global vision of consumer culture requires us to think about inequality and growth, poverty and standards of living, in new ways. Our challenge is to create the cultural climate in which ideas of moderation, of steady states and getting more from less will flourish. The signs are clear in nature—we cannot continue with business as usual.

REFERENCES

Adams, Laura. 2008. Globalization, Universalism, and Cultural Form. *Comparative Studies in Society and History* 50 (3): 614–640.

Adorno, Theodor W. 1991. *The Culture Industry: Selected Essays on Mass Culture.* London: Routledge.

Arnould, Eric, and Richard Wilk. 1984. Why Do the Natives Wear Adidas? *Advances in Consumer Research* 11:748–752.

Baker, Will. 1989. The Global Teenager. *Whole Earth Review* 65:2–35.

Baran, Paul. 1957. *The Political Economy of Growth.* New York: Monthly Review Press.

Burnham, John C. 1968. Historical Background for the Study of Personality. In *Handbook of Personality Theory and Research,* ed. Edgar Borgatta and William Lambert, 3–81. Chicago: Rand McNally and Co.

Cook, Ian, et al. 2004. Follow the Thing: Papaya. *Antipode* 36 (4): 642–664.

Diehl, Paul F. 2001. *The Politics of Global Governance: International Organizations in an Interdependent World.* Boulder, CO: Lynne Rienner Publishers.

Friedman, Jonathan. 1990. Being in the World: Globalization and Localization. *Theory, Culture and Society* 7:311–328.

———. 1992. The Past in the Future: History and the Politics of Identity. *American Anthropologist* 94 (4): 837–859.

Gross, Daniel, G. Eiten, N. Flowers, F. Leoi, M. Ritter and D. Werner. 1979. Ecology and Acculturation among Native Peoples of Central Brazil. *Science* 206:1043–1050.

Hannerz, Ulf. 1987. The World in Creolization. *Africa* 57 (4): 546–559.

Hartwick, Elaine. 2000. Toward a Geographical Politics of Consumption. *Environment and Planning A* 32:1177–1192.

Hobson, Kersty. 2003. Thinking Habits into Action: The Role of Knowledge and Process in Questioning Household Consumption Practices. *Local Environment* 8 (1): 95–112.

Hudson, Ian, and Mark Hudson. 2003. Removing the Veil?: Commodity Fetishism, Fair Trade and the Environment. *Organization and Environment* 16:413–430.

Huntington, Samuel P. 1996. *The Clash of Civilizations and the Remaking of World Order.* New York: Simon and Schuster.

Jackson, Tim 2009. *Prosperity without Growth? The Transition to a Sustainable Economy.* Commission on Sustainable Consumption.

Jankowiak, William, and Daniel Bradburd. 2007. *Drugs, Labor and Colonial Expansion.* Tucson: University of Arizona Press.

Linton, Ralph. 1936. *The Study of Man: An Introduction.* New York: D. Appleton-Century Company.

Lofdahl, Corey L. 2002. *Environmental Impacts of Globalization and Trade: A Systems Study.* Cambridge, MA: MIT Press.

Marx, Karl, and Friedrich Engels. 1848/1955. *The Communist Manifesto.* Ed. Samuel Beer. New York: Appleton-Century-Crofts.

Pieterse, Jan. 2003. *Globalization and Culture.* Lanham, MD: Rowman and Littlefield.

Princen, Thomas 2002. Distancing: Consumption and the Severing of Feedback. In *Confronting Consumption*, ed. T. Princen, Michael Maniates and Ken Conca, 103–132. Cambridge, MA: MIT Press.

Redclift, Michael. 1996. *Wasted: Counting the Costs of Global Consumption.* London: Earthscan Publications.

Ryan, John C., and Alan Thein Durning. 1997. *Stuff: The Secret Lives of Everyday Things.* Seattle: Northwest Environment Watch.

Sanne, Christer. 1995. The (Im)possibility of Sustainable Lifestyles. Conference proceedings, Ecology, Society, Economy, Université de Versailles, 23–25 May.

Schor, Juliet. 1998. *The Overspent American.* New York: Basic Books.

Shove, Elizabeth. 2003. *Comfort, Cleanliness and Convenience: The Social Organization of Normality.* Oxford: Berg.

United States Energy Information Administration. 2009. International Energy Outlook 2009. Report #: DOE/EIA-0484(2009). http://www.eia.doe.gov/oiaf/ieo/highlights.html.

Watson, James, ed. 1997. *Golden Arches East: McDonald's in East Asia.* Stanford, CA: Stanford University Press.

Whiting, Robert. 1977. *The Chrysanthemum and the Bat.* New York: Dodd, Mead, and Company.

Wilk, Richard. 2006. *Home Cooking in the Global Village: Caribbean Food from Buccaneers to Ecotourists.* Oxford: Berg Publishers.

———. 2007. Anchovy Sauce and Pickled Tripe: Exporting Civilized Food in the Colonial Atlantic World. In *Food Chains*, ed. Warren Belasco and Roger Horowitz. Philadelphia: University of Pennsylvania Press.

Wilks, Ivor. 1979. The Golden Stool and the Elephant Tail: An Essay on Wealth in Asante. *Research in Economic Anthropology* 2:1–36.

Wolf, Eric. 1982. *Europe and the People without History.* Berkeley: University of California Press.

4   Goods and Service Consumption in the Affluent Welfare State— Issues for the Future

Jan Owen Jansson

BACKGROUND AND MAIN QUESTION

Economics is the study of how supposedly insatiable wants can best be met, given that resources are scarce. As a number of basic wants are now approaching saturation, and further expansion of private consumption is increasingly spurred by "rivalry" rather than genuine needs (Layard 2005), it is high time to reconsider the conventional economics of consumer demand. This short chapter is just a start, probing into a vast new territory. On the basis of a brief description of long-term trends as well as more recent tendencies of private and public consumption development, the main challenges for an unconventional consumption policy are identified and discussed. Is the main idea of the welfare state necessarily counterproductive?

UNPRECEDENTED HIGH RATE OF ECONOMIC GROWTH AND RADICAL CHANGE IN THE COMPOSITION OF TOTAL CONSUMPTION OVER A CENTURY

The single most important economic development in the Western world during the last century is the high rate of growth of the output volumes of goods and services alike, which has been without parallel in all history of mankind. The fruits of the Industrial Revolution and all the great inventions during the eighteenth and nineteenth centuries were mainly reaped in the twentieth century, when technical progress accelerated. Real gross domestic product (GDP) increased nineteen times in Sweden, which taking the population increase into account means that GDP per capita has increased eleven times during the last century. This is almost twice as much as the development in the birth country of the Industrial Revolution (see Figure 4.1). Compared to the pace of the economic growth in the last two centuries, all other centuries were standing still.

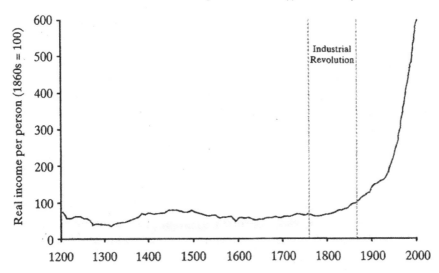

Figure 4.1 Real income per person in England, 1200–2000.
Source: Clark (2007).

The overriding positive effect of the great trend-break in the economic history of mankind is that most people in the developed countries now have enough to eat. The conquest of chronic malnutrition, which was virtually universal earlier, means, for example, that male manual workers in Britain on average have doubled their calorie intake from 858 kcal/day to 1783 kcal/day in two centuries (Fogel 1999).

A general feature of the transformation of society from poverty to prosperity is the thorough change in the composition of consumption from necessities to what was regarded as luxuries by ordinary people in times past and to many completely new goods and services. An interesting difference between the European so-called welfare states and the US is the more recent development regarding the basic welfare services. I will focus on this in the following discussion, since it reveals a difficult dilemma that most likely will be a main issue for the future.

WHAT REAL DIFFERENCE DOES USER FINANCING VERSUS TAX FINANCING MAKE?

Contrary to what one might have expected, and to what the designation "welfare state" indicates, medical care and education make up a substantially larger part of total consumption in the US than in the European welfare states. Among the EU member states the proportion of tax-financed consumption, that is, "public consumption", is the highest in Sweden (Sandelin 2009). If we look at the composition of private consumption, however, Sweden is close to the EU average. Therefore, a comparison of the long-term structural change in total consumption in the US and Sweden should be of general interest. What is the main difference in terms of real resource use for health and education between these two rich countries? The first has chosen a user-financing regime, the second a tax-financing regime for these services.

For the comparative study the data for the US are taken from Fogel (2000), where household consumption is traced back to 1875. A main purpose of this work was to show the growing importance of health and education. For this purpose Fogel expanded the family budget data by including also the tax-financed part of health and education services, which always have been appreciable, although never as important as the user-financed part in the US. It is the other way around in the Swedish case. For a comparison with Fogel's "expanded consumption" data, more easily available public consumption data have been supplemented by private consumption data for the small minority of user-financed health and education services in Sweden.[1]

As seen in Table 4.1 the basic material needs for food, clothing and shelter required 87 per cent of the household budget in both countries in 1875. In 1995 this share had gone down to 43 per cent in Sweden and to 30 per cent in the US. The main counterbalancing difference between the two countries is that health and education constituted a fifth in Sweden and a third in the US of total expanded consumption. And while this share has been stagnant for thirty years in Sweden, it is on the increase in the US (See Figure 4.4).

Table 4.1 Structural Change in Consumption in Sweden and the US between 1875 and 1995, Shares in Percentages

Main types of consumption	Sweden		USA		Long-run income elasticity
	1875	*1995*	*1875*	*1995*	
Food and drink	50	15	57	12	0.2
Clothes and shoes	10	3.5	14	4	0.3
Housing	27	24.5	16	14	0.7
Health and education	3	21.5	3	34	1.6
Other	10	35.5	10	36	1.1
TOTAL	100	100	100	100	1.0

Source for Sweden: Johansson (1967), Lindahl (1956), Krantz and Schön (2007); *Source for USA*: Fogel (2000).

The build-up of the system of welfare service provision in Sweden was relatively fast. It was made possible by a massive entry of women into the labour market and financed by successive tax rises from a tax rate (ratio of total taxes to GDP) of 20 per cent in 1950 to a tax rate of 50 per cent in 1980. Thereafter the tax rises have ceased. So has the increase in female participation in work outside the home,[2] as well as the increase in the welfare service provision. The "Swedish Welfare State" is no longer characterized by a comparatively large share of GDP going into health, education and care of children, elderly and disabled persons (HEC for short), but by the fact that HEC services are provided basically free of charge.

RECENT TENDENCIES IN THE ARCHETYPICAL WELFARE STATE

In Table 4.2 the more recent tendencies in total consumption in Sweden are indicated. Volume changes and prices changes are separated, which reveals that in real terms food and drink has increased slowly but somewhat more than other consumables. However, total expenditure on food and drink continues to make up a decreasing share of the household budget, since the nominal

Table 4.2   Total Consumption in Sweden: Composition and Recent Changes

Main types of consumption	Total expenditure 2006, billion SEK	Changes 1993–2006	
		volume	price
Food and drink	162	31%	8%
Other consumables	245	5%	46%
Dwellings	279	10%	26%
Other durables	250	122%	–11%
Private services	400	60%	30%
Total private (user-financed) consumption	1,336	38%	21%
Health	189	17%	60%
Education	183	16%	56%
Care	166	4%	63%
Collective services (Law and order, etc.)	224	–1%	39%
Total public (tax-financed) consumption	762	9%	55%
TOTAL CONSUMPTION	2,098	27%	38%

Source: National Accounts, Statistics Sweden.

prices of food and drink have increased considerably less than the general price level. The need for shelter, that is, a place to live, still requires a larger share of the household budget than all other household durables put together, but in real terms dwellings are the least expanding of the durable goods.

The two currently most expanding types of article in real terms are household durables and private services. The average price of the former has in fact decreased a little. Durables apart from dwellings now account for 19 per cent and private services for 30 per cent of total expenditure on private (user-financed) consumption in Sweden. Could the expanding demand for these two types of consumption be the main driving forces on the demand-side for economic growth in the future? Let us look closer at this development.

EXPANDING PRIVATE CONSUMPTION

Unsurprisingly, audio-visual equipment, telephones and computers account for the most striking real increase. Cell phones and computers have become everyone's possession in recent times.

A similar phenomenal increase was registered for cars in Europe in the 1950s and 1960s. Although total expenditure on car purchases has gone up by 155 per cent in real terms in Sweden from 1993 to 2006, the car fleet has expanded by just 15 per cent. It is mainly the quality of cars that has been upgraded. A sort of "number saturation" seems to be approaching; most purchases are replacements rather than new investments. This is typical of most durable goods in the process of maturity. In his presidential address to the American Economic Association, Robert Fogel stated that "we have

Table 4.3   Household Durables apart from Dwellings in Sweden: Composition and Recent Changes

Main types of household durable	Total expenditure, in 2006, billion SEK	Changes 1993–2006	
		Volume	Price
Clothes and shoes	67	52%	12%
Cars	50	155%	3%
Furniture	27	102%	11%
Audio-visual equipment, telephones, computers, etc.	26	800%	–78%
Boats, caravans, etc.	6	104%	52%
White goods	5	107%	6%

Source: National Accounts, Statistics Sweden.

become so rich that we are approaching saturation in the consumption not only of necessities, but of goods recently thought of as luxuries, or which were only dreams of science fiction during the first third of the twentieth century . . . On some items such as radios we seem to have reached supersaturation, since there is now more than one radio per ear (5.6 per household)" (1999, 6).

As regards private, user-financed consumer services, it should be observed that in a country like Sweden, where HEC is largely tax financed, there are no really dominant items. Total expenditure on any single type of service in Table 4.4 is not larger than 2 per cent of GDP. The rate of increase in telecom services is certainly impressive, but the total size (value) of this item is still less than a fourth of each one in the HEC trio. When the lower limit for inclusion in the list of Table 4.4 is set at two per mille of GDP, the currently much discussed "domestic service" is conspicuous by its absence. A hundred years ago domestic service was the main item among the consumer services. Tax breaks to stimulate cleaning firms as well as work by housepainters, carpenters, floor-layers, etcetera, which recently have been introduced in Sweden, seems to have had effect. The depressing fate of tailors, dressmakers, shoemakers, etcetera, in the present-day consumer society, where throw-away articles dominate, might be avoided.

Table 4.4   Private Services in Sweden: Composition and Recent Changes

| | Total expenditure in 2006, billion SEK | Changes 1993–2006 | |
User-financed services		Volume	Price
Restaurant, café, bar	66	50%	32%
Private health care	42	9%	137%
Bank services	42	49%	13%
Telecom	40	275%	–19%
Private child and eldercare, etc.	28	10%	133%
Transport services	27	30%	45%
Car maintenance and repair	25	32%	28%
Cultural entertainment	20	32%	66%
Sports entertainment	19	180%	32%
Hairdressing, beauty care	15	57%	45%
Insurance	15	–19%	55%
Package tours	14	51%	9%
Hotel and other lodgings	9	19%	63%
Repair of dwellings	6	113%	27%

Source: National Accounts, Statistics Sweden.

Recent tendencies indicate that besides telecom, sports entertainment and repair of dwellings are strong growth industries, showing volume increases which as percentages are many times greater than the rate of growth of total private consumption.

Tourism is supposed to be another strong growth industry, but its true size is notoriously difficult to measure. According to the Swedish national accounts, total expenditure on consumption abroad by Swedes was 59 billion SEK in 2006, and foreigners spent 69 billion SEK on consumption in Sweden. This is about the size of total expenditure by Swedes in Sweden on restaurant, bar and café services, that is about 2 per cent of GDP. Between 1993 and 2006 total expenditure by Swedish tourists abroad has roughly doubled in real terms, and that of foreign tourists in Sweden has increased two and a half times.

STAGNANT PUBLIC CONSUMPTION

The least expanding part of total consumption in Sweden in real terms is public tax-financed consumption, as seen in Table 4.2. The percentage increase in private user-financed consumption from 1993 to 2006 is more than six times greater than the increase in public consumption. Two underlying factors contribute to the relative stagnation of public consumption. Firstly, the relatively low rate of productivity growth for many services has resulted in ever-rising costs, a phenomenon known as Baumol's "cost-disease"; secondly, the tax financing applied in the welfare states has in more recent times led to a stagnant supply of resources to HEC.

Baumol identified the cost-disease when he investigated some vanishing culture services, as well as the "inner-city problem" in the US. Many municipal services are—like elsewhere—financed by local taxation in the US.

> The bulk of our municipal expenditures is devoted to education which offer very limited scope for cumulative increases in productivity. The same is true of police, of hospitals, of social services, and a variety of inspection services. Despite the use of the computer in medicine and in traffic planning, despite the use of closed circuit television and a variety of other devices there is no substitute for the personal attention of a physician or the presence of a police patrol in a crime-ridden neighbourhood.
>
> The upward trend in the real costs of municipal services cannot be expected to halt; inexorably and cumulatively, whether or not there is inflation, administrative mismanagement, or malfeasance, municipal budgets will almost certainly continue to mount in the future, just as they have been doing in the past. This is a trend for which no man and no group should be blamed, for there is nothing that can be done to stop it. (Baumol 1967, 423)

If you substitute public for "municipal", this description of the increasing problems of making ends meet fits the budget preparation at all levels of government in the welfare states today. Irrespective of how the economy as a whole is developing, the problems do not go away. Depending on how the public sector is organized, it may be the inner-city boroughs which are worst off in some countries, and in others, as in Sweden, it is the county councils, which are responsible for hospitals and public transport, and/or municipalities responsible for schools, child and eldercare.

The fact that public consumption finance is the main headache of local governments should not make us forget that there is also a positive factor at work. The relatively high income elasticity cited from the work by Robert Fogel (1999, 2000) in Table 4.1 is very noticeable in the US, where HEC is user financed to a large extent. It should also be mentioned that Fogel remarks in a footnote that "the elasticities are not adjusted for prices" (1999, 7). Since the prices of health and education services have increased significantly, the price-adjusted income elasticity is higher than shown for these expenditure categories, and it is the other way round for food, clothing and housing where relative prices have declined.

However, this high income elasticity cannot manifest itself in a regime where tax financing of HEC applies. Stagnant quality of HEC services in the welfare states is the main reason for undertaking the following consumption policy analysis, but it is not the only identifiable problem involved. Therefore, the policy analysis will start at a more general level by emphasizing the obvious, yet sometimes overlooked, fact that neither "economic growth" nor "export" (nor some other popular desiderata pointed out in economic policy discussion) should be the ultimate goal of the economy from a social point of view, but *consumption*. If the goal of maximum consumer want satisfaction were in conflict with the target of full employment, this goal should be modified. However, as is argued in the last section, there is no such conflict. On the contrary, the consumption policy advocated in the end would be perfectly compatible with an employment policy aimed at reducing unemployment among the young.

CONSUMPTION POLICY ANALYSIS: BASIC THEORY

In economics "resource allocation policy" is the technical term for what is discussed in the following sections. This marks the relevant policy area off from the policy areas addressed by "stabilization policy" and "income distribution policy". Here "consumption policy" is preferred because it more directly conveys that the ultimate goal is an allocation of the national resources that results in maximum want satisfaction.[3]

For an operationalization of these ideals, the pie chart in Figure 4.2 is helpful. The whole pie represents total expanded consumption, where do-it-yourself or household production ("self-service" for short in Figure 4.2) has been added to total consumption of goods and services produced in the formal economy and recorded in the national accounts. The size of the pieces of the pie roughly corresponds to the present total values of the constituent sub-sectors of the total expanded consumption.

Total service consumption besides self-service is first divided into two parts: private user-financed services (light grey area) and public, tax-financed services (non-shaded area). The latter is then divided into "pure public goods" and "merit goods" in accordance with standard terminology of economics.[4] The pure public goods include law and order, national defence, basic research, environmental enhancement and protection, and the merit goods are made up of HEC in the first place.

From a financial point of view, the salient feature of pure public goods is that they cannot be charged for; non-payers cannot be excluded from consuming the services concerned. Therefore, they have to be tax financed, if they are to be provided at all. Since "public goods" is a common designation of all services provided in the public sector, including "merit goods", pure public goods are from now on called "collective services". This indicates their main characteristic from an economic point of view: they are not divisible to meet the different demands of individual consumers, but are devoted to satisfying collective wants, for example, the want of a nation for lasting peace or the want of an urban community for fire protection.

Merit goods are "goods that are determined by government to be good for people regardless of whether people desire them for themselves or not" (Stiglitz and Walsh 2005, glossary A-6). Like the collective services they all prove to be immaterial services in practice. The salient feature of the welfare states is that the public choice resulting from a democratic political process

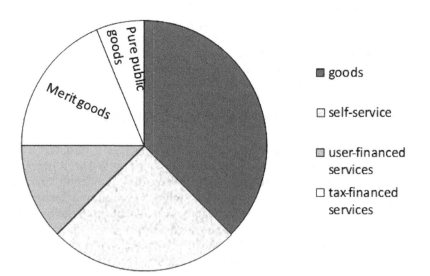

Figure 4.2 The expanded consumption.

is to provide HEC basically free of charge in spite of the fact that these services can be individually charged for; non-payers could be easily excluded if desired. From a welfare economic point of view this policy makes (individual) merit services and collective services similar in one important respect: they are consumed "in equal amounts". This is the nature of collective services, and is an acquired characteristic in the case of merit services by the political decision to provide the same (high) quality HEC services to all eligible consumers, basically free of charge. Then the driving force of rivalry in consumption is eliminated. This rivalry besets most private consumption and can make consumers' willingness to pay an exaggerated measure of the true benefit. This negative externality will be increasingly relevant in the affluent society, and it should strongly favour collective and merit services before private goods.

That the pie should be as large as possible, everybody could agree on. The difficulties in formulating a common goal appear when it comes to the allocation of resources between the sub-sectors given in Figure 4.2. Therefore, politicians often seem to think that a policy for maximum "economic growth" could make the difficult question of resource allocation superfluous. This is illusory. Economic growth cannot replace allocation policy (see further Jansson 2006). Maximizing the total value of the whole pie would be feasible and could be said to represent the optimal resource allocation, only if all goods and services were offered for prices equal to the marginal costs. In a mixed economy of the real world, however, the necessary conditions for a welfare maximum are approximately present for less than half the expanded consumption, at least in the welfare state. This lays a great responsibility on the consumption policymakers. The responsible politicians have to somehow decide and muster support for some trade-off between goods and services supplied on free markets and pure public and merit goods that are in the best public interest.

Taxation is the main policy instrument for consumption policy. Taxes are used in the first place for financing the public consumption, and secondly for private consumption demand management. In Sweden one-third of total consumption is tax financed, and tax breaks and surcharges are extensively used to stimulate or deter certain types of consumption, for example, alcohol and tobacco. Before the final discussion of public consumption policy, we will take a brief look at commodity tax policy vis-à-vis private user-financed services.

STIMULATION OF USER-FINANCED SERVICES

There are other allocation problems in the economy besides the provision of collective and merit goods, less fundamental perhaps, but tricky enough, in particular the problem due to the growing self-service sector in the high-tax economy. This problem has been discussed for a long time in the applied welfare economics literature and has recently become topical in the Swedish policy discourse.

As is illustrated in Figure 4.2, the user-financed service sector is squeezed between self-service and tax-financed services. One obvious consequence of being hard-pressed from the latter is the almost complete disappearance of user-financed hospitals and schools in the welfare states. Pressure from the other side, that is, competition from self-service in combination with sophisticated household capital goods, threatens to extinguish some traditional user-financed service enterprises, for example, travel agencies, removal firms and laundries. In view of the fact that durable goods including dwellings constitute a large part of total consumption, repair and maintenance of durables should be a service sector of great potential, that is, professions such as carpenters, house-painters, upholsterers, floor-layers, etcetera, could have a bright future. By substantial subsidization of work by these professionals, meant to neutralize the tax advantage of self-service for house repair and renovation, a more level playing field has been created by the Swedish government. A similar tax break has also been introduced for buying professional domestic services. This part of the general policy of stimulation of user-financed services is controversial, since it is feared that the past, conspicuously unequal society of gentlefolks and servants could reappear.

COLLECTIVE SERVICES AND THE
THEORY OF SOCIAL BALANCE

As was shown in Table 4.2, in the last two decades private consumption has in real terms been steadily increasing while public consumption has been almost stagnant, in particular collective services. In Sweden—in contrast to the US—the growth of HEC has also been sluggish. Consumer durables, except for dwellings, and certain private (user-financed) services have been very expansive. Are the needs for higher quality durables and various user-financed (private) services really more urgent in the affluent society than the needs for collective services like law and order and environmental protection, as well as improved quality of HEC services?

More than fifty years ago J. K. Galbraith in his famous book *The Afflu-ent Society* (1958) asked basically the same question with regard to the US economy. On the basis of "the theory of social balance" (chapter 17 in the second, revised edition) Galbraith gave a negative answer. His reasoning seems highly relevant today as regards collective services in the first place.

> The final problem of the productive society is what it produces. This manifests itself in an implacable tendency to provide an opulent supply of some things and a niggardly yield of others. This disparity carries to the point where it is a cause of social discomfort and social unhealth. The line which divides our area of wealth from our area of poverty is roughly that which divides privately produced and marketed goods and services from publicly rendered services. Our wealth in the first is

not only in startling contrast with the meagreness of the latter, but our wealth in privately produced goods is, to a marked degree, the cause of crisis in the supply of public services. For we have failed to see the importance, indeed the urgent need, of maintaining a balance between the two. (Galbraith 1970, 207)

Galbraith had in the first place local collective services in mind. He lamented over the:

> shortcomings in the elementary municipal and metropolitan services. The schools were old and overcrowded. The police force was under strength and underpaid. The parks and playgrounds were insufficient. Streets and empty lots were filthy, and the sanitation staff was under-equipped and in need of men. Access to the city by those who work there was uncertain and painful . . . Internal transportation was overcrowded, unhealthful, and dirty. So was the air. Parking on the streets should have been prohibited, and there was no space elsewhere. (1970, 207–208)

These problems were, in Galbraith's view, to a large extent caused by the growing affluence of certain private goods.

> The cars that could not be parked were being produced at an expanding rate. The children though without schools, subject in the playground to the affectionate interest of adults with odd tastes, and disposed to in-creasingly imaginative forms of delinquency were admirably equipped with television sets . . . The family which takes its mauve and cerise, air-conditioned, power-steered, and power-braked car out for a tour passes through cities that are badly paved, made hideous by litter, blighted buildings, bill-boards, and posts for wires that should long since been put underground. They pass on into a countryside that has been rendered largely invisible by commercial art. The goods which the latter advertise have an absolute priority in our value system. Such aesthetic considerations as a view of the countryside accordingly come second. On such matters we are consistent. (1970, 208)

Galbraith's main thesis is that the collective services will be undersup-plied simply because people dislike paying taxes much more than paying for items of private consumption of their own choice, and/or that, in par-ticular, Republican politicians oppose raising the necessary taxes (unless the national defence is concerned).

The policy corollary of Galbraith's reasoning is that the allocation of resources to collective services should at least keep abreast with the growth in the private goods to which they are complementary. In the Swedish welfare state, as seen in Table 4.2, collective services is the only main item showing a negative development in real terms in the period 1993–2006. The volume decrease of 1 per cent is not much, but compared to the volume increase in total private consumption of 38 per cent in the same period it stands out.

MERIT SERVICES

Galbraith did not say much about HEC services, which today account for the lion's share of the public consumption in the European welfare states. The reason was of course that these services now as then to a large extent are user financed in the US.[5] The build-up of the welfare states started after the publishing of *The Affluent Society*. Although HEC are strictly private services in the economic-theoretical sense, the HEC expansion in Europe was largely tax financed. The first question to consider is therefore: why is the tax-financing still prevailing?

FROM HOUSEHOLD TO INDIVIDUAL WANT SATISFACTION

Although poverty has been eliminated during a century of unprecedented economic growth, and total taxes have reached a level of 50 per cent of GDP, it is paradoxical that in Sweden, and many other similar countries, the need for additional taxes to finance merit service seems greater than ever. Really poor families hardly exist anymore, so one would think that the public intervention in the allocation of resources should be decreasing. That this has not happened is to a large extent explained by a change of focus from the household to the individual. Unlike traditional microeconomics, which is the study of the behaviour and market interactions of firms and households, the ideas behind the welfare state, as well as the implementation of women's emancipation, have made the concept of the traditional "household" obsolete as the basic unit in consumption demand analysis,[6] and in particular in welfare economics. The family is just as important a social construction as ever, but the concept of the household headed by the master/husband with complete authority over all household members belongs to the nineteenth century, at least in the Western world. Views on children are also profoundly different today. Long ago, children were regarded not only as beings with undeveloped faculties, but also with feelings of a more primitive kind, of less value than adults' feelings. Now full recognition has been established of children as individuals with individual wants in their own right. Individuals should replace households on the demand-side in normative economic analysis.

This does not mean that parents are no longer responsible for their children. The point is that in the welfare state the children, and other weak groups, should not be completely dependent on their families or other relatives. Parents' responsibilities are shared with society at large. Similarly, the responsibility for the elderly and for disabled people is shared by all of society. This is the key to understanding why a large part of total services could continue to be tax financed rather than user financed in a country growing richer and richer as a whole.

The lasting justification of tax-financed services is also more understandable in a life cycle perspective. Everybody belongs to the non-working half of the population at some stages in their life cycle. It can be argued that the distribution of goods and services over the lifetime of an individual is more relevant than the cross-section distribution of household incomes. In Figure 4.3, the giving to and taking from the public sector over the life cycle of a representative Swede are depicted.

The total delimited area above and the total delimited area below the age axis are equal. Over a lifetime in a stationary economy, a representative individual pays mainly in the form of taxes for the merit services consumed and the income transfers received as a child and as a young person and upon retirement.

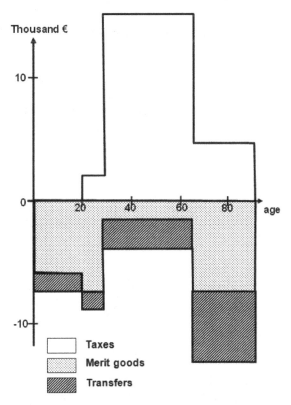

Figure 4.3 The economic life cycle of a representative individual.
Source: Söderström et al. (1999).

THE WELFARE STATE DILEMMA

What the ideologues behind the welfare state build-up did not foresee was that the tax financing of HEC would in the long run lead to a similar problem to that pointed out by Galbraith as regards pure collective service, but with a considerable time-lag. Most economists in those days thought instead that providing HEC free of charge would lead to excess demand and oversupply as the queuing could not be eliminated by raising prices ("the queue-up society").[7]

In view of the development of health and education services in the US, it can in retrospect be conjectured that if these services had been user financed also in the welfare states, with prices (health insurance premiums and tuition fees) differentiated with respect to the quality of service, substantially more resources would have been allocated at least to health and education in the HEC conglomerate than under the present regime of tax financing.

This does not mean that the tax-financing regime should be abandoned. Equality in respect of health care, basic education, child- and eldercare, which is obtained by offering these services equal for all according to need rather than purchasing power, is a great virtue. It is actually the main idea behind the welfare state. However, if the quality of these services cannot be maintained as long as the tax financing prevails, the welfare states are facing a most difficult dilemma. Do we have to choose, or is there a way out of this dilemma, so that both equality and quality of HEC services can be maintained?

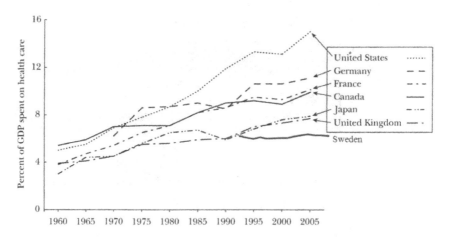

Figure 4.4　Percentage of GDP spent on health care for selected OECD countries.[8]
Source: OECD (2009).

The dilemma seems genuinely insoluble in the very long run, but with a planning horizon of twenty to thirty years an intermediate allocation policy, good enough for this period of time, seems possible and worth discussing. Who knows what decisive new circumstances will be present thirty years hence?

BETTER WELFARE SERVICES WITHOUT TAX AND/OR PRICE RISES: AN INTERMEDIATE SOLUTION THAT WILL BOOST TOTAL EMPLOYMENT AS A BONUS

It can be observed in Figure 4.3 that total transfer payments are almost of the same size as total expenditure on merit goods. This is the key point of the proposed policy redirection. Given the tax rate, public consumption could be boosted both by an employment surge which would be good in itself, and by changing the proportion of expenditure on public consumption and transfer payments. This can be done by and large without making any major group of individuals losers. Two main strands of the proposed policy are:

1. Boosting merit goods production requires more labour for HEC. Remember that during the last fifty years the trend in the rate of employment (employment per person) in Sweden increased noticeably only in the 1960s and 1970s, when a large number of women became employed in the public sector for the build-up of the welfare state. Now a similar employments surge could be brought about by a strong policy for HEC quality improvements—more personnel per patient, pupil, children in nurseries and old people in eldercare—in the first place by reducing the present regrettably high rate of unemployment among young people. This would imply a reduction of public expenditure on people of working age, corresponding to the reduced need for unemployment benefits, and additional tax revenue from previously unemployed persons. A commensurate increase in collective services and HEC for children and old people could be brought about.

2. In an economy with continuous productivity growth in the manufacturing industry it would be possible to successively reallocate labour from material goods production to services without reducing the output of material goods.[9] Financially, a break-even outcome would be obtained by freezing pensions, child allowances and possibly some other transfers as well. The net effect would be that the future increase in consumption mainly consists of tax-financed services. Retired people, families with children and possibly some other categories would by and large stay at the present level of material goods consumption for the following twenty to thirty years. This would successively make additional tax revenue available for collective and merit service provision

to those who would have to forgo increasing goods consumption. They would be compensated for this by more human eldercare, better schools and shorter waiting time for medical care.

NOTES

1. Useful national accounts for Sweden back to the nineteenth century were compiled in the 1930s by statisticians and economists including Karin Kock and Erik Lindahl. Their work was followed up by Olof Lindahl (1956), Östen Johansson (1967) and more recently by economic historians Olle Krantz and Lennart Schön. Their latest work, *Swedish Historical National Accounts 1800–2000*, presents time series of GDP and its main components for two centuries in both current and constant prices (Krantz and Schön 2007).
2. The rate of gainful employment for women is now the same as for men in Sweden, although work hours per day are still higher for men.
3. There are many less pervasive but nonetheless important problems that require consumption policy measures which are not taken up. Consumer protection and guidance for which the National Board of Consumer Policies (*Konsumentverket* in Sweden) is responsible are left out of consideration.
4. It is confusing that "goods" has two different meanings in different contexts in economics. On the one hand, material goods are contrasted to immaterial services, and on the other hand, in some cases "goods" include both material goods and immaterial services. This is the case in the highest degree as regards both public goods and merit goods. They got their names in spite of the fact that they are all services. In Figure 4.2 the standard terminology is adhered to, but in the following discussion it comes natural to me to speak about collective services and merit services.
5. The main exception is tax-financed municipal primary schools, which, as seen earlier, Galbraith included in his lamentation over the growing social imbalance. The quality difference between private and municipal schools is still a good example of Galbraith's fundamental thesis.
6. For a survey of theories of families, see Bergstrom (1997). A concrete example, where an individual rather than household approach makes a great deal of difference in demand analysis is car ownership forecasting models: see Jansson, Cardebring and Junghard (1986) and Jansson (1989).
7. Market-clearing prices are applied in the US but the topical problem there, which President Obama is wrestling with, is that the freedom of choice in the market for medical care has the result that some 20 per cent of Americans remain uninsured. If a reasonable minimum level of health insurance is made compulsory in the US, the tax financing of the system can be said to have increased, which would be abhorrent to some influential ideologists. Still the level of health insurance, and consequently the quality of service, would be open for choice, which should continue as a driving force, like in education, to boost the volume of medical care and other health-promoting services.
8. Note that EU member states Germany, France and Britain spend a larger proportion of GDP on health care than Sweden. As mentioned in the introduction, however, Sweden is at the top in the EU in terms of the total public consumption share of GDP.
9. This has been done with interest since 1960 in Sweden. From then on employment in goods production has been steadily on the decline, while the volume of goods production has been steadily growing.

REFERENCES

Baumol, William. 1967. Macroeconomics of Unbalanced Growth: The Anatomy of Urban Crisis. *American Economic Review* (June).

Bergstrom, Ted. 1997. A Survey of Theories of Families. In *Handbook of Population and Family Economics*, ed. M. Rosenzweig and O. Stark. Amsterdam: North-Holland.

Clark, Gregory. 2007. *A Farewell to Alms. A Brief Economic History of the World.* Princeton, NJ: Princeton University Press.

Fogel, Robert. 1999. Catching Up with the Economy. *American Economic Review* (March).

———. 2000. *The Fourth Great Awakening and the Future of Egalitarianism.* Chicago: University of Chicago Press.

Galbraith, John Kenneth. 1970. *The Affluent Society.* 2nd rev. ed. Harmondsworth: Pelican Books.

Jansson, Jan Owen. 1989. Car Demand Modelling and Forecasting—A New Approach. *Journal of Transport Economics and Policy* (May).

———. 2006. *The Economics of Services—Development and Policy.* Cheltenham: Edward Elgar.

Jansson, J. O., P. Cardebring and O. Junghard. 1986. *Personbilsinnehavet I Sverige 1950–2010. Linköping: VTI Rapport 301.*

Johansson, Östen. 1967. *The Gross Domestic Production of Sweden and Its Composition 1861–1955.* Stockholm: Almquist and Wicksell.

Krantz, Olle, and Lennart Schön. 2007. *Swedish Historical National Accounts 1800–2000. Lund Studies in Economic History 41.*

Layard, Richard. 2005. *Happiness—Lessons from a New Science.* New York: Penguin Books.

Lindahl, Olof. 1956. *Sveriges nationalprodukt 1861–1951. Meddelande från Konjunkturinstitutet, serie B:20.* Stockholm.

OECD. 2009. *Health Statistics.*

Sandelin, Bo. 2009. *Ekonomin i EU.* Stockholm: SNS Förlag.

Stiglitz, Joseph E., and Carl E. Walsh. 2005. *Economics.* 4th ed. New York: W. W. Norton.

Söderström, Lars, Anders Björklund, Per-Gunnar Edebalk and Agneta Kruse. 1999. *Välfärdspolitiska rådets rapport 1999: Från dagis till servicehus, välfärdspolitik i livets olika skeden.* Stockholm: SNS Förlag.

5   Consumption beyond Dualism[1]

Daniel Miller

INTRODUCTION

Is one of the problems with a social science perspective on consumption precisely that it is a social science? To be a social science assumes a commitment to some kind of collectivity, whether society, culture or the state, which is most commonly contrasted with various forms of individualism. So that sociology and anthropology oppose themselves to disciplines such as psychology or economics that tend to privilege the individual. For social science reduction to the individual is a problem or a sign of individualism (see, for example, Beck and Beck-Gernsheim 2001; Bourdieu 1977, 1979; Giddens 1991; Miller 2009a). In this chapter I want to show how the study of consumption as material culture may be a means to confront and repudiate this dualism. The power of this dualism is evident in the colloquial term *materialistic*. To call a person materialistic is to imply an orientation towards the commodities of modern capitalism at the expense of their proper orientation, which should be to other people.

The evidence I will use to refute this dualism comes largely from a recent book *The Comfort of Things* (Miller 2008), which examines how people cultivate material culture, particularly the objects of the home. The book presents thirty households almost all in and around a single street in South London, and examines in each case the relationship between the people who live there and the things they possess. The evidence presented there suggests that people are neither orientated towards individualism nor towards society. Instead most people live within a field of relationships to other persons and also to material things. One is not at the expense of the other; people who forge satisfactory relationships with things also tend to be the persons who forge satisfactory relationships to persons. Those who for whatever reason find it difficult to accomplish the former also find it difficult to accomplish the latter. There is little evidence to suggest any strong relationship to some larger communal entity such as society or even neighbourhood. Instead the emphasis is upon a few core relationships, the people and things that really matter to them. Kin, close friends, their home, a pet, but in some cases a computer game, fashion or a television program, around which form a much more extensive but shallower set of relationships.

The state and the political economy are just as important, but not because they tightly control permissible discourses as implied by Foucault, but because they do achieve something of the liberalism they espouse in creating conditions for the autonomous development of such relationships. Otherwise they have plenty to feed off in terms of the running of states, corporations and markets. Even the recent credit crunch and financial upheaval made almost no impact upon this downstream on the lives of people. They had more or less money, but rarely more or less core relationships. People deal with bureaucracy and taxation as they must. But as long as the state effectively provides education and health services and the market provides goods and entertainments, people may not even care that much about these transcendent forces. We do not seem to require any active allegiance to the abstractions of society or community. There are some vestiges of collectivity in the street, for instance, the church and the pub, but most people make limited use of these. They generally do not know their neighbours unless they live on the smaller side streets. These are random juxtapositions of households, determined by forces such as house prices, transport systems and proximity to work, school and leisure. The political economy and state determines these circumstances, but not how people live within them. They presume an increasingly accepted liberalism, which assumes that, inasmuch as actions do not result in any harm to others, people are free to be and do what the hell they want.

This amounts to a repudiation of much of Durkheim and the premise of social science. People do not need to believe in society; they may not bother to vote, treating politics more as a spectator sport, on a par with football. Their fundamental allegiance may be to Ireland or Jamaica, split between several locations; often unrelated to the place where they live and whose laws they obey. A gay couple, Simon and Jacques, who happen to be living in London at present, seem to regard Tallinn, the capital of Estonia, as in effect a distant London suburb, which they might choose to live in next since property prices are less than outer London. Marcia may go to a Catholic instead of a Pentecostal church because it is closer to her house, probably to the consternation of both branches of Christianity. People confound the rules of social science, and more importantly this doesn't seem to matter much.

But is the alternative actually liberalism which fetishizes the individual as against society? Is the alternative to society isolated individuals, defined through choices—whether of commodities or of a political party? Liberalism is also an ideology constructing the individual as the *other* to society; the individual representing a fundamental unit, the basic point of reference as opposed to God or society. In different ways, sociologists such as Nicholas Rose (1989), anthropologists such as Marilyn Strathern (1992) and philosophers such as Charles Taylor (1989) have explored the history of individualism and its consequences. But my evidence no more supports a belief in individuals than a belief in society. Most people regard being solely an individual as, largely speaking, a failure in life. There are some individuals in *The Comfort of Things*, such as Aidan the exhibitionist, for whom life as an individual is the project to which they devote themselves. Some of the younger participants tend to espouse individualism, at least in practice, while breaking away from their family. But, later on, most people seem to be individuals by default rather than by design. Many treasure some limited autonomy, but otherwise individualism is most fully equated with loneliness and a lack of relationships. The extreme cases tend to be elderly men.

Suppose we put to one side this dualism of society and the individual and instead turn to the people of this London street and ask them what matters in their lives. We would hear a surprisingly uniform response. It would focus upon whether or not they experienced a number of significant and fulfilling relationships. So I propose that we respect their insight, and also focus on such core relationships. When they say this they mainly have in mind relationships with other people. Their desire for good relationships with children, parents, the wider family, with lovers or spouses (sometimes lovers and spouses), with colleagues and with good and true friends. With some aspiration to the ethics of wider collectivities such as the nation, a workplace, the environment (or at least a football team). But there is another set of relationships which is not explicit but emerges through my decision to study it; their relationships with objects. An approach based on a dialectical theory explicated elsewhere (Miller 2009b) in which material objects are viewed as an integral and inseparable aspect of all relationships. People exist for us in and through their material presence. An advantage of this unusual perspective is that sometimes these apparently mute forms can be made to speak more easily and eloquently to the nature of relationships than can those with persons.

THE EVIDENCE

Sharon, for example, started out with certain key strategies designed to repudiate her parents. Her mother spent ages looking feminine or glamorous before even going out to the shops. Sharon, by contrast, played with the boys and ended up a champion body-builder. On the other hand, the fact that she was the youngest and smallest in her class could also explain the emphasis on strength and size. We could see the relationship to her parents, therefore, as completely incidental or essentially formative to her adoption of body-building. But most likely it is precisely because of the conjuncture of the two factors that this life trajectory become sustained. Most of what people come to be in life, seems in our material to be overdetermined, but meaning here simply multiply caused, not necessarily its technical use by Freud or Althusser.

Sharon also hated the way her parents hoarded and collected things. She notes that for them it was security while for her it is clutter. But then Sharon's life fell apart. She went through an appalling divorce after which her ex-husband either stole or destroyed her possessions. She ended up homeless, without work, living on the street with her baby. For three months she camped outside the local government offices, until eventually she was rehoused. Under these conditions, aspects of her parent's lives that she had repudiated came back to her as an integral part of herself. She started hoarding things, conscious now of the fragility of possession. Today she moves furniture and other things around her flat almost daily to confirm that she has returned to control over her own house. Yet she has successfully returned to the education she originally missed out on because of dyslexia to the extent that she is now a professional who trains social workers. Unusually for a social worker Sharon still does body-building and works at night as a bouncer, that is, someone who expels undesirables from clubs. She still refuses to engage with the kind of glamour she repudiated early on. She recalls a vision that took place when she was nine years old of a much older woman, dressed in pink and with pink lipstick and orange blusher. She claims this led to her sustained aversion to women dressing younger than their age. The vision fits her current condition, her daughter is now nine and Sharon is terrified about her dressing in sexually provocative ways.

This structure or order to her life has two main dimensions. The first is vertical and corresponds to a study of how events or circumstances build a narrative that is commonly first explicated around the relation to parental influence. This logic of biographical narrative is not simply a sequence of events; it is also in part an accounting for that order, as one thing literally leads to another. Whenever a person says this thing happened and then they did that, we have responsibility to decide the degree to which they are implying the cause of what they then did or became. This vertical dimension is cross-cut by a horizontal dimension which is the logic, what Bourdieu (1977) referred to as the homologies, between different areas of practice. This leads us to ask to what degree we can explain someone's way of dealing with one area of their life by virtue of its consistency with what otherwise might seem an entirely unrelated part of their life. The way they relate to their work sometimes seems reminiscent of the way they relate to lovers, or collections of glass.

Finally, one of the features that defines what we mean by "modern" lives is the degree of conscious reflection. We might quote the sociologist Giddens (1991) on the way people try and keep order in their narrative of their past as a means of legitimating their present. But then so could Sharon. She has probably read Giddens. But such academic accounts often assume that this self-consciousness creates in some measure a less immediate or authentic relationship to ourselves, a more abstract or ironic distancing, such that we could be said to be acting ourselves. But I saw no evidence that having read Giddens would lead Sharon to distance herself from her own behaviour, any more than traditional rationalization or legitimation of behaviour. The fact that she can explain the relationship between constantly moving furniture around and the way it clears her head, in much the same way as we would explain it, doesn't seem to diminish one iota the efficacy of her action in actually moving furniture or her need to do it. Just as her knowledge of why people need to hoard, that she describes as irrational, didn't at all save her from needing to hoard when her own circumstances fitted her theory of hoarding.

Malcolm's work fluctuates between Australia and the UK, but what he understands as his permanent address is his email, and the nearest thing to home is his laptop. Both his friendships and his work are largely organized by email, a place he constantly orders, returns to, cares for, and where in many respects "his head is". But to understand the intensity of this relationship to his laptop, we need to read the anthropologist Fred Myers (1986). Because, Myers notes, for many Aboriginal groups there is a tradition of avoiding the physical possessions of the deceased. Malcolm's mother was Australian Aboriginal and most of her possessions were indeed destroyed at her death. But he took from her a mission to locate and preserve the history of his family, including those once taken away from their parents. As he sees it, too much Aboriginal history is viewed as lying in police records; he wants a proper archive he will deposit in an Australian State archive.

Malcolm has an antipathy to things. He has given most of his inherited or childhood objects away. In his devotion to immateriality he prefers anything digital. He is getting into digital photographs; he downloads music and immediately throws out the covers. Very unusual for the street is that he even gives away his books after he has read them. One could relate this to his mobility, one could relate it to his interest in the potential of new technologies, one could relate it to this Aboriginal inheritance. There is more. His father sold antiques but the result was that as soon as he started becoming attached to things in his childhood, they would be sold, another possible source of his detachment from things. Once again then his personal habitus (Bourdieu 1977) is overdetermined. Even he can't decide how much his mobility is cause and effect. But the overall result, as he puts it, is that "I think I've set myself up to be out of touch with objects and things, so there's probably something psychological behind that." He has a more ambiguous relation to less tangible things like documents; sorting both his mothers and his own things into neat box files. But his real identification is with digital forms. He constantly updates and sorts his emails, which becomes the updating of his social relationships. In going through them he recalls all those friends he owes emails to.

One could try and stretch the Aboriginal inheritance. The laptop as a kind of digital dreamworld that connects current relationships with those of the dead, a place he comes in and out of, as more real than merely real life. He retains this intense concern with lineage, devoting much of his time to creating order out of kinship history. He seems obsessed that if he were to die, that thanks to constantly sorting his emails, he would leave a legacy that was archived and up to date, so no one would have to do the work he did recovering and ordering his ancestral lives. But for my purpose what he typifies is firstly the multiple determination of his cosmology. Both father and mother and his work come together as possible explanations. One could not claim to have predicted him, but given what we now know, this relationship to his laptop that at first seemed so bizarre can certainly make sense. It is an aesthetic, a material cosmology. One can see how the horizontal dimensions of order merge with vertical, the overdetermination in his background.

People's lives are anything but consistent. Quite the contrary, the juxtapositions of influences both past and present are quite bewilderingly mixed. But as with parents understanding children, a consistency appears in retrospect between the influences that are picked up on because they are compatible with present orders. The vertical is made consistent with the horizontal. We can observe this at any stage in life. As in the case of Peggy who drops a whole slew of childhood influences and brings to the foreground a completely different set when her life changes at sixty.

Today she would emphasize the significance of movement during her early childhood, the fact that her family lived in several different countries when she was a child. Yet for most of her life these early childhood experiences were pretty irrelevant and by no means dominated the way she behaved. It is only now in her sixties that everything gets reconfigured. She and her partner, Cyril, both had previous marriages and very different lives. But once they discovered each other they found a happiness and compatibility beyond anything they could have imagined. It is now in this new relationship that things about her background that previously were important because they gave her stability in difficult times and relationships can be safely disregarded, while earlier childhood influences become the source of a quite profound freedom that these sixty-year-olds experience. They have become part of a kind of cruise society whose primary interest is in how many places they can see in the world before they are too old to continue the quest. They have a fantastic new set of relationships across the world, with people constantly coming to stay in London and they staying in turn in far-flung lands. This is helped by the way they have consolidated their relationship with their own descendents, obligations they restrict to within a niche of time that doesn't much detract from their cruising. What they demonstrate is that, contrary to most psychology, a relationship at sixty may be just as formative as a relationship at six.

There is an important contrast between Malcolm and Peggy. In the case of Peggy, her relationship to objects and to the order of objects was essentially subservient to her relationship to particular people; everything has changed because of her meeting Cyril. But that is not true of Malcolm. He may well have entirely fulfilling relationships with people, but one senses an overriding concern with the way he needs to order his relationships to things, even if they are immaterial and digital forms intended to repudiate objects per se. Actually people, especially the deceased, become objects which need to be ordered as other objects. There is no sense in trying to privilege persons or objects on this street. The determinant relationship might be to a partner or parent, but it might be to cruising or clubbing or cars.

The mini analytical portraits I present here derive mostly from recording objects around the house or discussing them and their associated memories. We did not collect biographical narratives as such. It is my analysis that concludes that Peggy would have regarded a completely different set of earlier events as formative if we had met her at a different stage in her life. So although I am trying to construct explanations that would make sense to these participants, they are not necessarily their own ways of accounting for their actions and possessions.

Nevertheless, it often helps to start by focusing on parental socialization. Because however complex that relationship, and we find it just as rich and contradictory as that revealed in the psychoanalytical literature, it follows from the logic of vertical development that in some ways the relationship to one's parents is actually one's simplest ever relationship. Because all subsequent relationships include the contingency of the way they inflect prior relationships. Initially what are most common are both the systematic repudiation and/or systematic reproduction of parental models.

Take, for example, Marina's relation to McDonald's Happy Meals. For six years she took her three children every week to McDonald's to eat a Happy Meal and keep the toys produced in series that came free with them. If going on holiday she tried to make sure she went to the McDonald's at the airport so as not to miss out on the series as a whole. She is lyrical in her praise for both the toys and the place. She says, "I just think they are incredibly well made, such beautiful things and they're free, you get them with the meal. They are mass-produced to an exceptionally high standard." She also harps on about McDonald's itself, their baby-changing facilities, the way they encouraged breast-feeding, how she got to know the personnel, the reliability of their food, which she also claims is healthier than alternatives.

Why? Firstly it turns out that Marina (like Sharon) repudiates her parents through becoming a tomboy and then, in her case, training in engineering. Her parents were brought up in the colonial office in Africa, but without quite enough money to live up to their class pretensions. She feels she was neglected, given over like the other kids to their African nannies, but carefully trained to make sure they only ever said lavatory, never toilet. So at one level McDonald's is a repudiation of these class pretensions, of parents who would never go to McDonald's, and who treated their children so coldly. But there is more. These six years were sandwiched between this conflict with parents who she stopped speaking to and the recent unemployment of her husband, which means that while working she never has enough time to spend with her children. The McDonald's period was the only time that wasn't either alienated from the past or from the present.

Taking her kids to McDonald's, including the half-hour playing with the new toys, was for her almost the only moment of pure indulged motherhood, away from competing domestic tasks. These were precisely Happy Meals where her children learnt to care about, systematically collect, develop imagination and create perfect moments of family life. All her precise memories of her children's development are associated with obtaining specific toys, which still today come out as collections in the summer. McDonald's Happy Meals became an aesthetic totalization of her existence. She was delighted that her children regaled us with detailed stories evoked by these toys while we were sitting having tea. As such she exemplifies these same themes of overdetermination, an aesthetic and verticality.

Although for convenience I am often referring to individuals, actually the unit is commonly dyadic. Peggy makes no sense without Cyril, Malcolm without his laptop. With James and Quentin, a gay couple of thirty years standing, each exists largely in relation to the other. James may have failed in his arts career, but his charming juxtaposition of ornaments and other possessions, his aesthetic based on creative disorder, prevents Quentin from becoming enslaved to his own skilled use of memory and order. What determines each are the needs of the other.

Even when it comes to reproduction or repudiating parents the unit need not be an individual. Another house consists of four twenty- and thirty-somethings. They are typical post-university, completely unrelated, tenants. Yet they only make sense when taken as a collective. Each has issues and problems they have had to face up to, some deep and difficult. In response to this fragility, although without partners and children, they are all to some degree desperate to get back to the kinds of order and comfort represented by their original middle-class homes. In their collectivity of tennis, gardening or wine tasting they can construct what they need, which is the reproduction of the firmer foundations of their earlier life, in many ways making themselves appear more like fifty- or sixty-year-olds. But they cannot do this without the support of the others in that same household.

For anthropologists the vertical dimension is often anyway best seen more generically as background rather than just as parents. Take, for example, Marcia. One might look at her living room absolutely stuffed with ornaments and see this as her Caribbean inheritance. But such Caribbean displays that I studied in Trinidad and Jamaica tend to be full of objects that speak to close relationships; educational certificates or presents from grandchildren. On close inspection Marcia has no ornaments at all that speak to the existence of her husband, son or grandchildren. This turns out to be in part because of certain early influences of her respectable mother, a schoolteacher, and the self-reliance that came with poverty. A set of cultural rather than simply parental ways of being. The problem is that these cultural rules, such as respectability, which worked well in a Caribbean context were much less helpful to her in the isolation of South London and led to a defensive rejection of accepting anything from relationships and only integrating that which she obtained for herself. The problem for Marcia was that being rigidly true to her Caribbean roots ended up as tragically limiting when no longer in the Caribbean, because what would have confirmed her as a matriarch in the Caribbean left her completely isolated in the very different context of South London.

The horizontal dimension complements the vertical. At any given point of time what I am calling the aesthetic (by which I mean an individual habitus) is distributed through a series of relationships that may be homologous or systematically contradictory. Genres such as accumulated collections of ornaments, the friends one goes drinking with, holidays or neighbours. I will take just one example, the exploitation of the spatial order represented by the house itself. The kind of normative structure that Bourdieu presents to us of the Kabyle house, here becomes the often ad hoc aesthetic of particular houses which are ordered in relation to diverse practices.

Di, for example, like many others, wants to retain something of her parents' possessions as memories, but doesn't want these to undermine the autonomy she has carefully constructed for her own life. So when they move house she takes certain things, but keeps them not in the house, but in her garden shed. The shed is both near enough and far enough to exemplify the place in her life she wants her parents to inhabit. This matters because the most consistent relationship she has cultivated in her life is to the house itself. Starting from her hippy days the house became the repository of ethnic paraphernalia that stands also for her liberal attitudes reflected today by her working with immigrant children. Even her husband at their divorce knew he could not ask for things from this, their once shared, house. The house is full of her emotional repertoire. It has places to cry in, to have great sex in. She can look at a wall of tickets to rock gigs she has been to. But it's also her logistical base, without children, the object of her practice of care. The house links the very particular schema of emotions and pragmatism that is Di's aesthetic form.

A more extreme example comes when a house objectifies the values of its inhabitants with unrelenting aesthetic consistency. Designers whose house is a shrine to their cosmology. The house that proclaims there is no colour but cream. The house whose doctrine is that objects must express dynamism, not become museums. So on the wall are not pictures as in other houses but clothes hung as decorations, which can be changed over time. Thirty pairs of jeans are carefully ordered according the precise degree of wash, fade and distressing. A similarly overt cosmology is evident when one walks into a feng-shui house. It speaks to a life that insists no sentiment or other interest can disrupt the tyranny of calm order. Gifts from relatives, indeed all gifts, are carefully stowed away in unseen cupboards or given away. Light, the sound of fountains, rock and wood, all where they should be. Consistency resolving contradiction. This feng-shui is just as important as an antidote to his wife's stressful work as a management consultant as it is to his own work as an acupuncturist with an Eastern spiritual inflection.

CONCLUSIONS

The approach taken to these people is derived not from psychology, but from the way an anthropologist would present a society. For example, an anthropologist who conducted exemplary work on material culture was Annette Weiner. In *Inalienable Objects* (1991, 54–62), Weiner discusses a wide range of Maori objects, some of very general significance, some quite specific. She explores their different capacity of bones, stones and cloaks to represent the inalienable. Cloth, being ambiguous in its symbolism as a second skin, is good for mediating the transition from human to larger cultural reproduction. Henare (2005) describes Maori weaving ancestors together. This contrasts with the inalienability that might be suggested in stone. Objects may also represent an individual chief or warrior, have individual names or be buried with a particular person. So the term *society* may indicate the greater authority of social hierarchy, chiefly power or the authority of the sacred, but it can also connote a commitment to one relationship (Weiner 1991, 54).

This has resonance with my material from South London. On a bookshelf lies Grandfather's tin from the First World War. By now this tin simultaneously represents the specific grandfather, England and history itself. A ring is felt to be inalienable because of the deep love between one's parents, but also for the importance of love in general. A clock from one's grandparents' farm stands for roots in the countryside as well as them specifically. A print of one of the hero's of the IRA also stands for one's specific Irish roots within this cosmopolitan, but possibly hostile, social environment. Inalienability tends to pass within family when a man asks his wife to wear something he inherited from his grandmother.

All of this is as you might expect. But here, as with the Maori, people also create whole genres of the inalienable. An aesthetic that totalizes their lives on a par with social cosmology. Charlotte has systematically carried out a very large number of piercings followed by a series of tattoos, and simultaneously developed a clear philosophy of how these acts of self-construction contribute to her understanding but above all her control over her own life. She exemplifies both the vertical and horizontal dimensions. The vertical dimension starts once again from her relationship to her mother. This is not a simple repudiation; it was her mother's friend who first introduced her to piercing at the age of eleven. But she then appropriates this as a means of distancing. For example, when her mother said, "oh, but you're just trying to be the same as everyone else", she responded by searching out the most extreme and different piercings that for her said (her words): "I've got a piercing, but not because everyone else has that, but because nobody does, actually."

From this came her desire to establish complete mastery over memory itself. She established a fictive relationship to her past. Although born in London she associates herself completely with the country of origin of her lover. She has mastered the accent, had a flat built for her to move to when she has qualified and was already tattooing designs from that country before ever visiting it. As a lesbian she also feels that her sexuality is something she chooses and controls. Control for her means objectifying memory as a thing one can choose to attach or detach from the self. Every piercing represents a specific memory. Life consists of accumulating happy memories that are objectified in this way. So even if she is embarrassed by chasing boy bands as a teenager the memorabilia is retained as something happy at the time. Key piercings and then tattoos represent her best relationships.

With regard to the horizontal, Charlotte, just as Weiner or the Maori, carefully considers the precise materiality of each genre within which memory can be objectified. There is clothing she can throw away. Piercings have a potential transience, for example, when she moved to another part of London she says (her words): "I took out a lot of my bottom rings, so at that stage, and I think that was probably because I had left a lot of rubbish and a lot of people that were not doing me any good, like old memories behind, so I didn't need it any more." Abandoned rings from piercings are kept in a box, photographs of piercings and tattoos on her back allow her to recall a memory, but can't be as easily accessed as those she can look at when on the move. The placing matters, as with nipple piercing viewed the position closest to her heart. Each material form is used to extend and complement the others.

It is the tattoos that establish the full possibilities of the inalienable. They ensure that memories of the best relationships can never be excised. These include her relationship to the tattooist, a close friend who is practicing on Charlotte to obtain her professional qualification. Also her relationship to her lover through having identical tattoos. The memory is precise. Unlike others she will never have supplementary tattooing since this blurs the relationship to the particular time the tattoo was created. As with Weiner, she works out a material technology of inalienable memory. She can't understand people who tattoo for pattern itself rather than to establish the inalienable. She starts from an awareness of people such as her grandfather who lived to regret the tattoos of her youth, yet now has the complete confidence in her current total leg tattooing. She does understand the logic of those who tattoo a cross for a deceased love one, but remains consistent to her own systematic accretion of happy memories and relationships. Charlotte is not then just another person who does piercings and tattoos. In her early twenties she has a systematic cosmology of memory and objectification that is analogous with the way a society creates cosmologies of memory and objectification. At both levels we can study how the vertical relationships of time cross-cut the organizational horizontal relationships of space and specific material genre.

Such relationships rarely link directly to modern states and political economy, a financial crisis may barely impinge upon the relative autonomy of such cultural creativity. We merge cultural and parental influences, normative social orders and other ingredients, adding others as we go along. Such households may combine people from different points of origin or with very different concerns and tastes. They become more like societies creating cosmology more or less linked to wider religious and cultural norms. These are not, however, fragmented individuals but people who strive to create relationships to both people and things which give order, meaning and often moral adjudication to their lives; an order which, as it becomes familiar and repetitive, may also be a comfort to them. I have called this order an aesthetic, although it often remains tentative, contradictory, multiple and constantly changing. But then this is true, if on a different scale, of larger cosmologies and aesthetic orders, such as society or religion.

So the conclusions of this chapter are not intended to support either the ideology of the liberal market or its critics. Instead it shows the consequences of modern consumption within the heterogeneity and diversity of London households. A previous London street study (Miller 1995) examined quite the opposite phenomenon, demonstrating extraordinary generalizations about contemporary Londoners, even those who have migrated to London quite recently. It showed a ritual structure to shopping that applied to more or less anyone. Similarly, Murray (2009), working in Madrid, which is just as much a modern capital city as London, found a remarkable degree of homogeneity at this same level of household order. London happens to possess this heterogeneity; that is not my main point. Rather: whether in conditions of diversity or similarity, people are engaged not as individuals and not with society, but as a point within a network of core relationships. As such the study of consumption needs to repudiate these academic foundations and come closer to that which matters most to the people we study.

NOTES

1. Much of the content of this chapter is derived from two previous publications, Miller (2007) and Miller (2008).

REFERENCES

Beck, Urich, and Elisabeth Beck-Gernsheim. 2001. *Individualization*. London: Sage.
Bourdieu, Pierre. 1977. *Outline of a Theory of Practice*. Cambridge: Cambridge University Press.

————. 1979. *Distinction: A Social Critique of the Judgement of Taste*. London: Routledge and Kegan Paul.

Henare, Amiria. 2005. Nga Aho Tipuna (Ancestral Threads): Maori Cloaks from New Zealand. In *Clothing as Material Culture*, ed. S. Küchler and D. Miller, 121–138. Oxford: Berg.

Giddens, Anthony. 1991. *Modernity and Self-Identity*. Cambridge: Polity Press.

Miller, Daniel. 1995. *A Theory of Shopping*. Cambridge: Polity Press.

————. 2008. *The Comfort of Things*. Cambridge: Polity Press.

————, ed. 2009a. *Anthropology and the Individual*. Oxford: Berg.

————. 2009b. *Stuff*. Cambridge: Polity Press.

Murray, Marjorie. 2009. How Madrid Creates Individuals. In *Anthropology and the Individual*, ed. D. Miller, 83–98. Oxford: Berg.

Myers, Fred. 1986. *Pintupi Country, Pintupi Self*. Washington, DC: Smithsonian Institute Press.

Rose, Nikolas. 1989. *Inventing Ourselves*. Cambridge: Cambridge University Press.

Strathern, Marilyn. 1992. *After Nature: English Kinship in the Late Twentieth Century*. Cambridge: Cambridge University Press.

Taylor, Charles. 1989. *Sources of the Self: The Making of the Modern Identity*. Cambridge, MA: Harvard University Press.

Weiner, Annette. 1992. *Inalienable Possessions*. Berkeley: University of California Press.

Part III

Changing Consumer Roles

6 Selves as Objects of Consumption

Zygmunt Bauman

Emily Dubberley, author of *Brief Encounters: The Women's Guide to Casual Sex*, remarks that getting sex is now "like ordering a pizza . . . Now you can just go online and order genitalia". Flirting, making passes, laborious and protracted efforts to earn reciprocity from the beloved are no longer needed; there is no need to work hard for the partner's approval, no need to lean over backward in order to deserve and earn the partner's consent, to ingratiate oneself in her or his eyes, and to wait a long time, perhaps infinitely, for all those efforts to bring fruit. . . . That means, though, that gone are all such things that used to make a sexual encounter such an exciting event, because an uncertain event with an outcome hanging in the balance, and seeking such an event, was romantic, a risky and full of traps adventure. Something has been lost. . . .

But many men, and also as many women, are heard to be saying that what has been gained is worth the sacrifice. What has been gained, is *convenience*—cutting the effort to the absolute minimum; *speed*—shortening the distance between desire and its satisfaction; and *insurance against consequences*—which, like in the consequences' habit, are seldom fully anticipated and may turn nasty.

One website offering the prospect of quick and safe ("no strings attached") sex and boasting 2.5 million registered members advertises itself with the slogan: "Meet real sex partners tonight!" Another, with millions of members around the world, profiled mostly to the globetrotting part of the gay public, chose another slogan: "What you want, when you want it." There is a message only barely hidden in both slogans: sought-after products ready for consumption, consumption now, on the spot, desire in a package deal with its gratification, you are in charge. That message is sweet and soothing to the ears trained by millions of commercials (each one of us is forced/manoeuvred to watch more commercials in one year than our grandparents could see in their whole life)—commercials that now (unlike in our grandparents' time) promise joy to be instant like coffee or powdered soup ("just pour hot water"), and degrade/ridicule spatially and/or temporarily remote joys that need patience, sacrifice and a lot of goodwill, long training, cumbersome efforts and many trials with as many errors to be reached.

It all started perhaps with Margaret Thatcher's complaint against the National Health Service, and her explanation why she thought a free market for medical services to be better: "I want a doctor of my choice, at the time of my choice." Shortly afterwards the tools—the magic wands in the shape of the credit card—were invented, making Thatcher's dream become if not exactly true, then at least plausible and credible to many TV watchers, commercial readers and unsolicited mail recipients. Tools that brought the consumerist life philosophy within the reach of everybody who deserved the credit companies' attention and benevolence. Most importantly, tools that put within everybody's reach the life inspired and guided by the explosive precept hidden in Thatcher's succinct yet poignant declaration of faith: *my* choices order the world for me—regardless what choices other people might be fond of, are compelled or forced to make or are prevented from making. I am the sole subject in that world of mine (my *Lebenswelt*, the world as lived by me, the world that matters to me and I reckon with) and that position of mine transforms other (putative, putative) "subjects" into *objects*, *things* shaped and used by me according to *my* timing and *my* choice. . . .

Ancient and intemporal folk wisdom advises us "not to count your chickens before they are hatched". Well, the chicken of the new instant joy, what-is-there-for-me life strategy have by now been hatched in great profusion, a whole generation of them, and we have every right to start counting them. One such counting has been performed by psychotherapist Phillip Hodson, and his conclusions present the outcomes of the Internet phase of the ongoing sexual revolution as a rather mixed blessing. Hodson spotted the paradox of what he calls the "throwaway, instant gratification culture" (not universal as yet, but fast gaining converts), once it has been extended to embrace sexual intercourse: people who in one evening may flirt (electronically) with more people than their parents, not to mention their grandparents, could in their entire lives, find out sooner or later that like in the case of all other addictions the satisfaction they gain shrinks with every new dose of the drug. Were they to look closely at the evidence their experience supplies, they would also find out, retrospectively and much to their surprise and frustration, that the long, steady, consistent efforts of courtship and wooing, that slow and intricate labour needed to gain the intended partner's favour of which they can now read about only in old novels, were not the unnecessary, redundant, burdensome and irritating *obstacles* cluttering the way to the "thing itself" (as we are now made to believe), but important, perhaps even crucial, *ingredients* of that "thing", indeed of *all* things erotic and "sexy", of their charm and attraction. Greater *quantity* has been acquired at the cost of *quality*. Internet-mediated sex is, simply, not that "thing" which fascinated and enamoured our ancestors so much as to inspire them to scribble volumes of poetry in order to praise its delights, magnificence and glory, and prompt them to all but confuse marital bliss with heaven. And what Hodson, in agreement with a multitude of other researchers, found out as well is that rather than facilitating and speeding up the tying of human bonds, and rather than cutting down on the sum total of the tragedies of unfulfilled dreams, Internet-mediated sex results in stripping human partnerships of much of their allure and cuts down on the number of dreams.

Such bonds as are tied up with the Internet's help tend to be weaker and more perfunctory, more shallow and superficial than those laboriously built in the real, "offline" life—and for those reasons less (if at all) satisfying and coveted (less "valuable", as Georg Simmel pointed out a long time ago, the value of things tends to be measured by the size of the sacrifice needed to obtain them). *More people* can now "have sex" *more often*—but in parallel with the growth of those numbers grow the numbers of people living alone, suffering from loneliness and from excruciatingly painful feelings of abandonment. Such sufferers seek desperately to escape from that feeling, and are promised to find it in yet more online-supplied sex—only to realize that, far from satiating their hunger for human company, this particular Internet-cooked and Internet-served food only makes the loss of company more conspicuous and makes them feel yet more lonely and famished for warm human togetherness.

And there is another issue worth to be remembered when balancing the gains against the losses—particularly when the chances of ethically saturated human interactions are concerned. The online dating agencies (and yet more the instant-sex agencies) tend to introduce the would be one-night-stand partners through a catalogue in which the "available goods" are classified according to their selected marks, such as height, body types, ethnic origins, body type, body hair, etcetera (the filing methods vary depending on intended public, and its currently dominant ideas of "relevance")—so that the users (as if taking a leaf from Dr. Frankenstein, that clever if inadvertent producer of monsters) may patch together their chosen partner out of bits and pieces which they believe determine the quality of the "whole" and pleasures of sex (expecting *their* users to proceed in a similar manner). In the course of this process the human being somehow disappears from view: one no longer sees the forest beyond those trees. . . . Choosing one's partner from a catalogue of desirable looks and uses, following the way commodities are chosen from the catalogues of online commercial companies, perpetuates the myth which it itself originates and insinuates: that each one of us, humans, is not so much a "totality"—a person or personality whose unrepeatable worth lies all in her or his singularity and uniqueness—but a higgledy-piggledy collection of highly desirable and so sellable, or inferior and thus difficult to sell, attributes.

The reduction of humans into aggregates of traits, an act leading to the dissolution and vanishing from view of the gratification-seeker of the image of the other as an autonomous *subject*, is not of course of the online dating agencies' making. The agencies' way to proceed and lure customers wouldn't find such wide positive response as it does among their clients, if those clients were not primed already and prepared to view the world, including its human inhabitants, as a container of items and spare (separable and exchangeable) parts—what Kerstin Klein describes under the name of "molecular vision of life":

> Today, the "molecular vision of life" . . . has changed what "life itself" . . . is, or was. We can access it in altogether new ways, at the level of molecules, stem cells and genes, and we can do this in-vitro or ex vivo as well as in-vivo. We have technical possibilities at hand to engineer and enhance it to our desires, and we can create it, e.g. by the means of IVF, research cloning (somatic cell nuclear transfer, SCNT), synthetic biology etc. As these new technologies have transformed the western understanding of what it is to be a living thing . . . two transformations have taken place. One, in what it is to be a "living thing", and the other is a transformation of life into "value", into commodity and capital. This challenges us to rethink what notions like life and population mean and what they encompass, and the important point to make . . . is that this has changed our "bio-political imaginary of species-being" and of "life".[1]

Genetic engineering is the logical sequel, and increasingly also the moving engine of the "molecular vision of life". Craig Venter is a most (*the* most?) indefatigable warrior of the fast-expanding "genomist" army. His ambition to remake every detail of the human body into something else (better? More efficient? Or just different, novel?) grows with the insertion of every chromosome into any cell and eliminating any chromosome which the insertion will have made redundant. Offering his "guide to the future", alongside a few other frontline scientists (see the *Guardian* of 1 January 2009), he announces that the time has arrived to "convert billions of years (that is, 3.5 bn years of evolution) into decades and change not only conceptually how we view life but life itself". Philosopher Daniel Dennett sounds yet more intoxicated by yet more mind-boggling prospects: "When you no longer need to eat to stay alive, or procreate to have offspring, or locomote to have an adventure-packed life, when the residual instincts for these activities might be simply turned off by genetic tweaking, there may be no constant for human nature left at all". And, finally, Steven Pinker, a psychologist, crosses the remaining t's and dot the few neglected i's celebrating the advent of another, perhaps the ultimate, liberation "of man and consumer" (who in the present-day thinking and acting is replacing the French Revolution's vision of *l'homme et citoyen*): "This past year (2008) saw the introduction of direct-to-consumer genomics". Presumably, you would be now able to select *yourself* from a shop shelf, just as you've learned to select brands of sneakers or fashion accessories. . . . You can put paid once and for all to all those spiritual torments of the moral self, the unending and impossible to placate pangs of conscience, perpetual uncertainty as to whether all that needed to be done has been while what has been done was fully and truly for the good of those around you. It is all now about economy, stupid: instead of bending over backwards to assist the preservation and blossoming of the partner's uniqueness, it would be enough to purchase a ready-made replacement from the shelf, hopefully with a year-long guarantee attached. And if we are to believe Venter's assurance that "no constant will be left", you may also be able, once bored, to dump yourself and buy another "self", currently more fashionable and so more attractive and as yet less boring. Genome and genetic engineering as natural, obvious and ultimate crowning of the long, tortuous struggle for more consumer freedom.

Engineering human affairs is not, of course, the genomists' invention. The intention to engineer (indeed, to create a "new man") accompanied the modern order from its inception. Summing up more than a century of disperse but insistent efforts to design a setting more human friendly, more akin to human potential and more suitable to decent human life, Karl Mannheim concluded in 1929 that planning is the reconstruction of an historically developed society which is regulated more and more perfectly by mankind from certain central positions. The social engineer in the modern man believed, as Karl Popper suggested in 1945, that in accordance with our aims we can influence the history of man just as we changed the face of the earth (let me observe, though, that the comparison of changing human history with changing nature sounded obviously less portentous and spine-chilling in 1945 when it was written, that it is now—even if Popper was not particularly enthusiastic about the social engineering practiced at the time). With the benefit of hindsight, we may sum up the long series of modern social-engineering experiments in the following way: the sole most "effective" among them were also the most inhuman, cruel, atrocious and outrageous, with the Nazis and the Communists in the top positions, closely followed by the more recent (and current!) exercises in ethnic cleansing. Treating humanity as a garden crying for more beauty and harmony casts some humans inevitably into weeds. One undertaking in which social engineering fully and truly excelled was the extermination of human weeds.

Nothing seems, however, to discredit social engineering enough to eliminate it once and for all from the area of legitimate human dreams. Only a couple of years ago Francis Fukuyama (of the "end of history" fame) suggested that the last century's attempts to create a "new and improved" human race did not fail because they were ill-begotten and bound to flounder, but because no adequate means of fulfilling them were yet available: the means available then—education, propaganda, brainwashing—were primitive, half-baked, cottage-industry techniques of recycling humans, no match with the grandiosity of the task. Fukuyama hastened to console his readers that, finally, the adequate means are fast becoming, belatedly, available—and we can now put the creation of a new human race back on the agenda, this time with a guarantee of success. . . .

Fukuyama's pretension to the heritage of an essentially sound even if imperfect tradition seems nevertheless unwarranted, because a crucial variable in his version of the "new man" has been radically changed. What Fukuyama augurs is a project altogether different from *social* engineering—which in its intention, even if not in its practice, was a design for a habitat more hospitable to the human urge of self-improvement, self-perfection and self-assertion. Social engineering was to be an operation performed on human *society*, not its *individual* members (though the first boiled down in practice, as it had to, to the second). In tune with liquid-modern times, Fukuyama follows Peter Drucker in no longer expecting the salvation to come from *society*. The "salvation" in question meant for Fukuyama (to paraphrase Jean-Jacques Rousseau) forcing humans to be happy as individuals—as it did also for (to quote Pinker once more) "a number of new companies" that "have been launched", and for their clients, the "medical consumers". Now you will have to buy yourself the gene of your choice that will *force* you (no longer in the thrall of the biblical curses of "sweat of your brow" or "labour to bear children"!) to enjoy the kind of happiness of your choice.

To cut the long story short: like so many other aspects of human life, creation of the "new man" (or woman) has been since—in our kind of society—deregulated, individualized and subsidiarized ("outsourced") to the individuals, counterfactually presumed to be the sole legislators, executors and judges allowed inside their individual "life politics". It is inside that individually run life politics that remaking of the self, through dismantling and replacing one after another the ostensible "constants" of individual nature, has already become a favourite pastime, importunately and obtrusively pushed by consumer markets and glowingly praised and heartily recommended by their ubiquitous propaganda organs. The snag is, however, that remaking one's self, dumping the discarded identity and constructing a substitute, or the act of "being born again", remains to this day a by and large DIY job, time-and-energy consuming, often costing a lot of sweat and labour and always soaked with risks. Most of the time it is a chore, and sooner or later it tends to turn into a bore.

The main message of the consumer markets, fully and truly their meta-message (the message underpinning and rendering meaningful all other messages), is the indignity of all and any discomfort and inconvenience: delay of gratification, complexity of a task transcending the already possessed skills, tools and/or resources of its performers, and a combination of the two (a need to engage in long-term training and labour to make the gratification of desire feasible) are condemned a priori as unjustified and unjustifiable and above all unnecessary and avoidable. It is from the sinking and the absorption of that message by the would-be consumers that consumer markets draw most of their seductive powers. The multifaceted art of life could be, so the message goes, reduced to just one technique: that of wise and dedicated shopping. Goods and services on offer all focus, ultimately, on getting the practice of life-art free from all things and acts awkward, cumbersome, time-consuming, risk-ridden and uncertain of success, inconvenient and uncomfortable. It is the *effortlessness* of desire-satisfaction, a *short-cut* to the satisfaction of the desire that is sought, and hoped to be found, on shop shelves and commercial catalogues. If the life-long effort of identity construction and reconstruction is at present a chore and threatens to become a bore—why not replace that infuriatingly convoluted and skill-stretching task with the one-off, instant, undemanding and painless act of buying a gene? As Guy Browning, one of the wittiest *Guardian* columnists, summed up recently, tongue in cheek, the popular reception of the genomologists' feat: "Soon, you'll be able to view your own DNA on your iPod, and download other people's instead of the tedious and messy business of procreation."

Whether "natural" but suppressed, induced or artfully construed, desires are to the consumer markets what virgin lands are to farmers: a magnet, a promise of fast expansion and new profuse and comparatively effort-lessly obtainable riches. This is, by the way, normal practice of the medical and pharmaceutical industry: once reclassified as pathological, uncommer-cialized (and thus unprofitable) human conditions turn into territories for prospective (profitable) exploitation. And the occasions for such reclassi-fication crop up whenever RD departments bump across a new gadget or compound able to provide answers to heretofore unasked questions, the sequence of events conforming to the rule "here is the answer . . . What is the question?"

The promise of the credit card issuers, "take the waiting out of wanting", opened vast expanses of new virgin lands that for two or three decades, until their exhaustion, kept the consumer economy fabulously profitable and the wheels of economic growth (measured by the amount of money changing hands) well lubricated. "Taking the risk and the effort out of self-creation" may well open new expanses of virgin lands to do the same for the next few decades. Making yourself to the measure of your dreams, being made to your own order; this is, after all, what you always wanted, you only lacked thus far the means of making your dreams come true. Now the means are within reach. Now once more you may take the waiting (and the chore and the boredom) out of wanting—this time reaching the ultimate frontier of all drive to mastery: mastery of your own being. As Craig Venter juicily and seductively expressed it, by inserting a new chromosome into a cell and eliminating the existing chromosome you can just throw away and lose "all the characteristics of the original" and replace them with something altogether different, for once, fully and truly to your taste.

The stage of this particular drama is thoroughly modern. Modernity, let me repeat, was about adjusting the "is" of the world to the human-imagined "ought". Now as in its original phase, modernity invested the hope of doing it in the human species: we, the human species, will deploy our collective wisdom to collectively achieve mastery over fate. Only in its original phase it was the hereditary prince, charismatic leader or people representatives, with their powers of coercion institutionalized in the state, that stood for the "human species" able to accomplish collectively what humans individually go on trying with little prospect of attaining. In its present, individualized society of consumers, it is the consumer markets vested with powers of seduction that stand for the "human species"—slipping into the role vacated by the state or the "Great Society".

In *The Art of Life* I pointed out that in our society of consumers, with its tacit assumption that self-care, pursuit of one's own best interests and happiness is the prime duty and obligation of every human (indeed, the purpose of life), ethical demands (as understood in Emmanuel Levinas's sense of "being *for* others") need to justify themselves in terms of the benefit which the obedience to them brings to the well-being and the self-enhancement of the obedient. Ethical philosophers have tried hard, and still go on trying, to build a bridge connecting the two shores of the river of life: the *self*-interest, and the care for *others*. As is their habit, philosophers struggled to muster and articulate convincing arguments able or at least hoped to be able to resolve the apparent contradiction and settle the controversy beyond reasonable doubt—once and for all. Philosophers tried hard to demonstrate that the obedience to moral commandments is in the "self-interest" of the obedient; that the costs of being moral will be repaid with profits; that the others will repay being kind to them in the same currency; that caring for others and being good to others is, in short, a valuable, perhaps even indispensable part of his or her self-care. Some arguments were more ingenious than other, some were backed with more authority and so carried more persuasion, but all circled around the quasi-empirical, yet empirically untested, assumption that "if you are good to others, others will be good to you".

Despite all the efforts the empirical evidence was hard to come by—or, if anything, remained ambiguous. The assumption did not square well with the personal experience of too many people, who found all too often that it is the selfish, insensitive and cynical people who gather all the prizes while the tender-hearted, bighearted, compassionate people ready to sacrifice their peace and comfort for the sake of others time and again find themselves duped, spurned and pitied or ridiculed for their credulity and unwarranted (since remaining unreciprocated) trust. It was never too difficult to collect ample proofs for the suspicion that most gains tend to go to the self-concerned, while those concerned with the welfare of others are more often than not left to count their losses. Today, particularly, collecting such evidence gets perhaps easier by the day. As Lawrence Grossberg puts it: "it is increasingly difficult to locate places where it is possible to care about something enough, to have enough faith that it matters, so that one can actually make a commitment to it and invest oneself in it". Grossberg coins the name "ironic nihilism" for the kind of attitude whose carriers, if pressed, could have reported the reasoning behind their motives in the following way:

I know cheating is wrong and I know I am cheating, but that is the way things are, that is what reality is like. One knows that life, and every choice, is a scam, but the knowledge has become so universally accepted that there are no longer any alternatives. Everyone knows everyone cheats, so everyone cheats, and if I did not, I would in effect suffer for being honest.[2]

Other, yet more principal, reservations have been voiced against the philosopher's assumption. For instance: if you decide to be kind to others *because* you expect a reward for your kindness, if the hoped-for *reward* is the motive of your good deeds, if "being kind and good to others" is the result of calculating your probable gains and losses—is your way of acting really a manifestation of a *moral* stance, or rather one more case of mercenary, selfish behaviour? And a yet more profound, truly radical doubt: can goodness be a matter of argument, persuasion, "talking over", "bringing round", deciding that "it stands to reason"? Is goodness to others an outcome of a *rational* decision—and could it be therefore prompted by an appeal to reason? Can goodness be *taught*? Arguments supporting positive as much as negative answers to such questions have been advanced, no one, however, commanding so far uncontested authority. The jury is still out. . . .

As far as the popular, folk morality is concerned—it is torn between diverse and all too often incompatible messages flowing from sites whose authority is not much more stable and much less volatile than the position on a latest recording on the top-twenty list, a latest TV hit on the ratings league of most viewed shows, the latest paperback on the list of best sellers—or for that matter of any other commodity on the league tables of everything, or almost everything. And what daily experience stubbornly day in day out reconfirms is the blatant unenforceability of any moral principles. We are daily exposed to ever-new proofs of endemic corruption in high places, billions of dollars of public funds vanishing in private pockets, the pickpockets and shoplifters filling overcrowded prisons while the fat cat sellers of worthless assets and fraudulent old age pensions, or the runners of "pyramid selling", hardly ever find their way to the defendant benches—though if they do there are enough lawyers, chartered accountants and tax advisors who for a proper fee will promptly pull them out of trouble. It is for the victims of their greed that bankruptcy courts and jails are built so that they themselves can continue their business. As Polly Toynbee noted in the aftermath of the recent "credit crunch" (in the *Guardian* of 25 October 2008): "after being rescued from certain catastrophe, bankers are as full of hubris as ever; and the government is as eager as ever not to interfere." In a mind-boggling reversal of philosophers' moral teachings, all that dishonesty seems to be ultimately grounded in the safe bet on basic human decency and honesty: "Luckily for reckless capitalism, the poor are willing to work hard in essential jobs that don't pay a living wage, so they need to borrow: they are mostly honest and easily shamed by debt collectors. That's why banks go on lending to them, as most move heaven and earth to repay".

For a moral being (that is, a being who ate an apple from the Tree of Knowledge of Good and Evil and remembers its taste), the jarring contradiction between the widespread moral sense of right and wrong and the continuous spectacle of moral corruption create an atmosphere of acute "cognitive dissonance" (confrontation with two propositions impossible to reconcile)—just as does the previously mentioned contradiction between universalistic claims of ethical demand and disaggregation and volatility of moral authorities. As psychologists have repeatedly shown, cognitive dissonance generates an anxiety difficult to endure and live with without painful disruption to the ego-cohesion and incapacitating behavioural disturbance. The afflicted person is prompted to cut the knot—impossible to be untied as it should have been if only the dissonance-causing contradiction was not of aporetic nature. There are two principal manners of cutting the knot: fundamentalism and adiaphorization (that is, cutting off certain categories of action from the realm of deeds subject to moral evaluation, and transferring it to the grey area of "beyond good and evil"), and given the acute, indeed inflamed, state of the cognitive dissonance, both are likely to be widely and repeatedly deployed. In your frame, the first manner will be particularly closely associated with religious fundamentalism; the second with what you would be probably inclined to call scientific fundamentalism.

The fundamentalist way of escaping the double cognitive dissonance (of the postulated universality of ethical demand versus polycentrism and polyvocality of ethical authority, and of the prevailing moral sense versus experiential evidence of its ubiquitous violation) aims at removing an ethical code of choice from competition with other ideational systems; declaring the sources of authority, invoked by those alternative systems, invalid in the matters of morality; moving the ethical prescriptions and proscriptions to the realm of revealed knowledge, imparted by powers beyond human reach, and particularly beyond human capacity to resist or reform. In short, rendering the moral code immune to human interference; something like Basil Bernstein's "restricted code" pushed to the extreme—not only dismissing the counter-arguments already advanced, but banning a priori the very admissibility of argumentation and denying all need of justification besides the (impenetrable, unguessable, beyond human comprehension) will of the law-maker. In religion, those effects tend to be sought and achieved by removing the sources and the sanctions of authority beyond the realm of human experience (for instance, the voice from a burning bush heard solely by Moses on Mount Sinai, paradise and hell seen only by the dead or the last judgment to be experienced only at the Second Coming, that is, at the end of earthly history).

In theory, fundamentalism appeals to faith—the unquestionable, unswerving and unshakable faith: dogmatic faith. In social practice, fundamentalism relies on the density of inner-communal bonds and frequency of interaction—contrasted with paucity of external links and reduced communication with the world outside the communal borders: on locking the doors and blocking the windows. It also relies on a bid to embrace and incorporate the totality of life functions and servicing the totality of life needs. In theory, fundamentalism demands isolation from the market of ideas; in practice, separation from the marketplace of human interactions. It remains to be seen, though, how those demands will be met in the age of the World Wide Web, Internet and minicomputers—all those technical novelties having been already intensely deployed in the formation of (let me use this oxymoronic term for the lack of a better one) "virtual fundamentalisms". Will the new media prove once more to be the messages, and would they reject the purposes alien to the messages they are?

In Michel Houellebecq's *The Possibility of an Island* (thus far the greatest of dystopias attempting to unmask and put on record the inner demons of our deregulated, individualized, fragmented, episodic, privatized society of lonely consumers), the final sentences jotted down by Daniel 25th—the last (by his own choice) in the long (infinite in its original intention) series of cloned Daniels—the sentences meant to explain his decision to opt out from reiterating his monotonous (read: contingency and uncertainty free) and dull (dull because monotonous) way of being-in-the-world are:

> I had perhaps sixty years left to live; more that twenty thousand days that would be identical. I would avoid thought in the same way I would avoid suffering. The pitfalls of life were far behind me; I have now entered a peaceful space from which only the lethal process would separate me . . . I bathed for a long time under the sun and the starlight, and I felt nothing other than a lightly obscure and nutritive sensation . . . I was, I was no longer. Life was real.[3]

Somewhere in between these meditations, Daniel 25th concludes: "Happiness was not a possible horizon. The world had betrayed". In Houellebecq's rendering, this was to be the end. But what was the beginning? How had it all started?

Twenty-five clonings earlier, in the heady, intoxicating times of what you call the "epistemological transgression", and before the "First" and the "Second Decrease" of human population of the planet (code names for credit collapse? Or ecological collapse?)—catastrophes destined to transform whatever remained of the erstwhile human species into scattered gangs of cannibalistic savages, and to leave the memory of human past to the sole possession, guardianship and care of "neohumans": the endlessly self-cloning, "equipped with a reliable system of reproduction and an autonomous communication network" and "gathered in enclaves protected by a failsafe security system" in order to "shelter from destruction and pillage the whole sum of human knowledge" (a motive which Daniel 25th would *retrospectively* impute)—Daniel 1st (the last of Daniels born of a mother) noted in his diary:

> I no longer feel any hate in me, nothing to cling to any more, no more landmarks or clues . . . There is no longer any real world, no world, no human world, I am outside time, I no longer have any past or future, I have no more sadness, plans, nostalgia, loss or hope.

As Daniel 25th would also note twenty-five neohuman clones later, in a stark contradiction to his hypothesis as to the original motives of the whole affair, Daniel 1st was on that theme—of nostalgia for desire—"particularly eloquent". That nostalgia, as we are allowed to guess, more than anything else prompted him to embrace the offer of the ultimate New Beginning: of an endless string of resurrections/reincarnations/new births as cloned replicas of his preceding selves. No wonder the first of the series of cloned Daniels was allured by the offer, since "in real life", as he noted (read: in life he knew, the only life he could have known before infinite cloning became a realistic prospect), the chances of "new beginnings" grind (sooner rather than later!) to a halt: "Life begins at fifty, that's true; insomuch as it ends at forty". By all standards of happiness, first Daniel was an epitome of success: he was a darling of chattering classes, awash with money, always in the limelight, with a supply of female charms outgrowing his ability to consume. One fly in that sweet ointment which he bewailed, and bitterly, was the infuriating finality of it all: you might have played down or ignored the spectre of the end . . . till you were forty—not much longer than that, though! After all, the "happiness bit" needed to be cleansed of the worry about the end—just as the exhilaration brought by the state of intoxication must be uncontaminated by the prospect of imminent hangover. In the times of Daniel 1st—*our real time*, yours and mine—the pursuit of happiness rests on the assumption of its endless self-repetition: in this respect at least, our concept of "living for the sake of happiness and ever-greater happiness" is perhaps the archetype of the project of cloning, that high-tech, state of-the-art substitute for immortality.

But the prospect of unavoidable end worms its way towards you stealthily, without you noticing, and once you are between forty and fifty years of age it settles *here*, in the place you call "the present", catching you as a rule unprepared and baffled. After all, little if anything in your successful life taught you and drilled into you life in the end's vicinity. Suddenly, what you've been trained for and come to consider "life", that luxuriant stream of pleasures, runs thin and comes ever closer to drying up; Daniel remembers Schopenhauer's warning: "No one can see above himself." Fortunately for him, Isabelle, the eternally elusive object of his eternal desire, was still around (shortly before she disappears from life forever), and "at that moment Isabelle could see *above me*".

And what did Isabelle see? In her own words, she saw that "when you grow old you need to think of reassuring and gentle things. You need to imagine that something beautiful awaits us in heaven". And then she mused: we train ourselves for death—when we aren't too stupid; or too rich . . . Being too rich (or too stupid—but if you were that, then by definition of stupidity you wouldn't know anyway), you'd find it terribly difficult to imagine an end to serial pleasures; if you ever tried to imagine it, that is. Seeing comes in this case *before* the imagination takes off. The end must first stare you in the face before you find out how inconceivable (meaning, in fact, unendurable) it is.

In his twenty-fifth successive rebirth, Daniel would, however, note: "The joys of humans remain unknowable to us (neohumans), inversely, we cannot be torn apart by their sorrows. Our nights are no longer shaken by terror or by ecstasy. We live, however; we go through life, without joy and without mystery."

It was that discovery, as we are allowed to guess, that prompted Daniel 25th, twenty-four clones after his first resurrection, to revoke Daniel 1st's decision and to *choose* what Daniel 1st wished to *escape*: to surrender (reject, rather) his by-cloning-assured perpetuity/infinity of existence, and cut himself free off the future (i.e., of future rebirths of the same). "I was, like all neohumans, immune to boredom . . . I was . . . a long way from joy, and even from real peace: the sole fact of existing is already a misfortune. Departing from, at my own free will, the cycle of rebirth and deaths, I was making my way towards a simple nothingness, a pure absence of content." Daniel 25th himself pronounced that sentence (as there was no one around who there and then or in the future could do it for him)—the sentence of twenty thousand days in purgatory, a vision which he could describe best in the words borrowed from Samuel Beckett:

> there is only me, this evening, here, on earth, and a voice that makes no sound because it goes towards none . . . See what is happening here, where there's no one, where nothing happens . . . I know, there is no one here, neither me nor anyone else, but some things are better left unsaid, so I say nothing. Elsewhere perhaps, by all means, elsewhere . . . [But] what elsewhere can there be to this infinite here?[4]

Indeed—having imbibed all there was available to be devoured, and with nothing in the past, present or future safe from its omnivorous voracity—infinity equals *impossibility of an "elsewhere"*. And what the neohumans managed, tragically, to forget was that without some "elsewhere" beyond the lofty, self-contended, gratified yet lonely self, without a number of other selves around searching, inquiring, challenging and prodding and altogether piercing the steel armour of self-centred solitude, without a number of next corners or next mornings there is not, and can't be, humanity.

At least a kind of humanity as we all, including the writers and readers of dystopias, know it.

NOTES

1. Klein (2010).
2. Grossberg (2007).
3. Houellebecq (2006).
4. Beckett (1999, 20, 23, 32).

REFERENCES

Beckett, Samuel. 1999. *Texts for Nothing*. Richmond: John Calder.
Grossberg, Lawrence. 2007. Affect and Postmodernity in the Struggle over "American Modernity". In *Postmodernism: What Moment?*, ed. Pelagia Goulimari, 176–201. Manchester: Manchester University Press.
Houellebecq, Michel. 2006. *The Possibility of an Island*. Trans. Gavin Bowd. Phoenix.
Klein, Kerstin. 2010. Illiberal Biopolitics and "Embryonic Life": The Governance of Human Embryonic Stem Cell Research in China. In *Orientations of the Right and Value of Life*, ed. J. Yorke. Farnham: Ashgate.

7 Consumers as Citizens
Tensions and Synergies[1]

Frank Trentmann

INTRODUCTION

What is the impact of consumer culture on well-being and civic culture? The debate about this question tends to dead-end in two rival, polar-opposite points of view. One position focuses on the pathologies of affluence. The 2008–2009 recession has given this critique a new urgency—the crisis, it is said, demonstrates the moral bankruptcy and public as well as personal costs of our lifestyle addiction to shopping, brands and conspicuous consumption (Lawson 2009; Ashley 2008; Williams 2009). In instinct and direction, however, this view follows an older critique, reaching back to J. K. Galbraith's *The Affluent Society* (1958) and beyond (see also Bauman 2007, 1998). In this view, the spread of a seductive world of goods and of a consumerist lifestyle after the Second World War has had devastating civic, psychological and environmental consequences. Wealth and well-being became divorced, a disjuncture that has been traced in a variety of indicators, from those on happiness and declining membership in associations to those on the rise in recorded mental illness and divorce. An excess of choice, we are told, has made us sick and depressed. Consumerist habits and aspirations, from television watching to a drive for conspicuous consumption and ever bigger houses and cars, are blamed for eroding the family, associational life and political participation (Schor 1999; Schwartz 2005; Layard 2005; Offer 2006).

The second position proceeds from a different starting point, especially manifest in recent reforms of public services in the United Kingdom and elsewhere in Europe. Here, choice appears as a source of empowerment and democratic renewal. In this view, the welfare state has been overtaken by a more affluent consumer society which has made people more individualist, knowledgeable and demanding. Democracies need to adjust. Instead of treating them as passive clients, public services should treat citizens as active, informed customers (Blair 2002; for critiques, see Clarke et al. 2007; Bevir and Trentmann 2007b).

The 2008–2009 world recession is a convenient moment to revisit this dichotomy and to complicate it. Both positions tend to operate with far too unitary, simplified views of consumption and citizenship. Citizens do not always act for the public good and high political participation or voter turn-out is not in and of itself a sign of democratic health (in Weimar Germany it was not). Likewise, people consume for a whole variety of reasons, some self-centred or to assert status, some other-regarding, altruistic or part of sociability (gifts, buying organic food, recreation).

Critics and advocates of "consumerism" both share debatable core assumptions. They may disagree in their evaluation, but both tend to view the "consumer" as a utility-maximizing and self-regarding individual as opposed to an other-regarding "citizen". The world depression of 1929–1931 suggests that such a polarized perspective offers little guidance in today's hard times. The Wall Street crash of 1929 prompted a resurgence of consumer activism. Having less meant each dollar counted more. Spending became a patriotic act. J. M. Keynes urged housewives to go out and spend their pennies. This was more than a commercial rescue operation. Progressives on both sides of the Atlantic raised consumers to a level of full citizenship previously reserved for producers. Membership in the nation no longer required proof of making things but the ability to consume them. And this meant a civic obligation to provide for all, including dependents and those out of work. In the United States, the New Deal promoted a new wave of grass-root activism, with federal radio shows, shoppers reporting back to government about local "profiteers" and consumers pledging to support producers honouring the minimum wage. By its nature, the fragmented and diverse consumer interest found it difficult to match the more concentrated force of producers and retailers at the level of federal agencies. Still, the sense of civic inclusion and change in political atmosphere was palpable (Cohen 2003; Jacobs 2005; Glickman 2009).

For moral critics, the current recession is welcome news because its pains, they hope, will shake people out of their self-centred, consumerist lifestyle and steer them back towards a more balanced, civic-minded and responsible way of life. Again, past recessions suggest the limitations of thinking in such mutually exclusive and sequential terms. For one, there is no universal correlation between general affluence and private excess, or between recession and frugality. Americans were saving more in the booming 1950s than in the hard 1930s, not less—notwithstanding Galbraith's fears of Americans becoming addicted to credit. The sharp drop of the American savings rate is a feature peculiar to the 1980s and 1990s—not to consumerism in general—and stands in contrast to the stickier saving behaviour of continental Europeans in recent decades. In many parts of the globe, consumer lifestyles have expanded alongside high private savings rate—China today, South Korea until recently. Nor should we forget the enormous expansion of public spending—unprecedented in history— alongside the rise in private consumption during the decades of affluence after the Second World War. Affluence is not just about private pleasures. It also funded schools, hospitals, parks and libraries.

Second, recessions do not only force individuals to make short-term adjustments but have long-term generational effects. The Oakland Growth Study was a pioneering research project that followed children born in early 1920s California through the 1930s Depression into mature life after the Second World War and beyond. It was not the Depression as such that left a mark on their later attitudes to money and consumption but whether they had to manage money or not. Those who received allowances or who had some paid work as children in the 1930s (selling newspapers, peddling self-made ashtrays, etc.) were more likely to save regularly as adults in the 1950s than those who did not—put differently, to promote a more balanced attitude to money, attention today should turn less on reckless consumers and more on keeping young people in some form of paid work. The Depression also had a kind of material displacement effect. The more deprived they were in their childhood, the more young parents invested themselves in providing domestic comforts for their own families. For men who had suffered deprivation as children, leisure was less important than their career. Today, this shift brings to mind a stereotypical image of the suburban patriarchal family with automobile, fridge, TV and a woman stuck at home. It is fair to remember that this boost in private consumption also came with a higher aspirational mindset. Greater consumption went hand in hand with a vision of greater social mobility for the next generation. Young couples in the 1950s had higher educational and professional aspirations for their children than their own parents had had for them (Elder 1974/1999).

Until recently, theorists of citizenship have had little to say about consumption, and vice versa (Soper and Trentmann 2007; JCC 2007). This essentialist view of the consumer is often tied to a broader view of contemporary history. "Consumer society" is heralded or condemned as a new historical era and paradigm break, a new all-embracing social system that, after rising up in the United States in the mid-twentieth century, swept across Europe and other parts of the world. Both of these assumptions are debatable and offer poor guidance for reform today (Miller 1995; Brewer and Trentmann 2006; Trentmann 2009).

This chapter offers some fresh perspectives for a more constructive and historically nuanced approach to the role of consumers as citizens. Neither consumers nor consumer culture are an invention of the last half century. They have come in various guises with shifting consequences for civic culture and political engagement. Attention to this longer history helps to highlight the ongoing variety and complexity with which "ordinary people" combine the desire, purchase and use of goods and services with their lives as citizens and their ideas about well-being and justice. Far from being separate universes, consumption and citizenship have overlapped in the modern period. This chapter discusses the interaction between the two, highlighting synergies as well as tensions. It places current movements for ethical consumption in a longer perspective, offers a broader view of choice and consumer identity and evaluates the potential appeal to caring consumers in strategies for improving well-being and engagement.

CONSUMPTION AS A SITE OF CIVIC ACTIVISM

Fears that material goods and pleasures undermine community and civic-mindedness are as old as theories of citizenship themselves, and can be traced back across the modern period to ancient Greece (Davidson 1999; Horowitz 1992). Critics of consumerism often invoke a golden age of civil society and political engagement, contrasting it with a recent decline in associational life and a spread in political apathy. History does little to support the idea that once people start consuming more they cease to be interested in civic affairs. Interestingly, it was the eighteenth century that saw a parallel mushrooming of consumption and civil society. New goods and tastes—tea, sugar, cotton and porcelain—were important ingredients in an expanding sphere of sociability, clubs and associations. In many parts of Europe and North America, the rise in material standards of living and the spread of commercial culture in the late nineteenth and early twentieth centuries—the department store, early cinema, tourism and branded goods—occurred during the very period when political participation and movements for social and democratic rights expanded.

In the course of the nineteenth century, consumption emerged more directly as a terrain of social mobilization and civic activism. In the 1980s–1990s it became fashionable to look to "Fair Trade" and campaigns against sweatshops as signs of a new "moral economy". Rather than a new departure, these boycotts and buycotts are chapters in a longer history, especially pronounced in Britain and the United States, but with a transnational network of buyers' leagues also extending to France, Austria-Hungary and Germany.

Three episodes illustrate the different modes by which consumption fostered civic engagement. The first was the mass boycott of slave-grown sugar by shoppers on both sides of the Atlantic in the late eighteenth and early nineteenth centuries. These boycotts were especially important for women, giving them a public voice while they were still formally outside the political nation. A second form was battles over water and gas at the level of local politics, notably in Britain. In the 1860s–1880s, these produced the first consumer leagues. These leagues were pioneered by propertied, middle-class men who asserted their rights as consumers against commercial monopolies which, they insisted, were providing poor service at high prices. A third form was the million-strong mass movement for free trade on the eve of the First World War in Britain supported by a phalanx of radicals, liberals, feminists and organized consumers. For them, an open door—without any trade barriers and subsidies—stood for cheapness, civil society and peace (Sussman 2000; Trentmann 2008; Glickman 2009; Trentmann and Taylor 2006; Dubuisson-Quellier 2009).

Consumption, these three examples suggest, is flexible and modular, offering different social and ideological possibilities for civic engagement. In the anti-slavery boycotts, women did not adopt the formal voice of citizen but exploited the gendered ideal of woman as bearers of a higher morality to exert ethical pressure, placing them above the material pressures of the market.

In the conflicts over urban water supply, propertied men, by contrast, exploited their status as taxpaying citizens to press for greater account-ability in the provision of services—some wanted a public take-over, others even talked of a "water parliament". Water is an interesting case because it concerns a good that is radically different from bread, a dress and most other commodities sold in a shop. In Victorian Britain, it was ratepayers—mainly middle-class property owners—who paid for water through their local taxes. The amount they paid was a reflection of the value of their house—not the amount of water physically used. In addition to battles over public versus private supply, this arrangement was a source of deep conflict over prices, the quality of supply and the rights and entitlements of con-sumers. Initially, in the mid-nineteenth century, this meant that the people who organized in "consumer defence leagues" were middle-class proper-tied men. By the 1890s, the introduction of constant supply for all in cities like London began to broaden the identity of the consumer into the public interest. Droughts, like those of the mid-1890s, became rallying points for radicals and working-class housewives as well as middle-class shopkeepers and the well-off. Was not everyone a consumer entitled to plentiful, run-ning water, irrespective whether they owned their house or simply were tenants who did not pay local taxes? The new voice of consumer rights expanded the scope of politics beyond voting and formal participation: the material world of everyday life became politicized and questions of basic needs introduced early ideas of social citizenship (Trentmann and Taylor 2006; Taylor and Trentmann, forthcoming).

A generation later in Britain, by the 1890s, the language of the consumer had expanded well beyond propertied taxpayers to women and the public in general. The popular momentum for free trade at the time cemented the new status of consumers as the public interest. Free trade gave consumers cheap goods. But the interest in cheapness was also tied to ideals of civil society and democracy. Female consumers in the cooperative movement now gave the power of the purse a more direct political thrust. They might not have the vote, but by preventing special interests from putting tariffs on food, free trade recognized their interests as vital parts of the nation. Moreover, they argued, their wise and responsible exercise of choice in the marketplace demonstrated their capability to exercise choice at the ballot box too (Howe 1997; Trentmann 2008).

What these cases illustrate is the diverse, evolving use of consumption in civic movements. To avoid misunderstanding, the point is not to replace the moralistic critique of "consumerism" with an idealized picture of the unilinear rise and triumph of the consumer as a hero of civic empower-ment. Consumer behaviour can be selfish at times. Consumer movements, like other movements, have ideological blind spots. They carry power, and exclude as well as include. For example, many critics of the slave trade had no problem with imperial conquest as such. Many British free-traders, likewise, were firm believers in an imperial mission, blind to the realities of exploitation and suffering in the colonies. Consumer activists who championed the municipalization of services, by contrast, were naïve in believing that a public take-over would ensure more responsible, economic consumption habits. Material well-being—such as cheap and easy access to water—can have damaging results for the environment.

The point here is to emphasize that a narrow focus on the consumer as self-regarding, materialistic individual ignores the broader moral and political universe in which consumers come into being. Conversely, we must not idealize the virtues of political action which are, after all, not always public-spirited (Schudson 2007). Clearly, consumer engagement is not limited to individual choice—the Victorian water consumer leagues wanted public control, not choice and competition. Yet where choice is mobilized, as in the free trade campaign to defend access to cheap foreign goods, it is not only in the sense of individual desire. It can be part of a larger vision of social and international justice. Progressive liberals believed that free trade would create "citizen-consumers", giving them an active stake in civil society and teaching them to develop "higher", socially more responsible tastes that would express greater care about the well-being of producers.

CHOICE AND CARING

"Choice" has become a central bone of contention in the current battle over extending consumerism to public services. This debate is mainly conducted in terms of support or opposition to an economistic model of choice as an instrument of maximizing utility, popularly associated with neoclassical economics. Critics see it as a dangerous transfer of values and practices from the supermarket to hospitals, schools and public libraries. Supporters champion it as a way to empower users of public services as co-partners, giving them an opportunity to pick providers and influence treatments.

For a consideration of well-being and participation, it is helpful to retrieve a broader conception of choice. Some of the criticisms of choice are problematic. Of course, it is possible to point to the dozens of kinds of milk available today in a supermarket as an example of an impenetrable jungle of choice. Most consumers will easily single out one kind of service or another to show the "ridiculous" proliferation of choice, such as the many telephone inquiry services competing with each other after deregulation.

The problem with this critique is that it is partial and cannot be generalized. What seems an excess of choice and waste of time and effort to some people for some goods and services appears vital to others. We would, for example, not draw the conclusion that the proliferation of choice of, say, books or music on any given topic or genre has diminished well-being. We may find it challenging, even at times frustrating, to steer our way through the escalating number of publications, but our well-being, knowledge, social life and sense of self would not be enhanced if we just had two or three books or music recordings to choose from.

The idea of choice, therefore, needs to be disentangled from the narrow utilitarian version that has received so much attention in recent years. One alternative tradition is that of John Dewey, the pragmatist philosopher and educational reformer, and perhaps the most influential public intellectual in the United States in the inter-war years. For Dewey, all life was about choosing. Choice helped individuals to develop "the habits and impulses ... to make us sensitive, generous, imaginative, impartial in perceiving the tendency of our inchoate ... activities". Individuals, in this view, are not just calculating machines that measure short-term pleasures and pains. Rather they learn to use their memory and experience to cultivate long-term habits that make sense of their lives, connect past and present and raise their consciousness. In short, choice makes people more human by making them constantly aware of the meanings of their actions (Dewey 1922; Ryan 1995; Bevir and Trentmann 2007a).

This may sound abstract and philosophical. In fact, it underpinned the progressive reform principles of how children would be taught—learning by doing rather than being taught to. It also shaped the cultural hinterland of the Home Economics Movement, through which hundreds of thousands of young American women and men learned how to enhance their daily lives as consumers—what today would be included under "well-being". In addition to questions of price and quality, home economics taught people about a range of cultural as well as financial subjects, from health care and banking to art. People were considered more than "buyers". They were "consumers", who (in addition to making purchasing decisions) learnt to evaluate choices according to motives, values and ends. The aim was to train consumers to make choices that were not only about instant gratification or a good price but which would develop their personality and foster social affections and relationships. Choice, in this view, was a channel between individual growth and social well-being.

Choice can connect personal and social motives. One manifestation is the use of consumption as an expression of caring for others. The consumer cooperative movement was a large-scale phenomenon across the globe until the middle of the twentieth century, and continues to be so in some countries (Furlough and Strikwerda 1999). In recent years, caring has stretched from concern for producers to care for the land and animals. Consumers have flocked to a wide variety of so-called "alternative" food and consumption networks, stretching from local farmers' markets to organic allotment groups, all the way to Internet schemes for adopting sheep in the Abruzzi Mountains. Interestingly, one appeal behind farm shops and organic food box schemes is that shoppers feel it increases their choice, providing them with previously unknown vegetables like kallaloo (Kneafsey et al. 2008).

Knowledge and interest in organic food is not the preserve of the educated middle class. People think about the health of their family, the environment and distant farmers as well as price. For many disadvantaged consumers it is not values or attitudes but lack of income and absence of a diverse retail landscape that prevents them from expressing their caring motives.

PUBLIC CONNECTIONS

It is unhelpful to see political consumerism (consumer boycotts, anti-sweat-shop campaigns, fair trade) and more conventional forms of political behaviour (voting, political engagement at the local or national level) as a zero-sum game—one drawing energy away from the other. Historically, they have tended to be symbiotic rather than competitive or mutually exclusive. The white label campaigns of consumer leagues a century ago provided a political space for reform-minded middle-class women (Sklar 1998). In the United States, in the 1890s, the National Consumers' League introduced a white list and placed white labels on goods produced under fair labour standards, mobilizing consumer power to enforce better working conditions. Similar buyer leagues followed in Britain, Germany, France and the Netherlands. Caring for workers became the professional duty of the middle-class female consumer. Similarly, the New Deal in the United States and grass-root consumer mobilization reinforced each other. Encouraged by New Dealers in Washington, millions of volunteers went up and down the country signing up households to display the American eagle and pledge to buy only goods produced under fair labour conditions. Local consumers reported on profiteers and high prices, assisting a process of "state building from the bottom up" (Jacobs 1997; see also Cohen 2003).

Of course, political consumerism is not inherently virtuous, nor does it always feed into civic engagement. We should resist the temptation of glorifying the history of consumer movements as the forward march of progress, democracy and justice. Middle-class consumer leagues, for example, had a paternalistic or perhaps rather maternalistic strain; philanthropic middle-class shoppers looked down at workers as producers, never taking them seriously as consumers in their own right (Chessel 2003). As an expression of caring, the power of the purse could also be targeted for imperial and racist purposes. In empire shopping weeks in inter-war Britain, hundreds of thousands of conservative women urged housewives to express their imperial loyalties by buying sultanas and other goods from their white cousins in the empire rather than "dirty" fruit from Turks and other "inferior" races (Trentmann 2008). The testing agencies that have sprung up in post-war Europe have focused on safe, efficient consumer durables rather than formal political engagement (Hilton 2003, 2009). Still, there is no reason to presume that political consumerism and political activity more generally have ceased to be symbiotic in many instances in the contemporary world.

Recent research on one thousand young people in Stockholm, Brussels and Montreal who used boycotts, buycotts and other forms of political consumerism shows that most of them also have an above average degree of community engagement, act as volunteers and have a high degree of trust in their fellow citizens. They are not alienated from public life in general but from formal political institutions in particular. They might be skeptical citizens, but they are neither apathetic nor passive (Micheletti, Stolle and Hoogh 2003; Micheletti 2003; Boström et al. 2005; Barnett et al. 2005).

More generally, the degree of disengagement from the public world must not be exaggerated. A focus on formal associations distracts from the many more informal and mediated modes of engagement. Television, more than any other feature of consumer culture, has been blamed for a retreat from an active public sphere into a private world of passive, material comforts. In fact, we know surprisingly little about how people consume media and what consequences this has for their engagement with public affairs. One British study, conducted in 2004–2005, found that most people felt connected to the public world; 70 per cent felt they had a duty to keep up with public affairs, and many had a habit of watching the news regularly. Nor were they indifferent. Most people felt strongly about issues. The problem was lack of trust in formal political institutions: two-thirds were interested in politics, but over half felt they had no say in what their government did. In short, the problem is not political interest but a sense of powerlessness and a lack of trust in politicians (Couldry, Livingstone and Markham 2007).

How, then, can we create a virtuous circle between well-being, engagement and participation? An older communitarian tradition tends to imagine a linear flow of cause and effect: materialism and commercial culture saps engagement which then results in diminished participation in public life. The preceding discussion suggests a different view. The spread of material goods and lifestyles may have transformed the issues and forms of engagement but they have not extinguished them. As far as regular political participation is concerned, the problem lies between existing levels of engagement and an area of formal politics that is seen as distant, exclusive and untrustworthy.

To what degree has the "consumerist" reform strategy of injecting "choice" into public services helped to overcome this legitimacy deficit? Has the appeal to "consumers" or "customers" of public services like medical care, social housing or care for the elderly given people a greater sense of belonging and empowerment? Interestingly, recent research from the United Kingdom shows the considerable gulf between government rhetoric of choice, on the one hand, and identities and practices on the ground, on the other. The "consumer" remains an ambivalent, shifting identity. The vast majority of people (local users of services as well as providers) disliked

the language of the consumer in public services—some felt it was importing a radically different world of the supermarket into the life of the community. People did want better services, but this included a concern for the
needs of others, not just their own. Voice matters as much as choice. Many
local authorities lacked the different kinds of channels to be heard that
citizens were looking for. The clash of languages between "consumer" and
"community" suggests that for well-being and engagement to be joined in a
virtuous transfer with participation, governments need to do much more to
listen to people on the ground and to take their local knowledge, identities
and ways of managing everyday life seriously. A blunt, universal reference
to "the consumer" is unhelpful here. Providers and policymakers do well to
recognize the many different meanings and identities users attach to consumption and the use of services (Clarke et al. 2007; Birchall and Simmons
2004; Bevir and Trentmann 2007b).

CONCLUSION

In the last two decades, consumption and choice have become significant
sites of political projects for enhancing well-being, people power and social
and international ethics. These have ranged from consumerist reforms of
public services to movements for fair trade and responsible consumption.
Public debate would do well to recognize that this appeal to the consumer
is not an entirely new phenomenon. The turn to the consumer as a political actor is not the invention of contemporary consumer culture, nor the
result of some "advanced liberal governmentality". It has a longer history
in social movements and battles for citizenship. This rich past reveals the
potential of consumption as a terrain of engagement, and of goods, tastes
and lifestyles, to articulate questions about public inclusion and account-
ability as well as about social ethics and responsibility towards others.

One historical constellation in this longer history of consumer politics
bears directly on the current economic crisis, that is, the battle of consum-
er-citizens as taxpayers over water, gas and other utilities. Consumers, it
cannot be stressed too strongly, were not always just individual shoppers.
At crucial moments, they rallied together as taxpayers, such as the middle-
class citizens in Victorian cities who argued that, as citizens who paid their
annual rates, they had rights as consumers vis-à-vis monopoly providers
of gas and water. Some of these battles concerned prices, others quality of
supply. They raised thorny questions of accountability. Once taxes were
handed over to private companies, how was the interest of consumers to
be protected? This, in essence, is one question of today's global financial
crisis that has not received the attention it deserves. Consumers, as taxpayers, have handed over an unprecedented cheque of billions and billions of
pounds, dollars, marks and krona to big banks that were facing meltdown.
In addition to whether this was the right (or wrong) economic medicine,

this intervention raises profound questions of accountability, rights and representations. How are the views and interests of these millions of small citizen-consumers and shareholders to be guarded? A broader, historically more sensitive understanding of the consumer as citizen is one step toward giving this question the political attention it deserves.

A longer historical perspective, finally, alerts us to the danger of seeing the consumer as an all-embracing identity or exclusive form of political practice. It would be unwise to simply reject consumers and choice as instruments of individualist materialism. But equally it would be foolish to idealize them and turn them into a new political toolkit fit for all occasions. In their everyday lives, past and present, people try to enhance their well-being through a variety of channels and forms of engagement. Choice and consumer empowerment is felt to be appropriate and desirable in some contexts, not in others. To advance engagement with citizens, any strategy for well-being should recognize the potential as well as the limits of choice.

NOTES

1. This chapter draws on my contribution to the Council of Europe's 2008 report "Rethinking Consumer Behaviour for the Well-Being of All". I am grateful to Gilda Farrell and the Council of Europe for kind permission to reuse material.

REFERENCES

Ashley, Jackie. 2008. The Recession Means We Must Do Politics Differently. *Guardian*, 27 October.

Barnett, Clive, Nick Clarke, Paul Clock and Alice Malpass. 2005. The Political Ethics of Consumerism. *Consumer Policy Review* 15 (2): 2–8.

Bauman, Zygmunt. 1998. *Work, Consumerism and the New Poor*. Buckingham: Open University Press.

———. 2007. *Consuming Life*. Polity Press.

Bevir, Mark, and Frank Trentmann. 2007a. Civic Choices: Retrieving Perspectives on Rationality, Consumption, and Citizenship. In *Governance, Citizens, and Consumers: Agency and Resistance in Contemporary Politics*, ed. M. Bevir and F. Trentmann, 19–33. Basingstoke: Palgrave Macmillan.

———, eds. 2007b. *Governance, Citizens, and Consumers: Agency and Resistance in Contemporary Politics*. Basingstoke: Palgrave Macmillan.

Birchall, Johnston, and Richard Simmons. 2004. *User Power: The Participation of Users in Public Services*. London: National Consumer Council.

Blair, Tony. 2002. *The Courage of Our Convictions: Why Reform of the Public Services is the Route to Social Justice*. London: The Fabian Society.

Boström, Magnus, Andreas Føllesdal, Mikael Klintman, Michele Micheletti and Mads P. Sørensen. 2005. *Political Consumerism: Its Motivations, Power, and Conditions in the Nordic Countries and Elsewhere*. København: Nordisk Ministerråd.

Brewer, John, and Frank Trentmann, eds. 2006. *Consuming Cultures, Global Perspectives*. Oxford: Berg.

Chessel, Marie-Emmanuelle. 2003. Aux Origines de la Consommation Engagée: La Ligue Sociale d'Acheteurs (1902–1914). *Vingtième Siècle. Revue d'Histoire* 77:95–108.

Clarke, John, Janet E. Newman, Nick Smith, Elizabeth Vidler and Louise Westmarland. 2007. *Creating Citizen-Consumers: Changing Publics and Changing Public Services.* London: Sage.

Cohen, Lizabeth. 2003. *A Consumer's Republic: The Politics of Mass Consumption in Postwar America.* New York: Alfred A. Knopf.

Couldry, Nick, Sonia Livingstone and Tim Markham. 2007. *Media Consumption and Public Engagement: Beyond the Presumption of Attention.* Basingstoke: Palgrave Macmillan.

Davidson, James. 1999. *Courtesans and Fishcakes: The Consuming Passions of Classical Athens.* New York: HarperPerennial.

Dewey, John. 1922. *Human Nature and Conduct: An Introduction to Social Psychology.* New York: Henry Holt and Company.

Dubuisson-Quellier, Sophie. 2009. *La Consommation Engagée.* Paris.

Elder, Glen H. 1974/1999. *Children of the Great Depression: Social Change in Life Experience.*

Furlough, Ellen, and Carl Strikwerda, eds. 1999. *Consumers against Capitalism? Consumer Cooperation in Europe, North America, and Japan, 1840–1990.* Lanham and Oxford: Rowman and Littlefield.

Galbraith, John Kenneth. 1958. *The Affluent Society.* New York: The New American Library.

Glickman, Lawrence. 2009. *Buying Power: A History of Consumer Activism in America.* Chicago.

Hilton, Matthew. 2003. *Consumerism in Twentieth-Century Britain.* Cambridge: Cambridge University Press.

———. 2009. *Prosperity for All? Consumer Activism in an Era of Globalization.* Ithaca, NY: Cornell University Press.

Horowitz, Daniel. 1992. *The Morality of Spending: Attitudes towards the Consumer Society in America, 1875–1940.* Chicago: Ivan R. Dee.

Howe, Anthony. 1997. *Free Trade and Liberal England 1846–1946.* Oxford: Clarendon Press.

Jacobs, Meg. 1997. "How about Some Meat": The Office of Price Administration, Consumption Politics, and State Building from the Bottom Up, 1941–1946. *Journal of American History* 84 (3): 910–941.

———. 2005. *Pocketbook Politics: Economic Citizenship in Twentieth-Century America.* Princeton, NJ: Princeton University Press.

JCC. 2007. Special Issue: Consumption and Citizenship. *Journal of Consumer Culture* 7 (2).

Kneafsey, Moya, Lewis Holloway, Laura Venn, Elizabeth Dowler and Helena Tuomainen. 2008. *Alternative Food Networks: Reconnecting Producers, Consumers and Food?* Oxford.

Lawson, Neal. 2009. *All Consuming: How Shopping Got Us into This Mess and How We Can Find Our Way Out.* London: Penguin.

Layard, Richard. 2005. *Happiness: Lessons from a New Science.* New York: Penguin Press.

Micheletti, Michele. 2003. *Political Virtue and Shopping: Individuals, Consumerism, and Collective Action.* New York and Basingstoke: Palgrave Macmillan.

Micheletti, M., D. Stolle and M. Hoogh. 2003. Zwischen Markt und Zivilgesellschaft: Politischer Konsum als bürgerliches Engagement. In *Zivilgesellschaft— national und transational,* ed. D. Gosewinkel, D. Rucht, W. Van den Daele and J. Kocka, 151–171. Berlin: WZB.

Miller, Daniel. Ed. 1995. *Acknowledging Consumption: A Review of New Studies*. London: Routledge.

Offer, Avner. 2006. *The Challenge of Affluence: Self-Control and Well-Being in the United States and Britain since 1950*. Oxford: Oxford University Press.

Ryan, Alan. 1995. *John Dewey and the High Tide of American Liberalism*. New York.

Schor, Juliet B. 1999. *The Overspent American: Why We Want What We Don't Need*. New York: HarperPerennial.

Schudson, Michael. 2007. Citizens, Consumers, and the Good Society. *Annals of the American Academy of Political and Social Science* 611:236–249.

Schwartz, Barry. 2005. *The Paradox of Choice: Why More is Less*. New York: Harper Collins.

Sklar, K. Kish. 1998. The Consumers' White Label Campaign of the National Consumers' League, 1898–1918. In *Getting and Spending: European and American Consumer Societies in the Twentieth Century*, ed. Susan Strasser, Charles McGovern and Matthias Judt. Cambridge: Cambridge University Press.

Soper, Kate, and Frank Trentmann, eds. 2007. *Citizenship and Consumption*. Basingstoke: Palgrave Macmillan.

Sussman, Charlotte. 2000. *Consuming Anxieties: Consumer Protest, Gender and British Slavery, 1713–1833*. Stanford, CA: Stanford University Press.

Taylor, Vanessa, and Frank Trentmann. Forthcoming. Liquid Politics: Water and the Politics of Everyday Life in the Modern City. *Past and Present*.

Trentmann, Frank. 2008. *Free Trade Nation: Commerce, Consumption, and Civil Society in Modern Britain*. Oxford: Oxford University Press.

———. 2009. The Long History of Contemporary Consumer Society: Chronologies, Practices, and Politics in Modern Europe. *Archiv für Sozialgeschichte* 49:107–128.

Trentmann, Frank, and Vanessa Taylor. 2006. From Users to Consumers: Water Politics in Nineteenth-Century London. In *The Making of the Consumer*, ed. Frank Trentmann, 53–79.

Williams, Rowan. 2009. Easter Sermon. *Guardian*, 13 April, 6.

8 Political Consumption Revisited

Should We Resist "Consumers' Resistance"?

Franck Cochoy[1]

The mundane views about market issues are contradictory. On the one hand, the market economy is often seen as a natural fact that is—or should be—affected by political regulations. On the other, the market phenomenon is often presented as a force coming from the outside that tries to penetrate and reduce the strength of our political society. Both views share the idea that market and politics are two conflicting entities. Politics may be used to fight market phenomena: see, for instance, the long tradition of the consumerist critique, from the denunciation of the one-dimensional realm of consumption (Marcuse 1960) to the claim for "no logo" (Klein 2000). But reversely, market behaviour may also be used as a trick to promote political values: see the idea of "political consumerism" which proposes to use market behaviour as an "individualized form of collective action". Consumers are urged to forward some collective ideals (sustainable development, ecological concern, fair trade) through their individual market decisions, either through boycotts or buycotts (Micheletti 2003). In this chapter, I would like to revisit, along with Callon (2007), the opposition between market and politics these strategies rest on. First, I will draw on a few historical facts to show that contemporary political consumerism is strongly connected to a long-term articulation between consumer and political issues. Second, I will focus on the micro level of consumer behaviour to show that the idea of a consumers' political "resistance" to market forces should not be reduced to the emergence of alternative forms of consumption, but rather seen as an excellent notion to encompass the growing elusiveness of shopping behaviour (Ekström and Brembeck 2004).[2]

Recent works surveyed how market actors developed a political critique and reform of market realities, both on the supply side, with the call for sustainable development and Corporate Social Responsibility (Vogel 2005) and on the demand-side, with the different forms of political consumption and consumer resistance—culture jamming, fair trade, slow food, etc. (Micheletti 2003; Roux 2007; Dubuisson-Quellier 2009). The project of "politicizing the market" rests on a double hypothesis: first, it implicitly suggests the existence of a prior state of a market deprived of any political dimension; second, it also points at a favourable context for its politicization.

In other words, many political consumerists see their movements as "new" and as an adequate answer of some recent transformations of the economy. Obviously, the recent financial and economic crisis, in deepening the gap between wealthy and poor countries and, inside each country, between the wealthiest and the poorest people, works as a clear call for fair trade and social responsibility.

The first hypothesis does not stand up to the facts, as the scholars who dealt with such questions have shown. For instance, boycotts and buycotts were used as a means to fight against slavery or to promote civil rights of black people in the United States. They were also used as part of the non-violent opposition to English colonialism of Gandhi, or as a weapon against the apartheid regime in South Africa (Micheletti 2003). Moreover, one may trace some more troubling and ancient analogies between the discourse of the activists who promote fair trade and the discourse of women consumer leagues of the end of the nineteenth century and beginning of the twentieth century in the United States (Glickman 2009) as well as in Europe (Chessel 2006). Yesterday, like today, activists fought for the use of consumption as a means to improve labour conditions, through boycotts, labels, "white lists" of companies or products that respected workers' rights and should thus be encouraged with purchases (buycotts). Yesterday, like today, the market was presented as a way to forward some causes that states were slow to deal with. At the time of the "Progressive Era", the initiatives of socially conscious activists were largely aimed at counterbalancing at the local level the relative failure to act of the governments of that time.

But if the initiatives of yesterday and today are to a large extent comparable, does not the knowledge of old movements help adopting the proper view about today's issues? The decline of political consumerism of the past century probably largely relies on how "standard" political institutions eventually proved capable to handle the problems at stake: the twentieth century witnessed the setting of fraud legislation (see the US "Pure Food Drug and Act" of 1906 or its French and Swedish equivalent in 1905), social insurances, statistical bureaus and instruments, market regulation, welfare state, etcetera. For instance, the anti-fraud regulation dealt with the dangers arising from the information asymmetries between manufacturers and consumers (Cochoy 2005). Later, other institutions that were a priori less concerned with consumption issues took responsibility for the societal problems that consumer movements ceaselessly identified behind the marketing of products: health and safety issues, labour force exploitation, government's weakness in terms of market knowledge and regulation. In so doing, these institutions lessened the need for a political action at the level of individual purchases. The recollection of these past evolutions should prevent us from concluding too fast that states are unable to overcome some problems that may well rely on a temporary powerlessness of political authorities.

Here comes the second hypothesis along which contemporary consumerism is linked to the larger context of "globalization". The development (or rather renewal) of political consumption is unanimously attributed to our contemporary globalized world. Globalization is supposed to weaken the efficiency of national governmental and legal systems. It thus would legitimate the advent of new modes of regulations based on private initiatives, like political consumption, codes of conducts, labels and certification schemes which are meant to guarantee the ethical, socially responsible or "environment-friendly" character of products. The weakness of intergovernmental efforts to renew and strengthen the rules and institutions of global financial markets after the recent crisis or to adopt some clear and efficient commitments to reduce gas emissions tends to favour private "street-level" initiatives as the only means to act and overcome the paralysis of public bodies. The question raised by such movements is less that of their aims—who would deny the necessity to defend the environment, social rights and human solidarity?—than that of the means to reach them. The will to promote "market-based governance" relies on the idea that government, state and classic public authorities fail to act properly. But if there is little doubt that international institutions face a crisis (which is probably more political than financial and environmental only), the question remains open if such difficulties call for an abandonment of politics to market mechanisms, or rather for a necessary renewal of public institutions at the global level.

Bruno Latour (1999) and Michel Callon (2007) have shown to what extent the problems raised by the introduction of non-human agencies into democracy (AIDS virus, hole in the ozone layer, global warming) call for the invention of new forms of political representation, new expertise and new institutions. Symmetrically, one can wonder if the proliferation of humans into the market dynamics does not call for the same type of transformation. In the same way that politics should not be delegated to scientists each time that a problem arises on the nature side, it should not be abandoned to the market each time that a difficulty emerges in the economy. The invention of the new hybrid institutions Latour calls for has already started in the realm of environmental issues, with the inscription of the precautionary principle in the French Constitution, the development of new type of democratic deliberation in "hybrid forums" (Callon, Lascoumes and Barthe 2001), the intervention of the Kyoto Protocol and later the IPCC at the international level, and so on. In the economic and social spheres, the question is now to know if markets need the morale discourse embedded in voluntary charts and labels, or rather some enlarged and renewed procedures and institutions that may legitimate the action of new agencies, police, inspection and standardization bodies liable to sustain some decisions taken collectively and according to the rules.

What is true at a worldwide scale is also true at the local level of consumer actions. The good idea in political consumerism is to show that politics is not only a matter of remote political action, but that it may also rest on local individual behaviour. However, we should look closer at the close action of "resistant" consumers. What is political in ordinary consumption? To what do consumers resist? And what does "consumer resistance" mean? I would like to stress two points which may help us to take a better measurement of political consumption.

First, "political consumerists" are groups of activists that have long evidenced some difficulties in bringing the masses with them. If we give to the notion of "resistance" the meaning it has in electricity, and if we have to choose between consumers' "resistance" or "non-resistance", we should rather admit that in most cases consumers are excellent conductors of the market current! The consumers who prove capable or anxious to resist the market represent an epiphenomenon. See, for instance, the market share of fair trade coffee, which is yet the emblematic product of this type of alternative goods. This market share oscillates between 3 and 12 per cent in European countries, and it represents 0.2 per cent only of the American coffee market (Vogel 2005). And even when political consumption seems to be successful, this does not go without ambiguities.

Why such a pessimistic statement? Why do consumers prove so unable to resist market seductions? The economist Bernard Ruffieux (2004) recently gave two suggestive answers to these questions. The first answer is that of a "framing effect": since market situations orient the consumers' eyes towards objects rather than towards their fellow consumers, the same situations "loosen" the moral constraint while exciting the propensity towards hedonistic consumer behaviour. The second answer is that of the "under additivity" of preferences:

> When a consumer learns that a product is certified "free of GMOs", she increases her propensity to pay. But if the same consumer later learns that this product is also an organic one, she does not increase her propensity to pay in the same proportion than for a product for which she has not paid already for an "alter" dimension. Thus, the propensity to pay for the collectivity or for others on markets is very fast *saturated*. (Ruffieux 2004; my translation)

But even when consumers pay for the "political" products, it is not sure that they do so because of this property. See the promotional label of a French mass retailer reproduced in Figure 8.1. On the one hand, this label allusively sells fair trade coffee on its top part ("Ground coffee Max Havelaar GOLDEN FILTER"): if the consumer wants to know what "Max Havelaar" means, she has either to know it already or make the effort to refer to some details written further on the coffee package. On the other hand and by contrast, the same label very explicitly promotes a price advantage on its bottom part ("save 0€50 on your consumer loyalty program").

Figure 8.1   "Ground coffee Max Havelaar: save 0€50 on your consumer loyalty program".

This label shows that consumers do not resist alone, but rather with some discourses in kit form which are provided to them to do so: their supposed resistance may thus be more the effect of some efforts which come from the outside than the result of a sovereign decision of their own will.

Second, resisting actions should be taken cautiously. Let's cite the example of Philip Morris. This cigarette manufacturer pretends to firmly resist its own temptation to sell tobacco to young consumers. In order to meet that objective, it develops some programs aimed at teaching young consumers how to resist its own products. Notably, the brand voluntarily writes on its cigarette packaging the warning: "for adults only". But one wonders if this rhetoric presented as part of the corporate social responsibility policy of the company is not a very astute means for the manufacturer to display its virtue while stimulating at the same time the behaviour it pretends to prevent. Teenagers, as we all know, are dreaming of quitting their minor status to join that of adults. In order to succeed, they very often tend to adopt the behaviours that are presented to them as the privilege of older people (Cochoy, Le Daniel and Crave 2009). These observations lead us to rethink and broaden the notion of consumer resistance first to better account for the forms of political consumption, second to explore other fields which are as political as the former ones but which tend to be neglected. In this respect, I would like to submit three proposals.

The first proposal is to admit that the Berlin Wall that is supposed to divide standard consumption from alternative consumption fell, or perhaps never existed. There may be no alternative to the market. In order to develop themselves, the so-called forms of "alternative" consumption have no other means than borrowing their resources from the same ordinary market they want to refuse. Slow Food pretends to sell the products directly, "without packaging of any kind", but as we may see it in Figure 8.2, this is said from a wonderfully packaged website! The electronic interface puts forward a brand ("Slow Food"), a logo (a little white snail on a yellow background), a symbolic representation of the product (the photograph of a fresh apple), varied descriptive information and so on.

Even activists behave more like standard consumers who take their share of the marketing process than like "alternative" consumers: like shoppers in self-service settings, they sort their waste; they drive kilometres to go to the local farmer, etcetera (Dubuisson-Quellier and Lamine 2008). Here is the paradox: consumers have all the more chances to resist efficiently to the market when they succumb to its very logic, wants and techniques. As a consequence, the consumers who think they are resisting the market in adopting the so-called alternative ways of consumption show the same docility and weakness in front of market devices as their supposed less politically aware counterparts.

The second proposal stems from the first one: mundane consumption is as much political as alternative consumption. As soon as one admits that resistance varies a lot depending on its object, as soon as one breaks away from the nice consensus about what consumers are supposed to resist, things become different. Resistance is in fact at stake in every market situation. Each consumer resists more or less the products offered to her. Resistance follows the logic of the greatest slope: one resists a product to yield to another. As soon as the object of resistance is open, the more resistant consumers are not the ones who refuse standard products and market devices, but those whose motivations are the most elusive. From this point of view, the most paroxysmic form of resistance is that of children, which is well known as "pester power" (Procter and Richards 2002). See, for instance, a commercial for the Zazoo condoms.[3] This commercial stages a scene in a supermarket. A little boy, eager to obtain the candy his father refuses him, after several

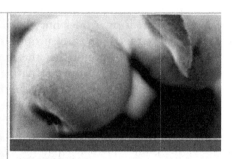

- **HOME**
- **HOW TO LIVE SLOW**
- **ABOUT US**
- **JOIN SLOW FOOD**
- **LOCAL CHAPTERS**
- **OUR PROGRAMS**
- **EVENTS**
- **BLOG**
- **GENERAL STORE**
- **PRESS**
- **SUPPORT**

Find Slow Food
in your area

Choose a state   ▾

Take Action!

Support food labeling that actually matters. Tell your congressperson that you care about mandatory identification of genetically modified foods. Visit www.ga3.org/campaign/ Label_GE_Food to send the message.

Don't settle for "greenwashed" packaging on unsustainable products. Get your food straight from the source without packaging of any kind. Buy direct from your local farmers by joining a CSA, co-op, or shopping at a farmer's market (visit www.localharvest.org/ organic-farms/ to find one near you).

Figure 8.2   http://www.slowfoodusa.org/change/01–17–07_take_action.html (consulted in May 2008).

unsuccessful attempts to place the candy in the family shopping cart, ends up throwing an appalling tantrum that puts all the clientele in turmoil and brings shame and powerlessness upon his poor father. The scene closes with this logic caption: "[if you don't want to live such a scene] use condoms". One cannot resist resisting consumers, except with the help of those condoms the story tries to sell.

Figure 8.3 Zazoo condoms (video capture).

This ad, beyond its humorous character, is rich in very serious lessons. First, it shows to what extent the political aspect of consumption depends not only on the relationship between market capitalism and vigilant consumers, but also on the interaction between individual consumers themselves, whoever they are. Who is resisting in the ad? The father, who refuses his son's choice? Or the son, who refuses his father's authority? Both of course. The confrontation between the two attitudes remind us that beside classic forms of activist commitment there exist a highly mundane kind of political debate between children who like candy and parents who think these products are bad for their children's teeth . . . or for their own purse (Cochoy and Grandclément 2005; Cochoy 2008a). Parents–children ordinary "commitments" around consumption issues form a very rich political society in itself, which deserves the same ethnographic scrutiny than adult explicit political commitments (Brembeck 2007). On a broader scale, there also exists a larger opposition between the consumers who demand greener or more ethical products, and others who on the contrary like shining and smooth fruits and vegetables, cheaper products and so on. Now the latter participate in market citizenship as well as the former: political commitment is not the privilege of one particular type of product or consumer. In other words, one should not confuse citizenship and activism. Politics, far from being a substance attached to some particular products or actors, rather designates the relationship that stems from the confrontation between all the entities—objects and people—implied in the market game.

A last question emerges. What do consumers resist? In the Zazoo ad, resistance is less oriented toward the refusal of products than toward the consumer himself, after an absurd radicalization of critique: in this ad, there is no other way to resist consumption society than resisting society itself, through the avoidance of the very existence of future consumers. The final coup de théâtre—"use condoms"!—is two-sided, since it reveals in the same gesture the critique and its use in marketing: the refusal of consumption society is the argument that is put forward to push us into the consumption . . . of condoms. The more resistant entity in this ad is neither the father nor the son, but the latex envelope which is aimed at helping us to get rid of the alternative between abstinence (resisting love) and descendants (resisting resistant children). Zazoo advertising campaign promotes the market through its radical denunciation. It points by antiphrasis to the impassable character of the market society, and more positively it designates the extreme richness of its political dimensions. Indeed, the ad underlines that there is no "one-dimensional" resistance, but rather that the latter is distributed among all market devices, products, actors and professionals.

The third proposal consists in questioning the very meaning of the resistance idea. Resisting is refusing. But refusing does not restrict itself to rejection; on the contrary, it often hides a very strong adhesion. Resisting the market is very often resisting oneself. It is this double resistance to the market and oneself that the consumerist press refers to when it humorously encourages consumers to cling to their shopping list, to take a basket rather than a shopping cart, to let the children at home, etcetera (Aldridge 1994, quoted in Mallard 2007). Here, we meet the figure of Ulysses who asks his sailors to tie him to the mast of his ship so that he may listen to the song of the sirens and resist their seduction. Jon Elster (1979) placed this legend as the center of his analysis of the weakness of will, i.e., the failure of anyone to stick to the decisions made, the difficulty to sacrifice one's immediate pleasure for a future well-being. For Elster, the only way to overcome this kind of weakness is to act like Ulysses: we should not rely on an internal moral force which is most of the time illusionary; rather, we have to delegate the exercise of our will to external people and devices. Indeed, the latter are the only entities which are capable of reminding us of our commitments, if necessary in returning them against ourselves. This framework is very suggestive, since at a larger level it also questions the ability of single actors to carry on their individual projects and the necessity to "delegate" this will to some kind of larger encompassing devices. Applied to political consumerism, this means that we should not expect too much of individualized political commitment, but rather rely at the same time on classic "public" regulation (Cochoy 2009).

But on marketplaces, people follow a similar yet different pattern than the one of Ulysses. The pattern is similar to the extent that the consumer's resistance is often an equipped one. But it is different to the extent that market resistance is much more complex than the scene described in the *Odyssey*. On the market scene, we may observe some devices which assist the resistance of the consumer . . . in order to overcome it. More precisely, there are two kinds of such devices. The first kind is aimed at rendering consumption reversible, in the hope that the reversibility option will favour the commitment of the consumer in a choice process: see "no purchase exit" or "satisfied or reimbursed" devices (respectively special gates and signs in the shops).[4] The second kind of device is aimed at favouring the partial consumption of products (self-service, window-shopping, sampling and tasting) in the hope that a first "free" consumption act will favour subsequent real purchases. Today, there are no more Ulysses, the ship and its mast on the one side, the sea, the sirens and their seduction on the other one. In contemporary market scenes, all these elements are tightly intertwined in "captation" devices[5] (Cochoy 2007): like the mast, these devices offer to the consumer some anchor points which help her not to buy anything (the situation is staged to favour the free consumption of products). But like the sirens, the same devices play on the former anchorage points in order to attract the consumer (the free access works as a commercial argument). All in all, everything looks as if the sirens provide Ulysses with both a mast and loose cords so that he may freely swim with them while at the same time not approaching them too close or too fast, in the hope to give him a chance not to be afraid anymore and thus embrace them later on. Therefore, and against any expectations, such market "captation devices" are inextricably seduction and resistance tools. See, for instance, a famous advertisement of the French retailer of cultural products "La FNAC". The video stages Jean-Luc, a young man sitting down who reads books in the shop for free, without being bothered by anyone, year after year. His life in the shop is shown with the ongoing subtitle: "Introducing Jean-Luc/He's been coming to the Fnac bookstore since he was kid/Through us, he discovered his craze for comics/science fiction and thrillers/Jean-Luc very often comes to the Fnac/All our salesmen have known and advised him for years/He's the first to know about new releases/But today, what would make us happy, at the Fnac/is that Jean-Luc at last purchased something." And the ad ends up with the FNAC's logo with the following motto: "We have the books. You have the rights."[6] Helping the consumer to resist, rendering her choices reversible or partial, has become the best means to overcome the very resistance of the consumers to market seductions.

We now understand better why we should be cautious before abandoning politics to market actors. As we have seen, there are two main reasons for being careful. On the one hand, the recent development of political consumption is the symptom of a lack of some international regulations of markets that should be fixed rather than abandoned. On the other hand, it would be a mistake to think that the market may be politicized since it already is and always has been. In times of crisis, the problem that market and government actors have to solve is to rethink the articulation between both the economic side and the public side of the same political and market reality.

In order to move into that direction, I will (like in the past) stress the virtues of vices. But instead of giving this idea its traditional Smithian

Figure 8.4   Jean Luc at the FNAC (video capture).

meaning (in which the free interaction of private vices—or individualized political virtues!—may lead to the miraculous advent of public
good) I would like to give it a Durkheimian sense, in which the poison
of vice, like a vaccine, is the best way to invigorate the social body and
the political direction of the economy.[7] I would like to believe in the
inventiveness of the market. The extraordinary jubilation, cleverness
and mischievousness of market actors—whose vice is the main virtue—
may well lead public actors and citizens to reinvent their action, the
law and eventually the inner workings of our "res-publica" (Latour and
Weibel 2005).

NOTES

1. Professor of sociology at the University of Toulouse/CERTOP-CNRS (cochoy@univ-tlse2.fr); visiting Professor at School of Business, Economics and Law of the University of Gothenburg (Franck.Cochoy@cfk.gu.se). I benefited from the material and intellectual support of this latter institution when writing this chapter.
2. This chapter borrows some elements from Cochoy (2008b, 2009).
3. This commercial can be viewed at the following address: http://www.kewego. fr/video/iLyROoaftYbh.html. I thank Ellen Hertz who made me aware of this 2003 ad. It received a silver lion at the Cannes International Advertising Festival, a "Golden Shark" award at the "Shark Awards" at Kinsale/Ireland and a gold award at "Eurobest 2003" (http://www.zazoo.be/).
4. I proposed elsewhere to call these devices "faire laissez-faire" devices, since they are aimed at carefully building and setting (faire) the dream of a free market (laissez-faire) (Cochoy 2007).
5. I have defined elsewhere a "captation" device (from the French *capter*: attracting, seducing without violence) as an instrument which attempts to profit from dispositions that one attributes to persons in order to shift their trajectories, to remove them from the external space and exercise control over them (see, for instance, a loyalty card, which plays on calculation to shift consumers from competition to routine; Cochoy 2007).
6. The full video may be watched at: http://videosostav.ru/video/9420a39a955 3d6518291bd925c0f9308/.
7. As we know, Durkheim saw crime as a necessary and possibly healthy factor in social life, since it helps society to better know and reaffirm its most fundamental values.

REFERENCES

Aldridge, Alan. 1994. The Construction of Rational Consumption. In Which? Magazine: The more Blobs the Better? *Sociology* 28 (4): 899–912.
Brembeck, Helen. 2007. To Consume and Be Consumed. In *Little Monsters: (De) coupling Assemblages of Consumption*, ed. Helen Brembeck, Karin Ekström and Magnus Mörck, 67–86. Berlin: Lit Verlag.
Callon, Michel. 2007. An Essay on the Growing Contribution of Economic Markets to the Proliferation of the Social. *Theory, Culture and Society* 24 (7–8): 139–163.
Callon, Michel, Pierre Lascoumes and Yannick Barthe. 2001. *Agir dans un monde incertain, essai sur la démocratie technique*. Paris: Seuil.
Chessel, Marie-Emmanuelle. 2006. Consumers' Leagues in France: A Transatlantic Perspective. In The Expert Consumer. Associations and Professionals in Consumer Society, ed. Alain Chatriot, Marie-Emmanuelle Chessel and Matthew Hilton, 53–69. London: Ashgate.
Cochoy, Franck. 2005. A Short History of "Customers", or the Gradual Standardization of Markets and Organizations. *Sociologie du travail* 47 (Supplement 1, December): e36–e56.
———. 2007. A Brief Theory of the "Captation" of Publics: Understanding the Market with Little Red Riding Hood. *Theory, Culture and Society* 24 (7–8): 213–233.
———. 2008a. Calculation, Qualculation, Calqulation: Shopping Cart's Arithmetic, Equipped Cognition and Clustered Consumers. *Marketing Theory, Special Issue on Markets Forms and Marketing Practices* 8 (1): 15–44.

———. 2008b. Faut-il abandonner la politique aux marchés ? Réflexions autour de la consommation engagée. *Revue française de socio-économie* 1 (1er semestre): 107–129.

———. 2009. Entre agence et dispositifs: les apories du concept de résistance. In *Consommation et Résistances des consommateurs*, ed. Dominique Roux. Paris: Economica.

Cochoy, Franck, and Catherine Grandclément. 2005. Publicizing Goldilocks' Choice at the Supermarket: The Political Work of Product Packs, Carts and Talk. In *Making Things Public: Atmospheres of Democracy*, ed. Bruno Latour and Peter Weibel, 646–659. Cambridge, MA: MIT Press.

Cochoy, F., L. Le Daniel and J. Crave. 2009. The Big Red Chevron and the 282 Little Kids. On Packaging as a Way to Combine Global Marketing and Local "Market-Things". CERTOP/University of Toulouse, Working Paper.

Dubuisson-Quellier, Sophie. 2009. *La consommation engagée*. Paris: Presses de Sciences Po.

Dubuisson-Quellier, Sophie, and Claire Lamine. 2008. Consumer Involvement in Fair Trade and Local Food Systems: Delegation and Empowerment Regimes. *GeoJournal* 73 (1): 55–65.

Ekström, Karin, and Helen Brembeck, eds. 2004. *Elusive Consumption*. Oxford and New York: Berg Publisher.

Elster, Jon. 1979. *Ulysses and the Sirens*. Cambridge: Cambridge University Press.

Glickman, Lawrence B. 2009. *Buying Power: A History of Consumer Activism in America*. Chicago: University of Chicago Press.

Klein, Naomi. 2000. *No Logo, Taking Aim at the Brand Bullies*. New York: Picador.

Latour, Bruno, and Peter Weibel, eds. 2005. *Making Things Public: Atmospheres of Democracy*. Cambridge, MA: MIT Press.

Mallard, Alexandre. 2007. Evaluating Telecommunication Products and Services: Consumerist Tests as Economic Experiments. In *Market Devices*, ed. Michel Callon, Yuval Millo and Fabian Muniesa, 152–172. London: Blackwell.

Marcuse, Herbert. 1964. *One Dimensional Man*. Boston: Beacon Press.

Micheletti, Michele. 2003. *Political Virtue and Shopping: Individuals, Consumerism, and Collective Action*. Palgrave: Macmillan.

Procter, J., and M. Richards. 2002. Word-of-Mouth Marketing: Beyond Pester Power. *Young Consumers: Insight and Ideas for Responsible Marketers* 3 (3): 3–11.

Roux, Dominique. 2007. Ordinary Resistance as a Parasitic Form of Action: A Dialogical Analysis of Consumer/Firm Relations. *In Advances in Consumer Research*, ed. Gavan Fitzsimons and Vicki Morwitz, 602–609. http://perso.orange.fr/dominique.roux/Roux_ACR_2007_published.pdf.

Ruffieux, Bernard. 2004. Le nouveau citoyen consommateur: Que peut-on en attendre en termes d'efficacité économique? *Sciences de la société* (mai): 93–117.

Vogel, David. 2005. *The Market for Virtue. The Potential and Limits of Corporate Social Responsibility*. Washington, DC: Brookings Institution Press.

9 Communities of Purpose

John W. Schouten and Diane M. Martin

Adherents of the school of Consumer Culture Theory (Arnould and Thompson 2005) hold that modern culture is forged as much in the marketplace as it in schools, churches or other institutions. In modern Western society the building blocks of material culture virtually all are mass-produced and sold, and it's primarily in our selection and composition of them that we, as consumers, piece together lives that, although in some ways unique, and occasionally flamboyant, nonetheless bear recognizable patterns of function and style. Culture, at levels ranging from macro to micro, provides the rules and tools for sense making. Consumers act with agency, but our agency and our imaginations, and therefore the patterns we create, are limited by the cultural frameworks we inhabit (Archer 1988). Even when we choose to break or redefine cultural rules, we do so in patterned, recognizable ways with resources found in the marketplace.

The macro- and micro-cultural forces that create the rules and tools of sense making (Weick 1979, 1995), identity construction (Belk 1988; Côté 1996) and personal narrative (Riessman 1993; Thompson, Locander and Pollio 1989) among people in society are constantly changing. This chapter deals with consumption communities amid those changing forces. Through various manifestations of community among motorcyclists over nearly two decades we reflect on the influences of cultural change. Then, just when you think this is all about motorcyclists, we'll make a hard left turn into the new and little-studied territory of communities of purpose.

CONSUMPTION COMMUNITIES REDUX

A strong thread running through marketing and consumer behaviour literature examines the patterned behaviours of various consumer communities. The publication of "An Ethnography of the New Bikers" (Schouten and McAlexander 1995) arguably marked the beginning of the intense scholarly interest in consumer collectives. As both consumers and producers of cultural meaning, the New Bikers organized key aspects of their lives and identities around a particular brand, Harley-Davidson, and its consumption, developing a consumer subculture, defined as a "distinctive subgroup of society that self-selects on the basis of shared commitments to a particular product class, brand or consumption activity" complete with, "an identifiable, hierarchical social structure; a unique ethos, or set of shared beliefs and values; and unique jargons, rituals, and modes of symbolic expression" (Schouten and McAlexander 1995, 43).

In their devotion to a single brand, the New Bikers also happened fit the definition of a brand community offered by Muniz and O'Guinn (2001, 412) as "a specialized, non-geographically bound community, based on a structured set of social relations among admirers of a brand" who exhibit consciousness of kind, shared rituals and traditions and a sense of moral responsibility to the brand. And in support of McAlexander, Schouten and Koenig's (2002) expanded model of a brand community, the New Bikers experienced and maintained strong relationships not only with the brand and each other, but also with their own motorcycles and with the company that manufactured them.

It is actually quite rare for a consumer subculture also to be a brand community, and vice versa. Most consumer subcultures form around and define themselves by certain activities or lifestyles, which in turn are supported by multiple brands. Those brands may compete for share and prestige within the subculture and, yet, all be viewed within the subculture as acceptable alternatives. For most consumer subcultures their brand identity is their activity or practice. Think "fly-fishers" rather than "Orvisians" or "Shakespeareans". Think "surfers", not "Billabongers" or "Hurleyites". Branded products are used, endorsed and legitimized according to what they bring to the party. In their emphasis on socialization and hierarchy, most consumer subcultures are more akin to communities of practice with their systems of apprenticeship and mentoring (Lave and Wenger 1991) than they are to brand communities.

Brand communities, alternatively, place primacy on the brand. Practice isn't irrelevant, but it also doesn't hew to a strict ideology of consumption or support a hierarchical social structure in the manner of a subculture. Practice in a brand community is more heterogeneous. Take the Apple community, for example. The brand is favoured, even to fetishism, in multiple and diverse communities of practice with no unifying status hierarchy or ideology of consumption beyond the superiority of Apple (Muniz and O'Guinn 2001). Consumer subcultures are interesting because their deep commitment to particular practices generates innovation in technology, style, use and brands. Brand communities are interesting because their extraordinary commitment to brands has managerial relevance. Cultivating a brand community generates loyalty and a whole host of marketing benefits (McAlexander, Schouten and Koenig 2002).

A possible challenge to the value of brand communities is a growing cultural discontent with marketing and branding (Klein 2002).

PATTERNS OF CHANGE

The New Bikers of the late 1980s and early 1990s exemplified a consumer subculture, but by the end of the 1990s they looked more like a brand community or a mosaic of microcultures (Schouten, Martin and McAlexander 2007; Thompson and Troester 2002). As has been the case with other consumer subcultures (Blair and Hatala 1991; McCracken 1986), the edgy, countercultural appeal of the New Bikers brought them notoriety and popularity. It became fashionable to ride a Harley. The stylishness was exploited, accelerated and commercialized by media, including the movie industry, and by Harley-Davidson Inc., for which the cultural phenomenon of the New Bikers meant unprecedented growth in sales, profits, stock prices and prestige. Thousands of new riders joined the Harley parade every month over several years. Many of them found the orthodoxy of the corporate-sponsored Harley Owners Group (HOG), or the microcultures of HOG's local chapters, to be unsatisfying, stifling or irrelevant, and they began to form alternative rider groups. The authority of "authentic" keepers of the subculture flame began to erode as alternative authenticities began to emerge (Kates 2002; Thompson and Coskuner-Balli 2007).

A critical re-inquiry into the subculture as experienced and expressed by growing numbers of women riders (Martin, Schouten and McAlexander 2006) showed that the core values of freedom, Americanism and machismo still held nominal sway, but that they meant different things to women than they did to white men. Women's sense of freedom, for example, was shaped by different cultural constraints and power structures than those faced by men. Women exercised freedom from limiting femininities, and they used machismo to push and expand the boundaries of gendered consumption. Similarly, the authors' more limited ethnographic interviews with African-American and Latino bikers, also having increased in numbers and achieved critical mass in pockets of the US, revealed still different overlays of meaning on the familiar language of Harley-Davidson ownership and ridership. Once again, against backgrounds of different cultural constraints, milieus and trends, the meanings of such New Biker values as freedom, Americanism and machismo also got redefined.

As a brand community without a unifying ideology of consumption, Harley-Davidson owners continue to display incredible loyalty. However, even among Harley owners the assumption of Harley-Davidson superiority and the brand's presumed position at the top of motorcyclists' collective ladder of aspiration has greatly diminished. Through the 1990s the entire motorcycle industry in North America benefited from a renaissance driven by the popularity of Harley-Davidson. Dubbed "come-backers" by Harley-

Davidson Inc., large numbers of former riders, most of whom were empty-nest baby boomers, rediscovered the joy of riding. For these consumers the Harley became the re-entry vehicle to the world of motorcycles. Once back in the saddle, however, many riders began to appreciate the qualities of other types and brands of bikes, including Japanese sport bikes, Italian exotics, such as Ducati, and the reborn British Triumph. Some riders left Harley ownership completely, while others simply added non-Harleys to their garages. The xenophobic days of bikers bashing (literally and figuratively) Japanese motorcycles have long ago faded, along with other quaint countercultural practices, such as removing muffler baffles to create the loudest possible exhaust sound.

The revitalized market for motorcycles has matured. A broader community of motorcyclists has subsumed subcultures and brand communities. The hand wave of acknowledgement that Harley riders once reserved only for other members of their tribe is now extended to all motorcyclists. The community grows more and more heterogeneous, enough so that its fragmentation into microcultures (Thompson and Troester 2002) accommodates any kind of rider—from minibike aficionados to iron-butt tourers, to road racers and squids, to dirt riders, to economizing commuters, to scooter fans, to chopper customizers—with no systematic prejudices against any mode or style of motorcycle ridership.

MOTORCYCLIST COLLIDES WITH ENVIRONMENTALIST

Although it may sound like a lurid headline from a local newspaper, the collision referenced in the subject heading is figurative. It refers to an unexpected trend wherein a few hardcore motorcyclists are embracing a goal of carbon neutrality. In the October 2009 issue of *Motorcyclist*, a popular, mainstream motorcycle magazine, the dominant theme, cover shot and lead story were summarized by the headline "Going Green". The bastion of internal combustion passion that is *Motorcyclist* devoted no fewer than fifteen articles and the majority of its prime real estate to electric and alternative-fuel machines. With the possible exception of a hybrid-electric three-wheeled scooter from Piaggio, none of the so-called green machines is manufactured by a major motorcycle company. All the players are pushing technology in innovative ways. And all of them were avid motorcyclists long before they discovered interests in zero-emission power plants. Legitimizing the experiments with electric motorcycles was the venerated, century-old road race, the Isle of Man TT. The first ever eco-version of the race, the TTXGP, drew registrations from sixty teams in fifteen countries (Frank 2009).

It's not the fact of an electric motorcycle that's particularly alarming. People have fooled around with electric bikes before. But for seasoned motorcycle road racers to compete on thirty-horsepower electric bikes is almost tantamount to Crips and Bloods (rival urban street gangs) competing in a pie-baking contest. It doesn't compute. That is, not unless you factor in one of the most sweepingly radical cultural changes since the postwar expansions of suburbia.

The environmental movement has been, until sometime in the beginning of the twenty-first century, something of a loose confederacy of consumption microcultures and countercultural activist groups. In the 1960s, when Rachel Carson's (1962) *Silent Spring* hit the bookstores with news about the health risks posed by DDT and other chemicals, environmentalism was a curiosity. The chemical industry reviled Carson, and many politicians branded her an alarmist. But others, like Senator Gaylord Nelson of Wisconsin, were listening. Grass-roots citizen groups began organizing around concern for the condition of the natural environment. In 1970, Senator Nelson's first Earth Day celebration provided a platform for millions of environmentally inclined citizens. In his own words:

> At a conference in Seattle in September 1969, I announced that in the spring of 1970 there would be a nationwide grassroots demonstration on behalf of the environment and invited everyone to participate. The wire services carried the story from coast to coast. The response was electric. It took off like gangbusters. Telegrams, letters, and telephone inquiries poured in from all across the country. The American people finally had a forum to express its concern about what was happening to the land, rivers, lakes, and air—and they did so with spectacular exuberance. For the next four months, two members of my Senate staff, Linda Billings and John Heritage, managed Earth Day affairs out of my Senate office. . . . Earth Day worked because of the spontaneous response at the grassroots level. We had neither the time nor resources to organize 20 million demonstrators and the thousands of schools and local communities that participated. That was the remarkable thing about Earth Day. It organized itself. (Nelson 2009)

Two things pop from the senator's statement. One is that Earth Day practically organized itself. This is a theme we'll come back to. The other is that, despite the primitive state of the media in 1969 (No Internet! No Facebook!), a massive, non-geographically centred community was able to assemble with a feeling of shared purpose and the possibility of having an impact on the national psyche. Building on the Earth Day momentum, pre-existing non-governmental organizations (NGOs), such as the Sierra Club, the National Wildlife Federation, the World Wildlife Fund, the Nature Conservancy, Friends of the Earth and the Natural Resources Defense Council, attracted more supporters and established stronger beachheads in a war with industry and lobbyists over battlegrounds in skies, waterways, forests, deserts and wetlands all across the country. From 1970 to the mid-1980s businesses generally resisted integrating environmental concerns into their business models (Walley and Whitehead 1994), preferring instead to lobby against environmental legislation.

Against the virtual stalemate between industry and environmental activists, many consumers have continued to find their own ways to live more healthfully and sustainably, and in doing so they've tended to organize into communities (Seyfang 2009). These aren't brand communities. They tend to eschew corporate brands or downplay their importance. Some may hold strict ideologies of consumption and form the hierarchical structures of subculture; but more do not. Instead, they are individuals or microcultures in a loosely organized, dynamic movement focused on "living our alternatives into being" (Klein 2002, 458). They also aren't communities of practice; their practices are too diverse. Participating in the movement in their own ways are vegans, freegans, vegetarians and organic gardeners; purchasers of renewable power, bicycle commuters and advocates of public transportation; kids, moms, dads and grandparents; CEOs, managers and labourers; teachers and students; buyers and suppliers and suppliers' suppliers. What unites these diverse groups isn't what they do or how they live. It's what they are trying to achieve.

HYPERORGANIZATION AND COMMUNITIES OF PURPOSE

Whether they organize in neighbourhood gardens, in cooperatives, in living rooms or in cyberspace, communities of purpose form and collaborate to achieve specific goals. Their purpose may be to change a zoning law, to make a campus safer or to make a workplace more equitable. They may focus on health care benefits in the workplace or on a single, critical operation for an uninsured child. They may be trying to save entire species from extinction or a single tree from the axe. The importance of communities of purpose to cultural change is highlighted nowhere more clearly than in Paul Hawken's (2007) book, *Blessed Unrest*, in which he grapples with the phenomenon he describes as a global web of "coherent, organic, self-organized congregations involving tens of millions of people dedicated to change" (4). By Hawken's estimate, there are over a million organizations in the world devoted to ecological sustainability and social justice. And once again, echoing Senator Nelson, we see a reference to self-organization.

As important as it is to understand as the nature of communities of purpose, it is equally important to understand the social dynamics that bring them about. In applying the principles of sense making and organizational communication (Weick 1979, 1995; McPhee and Zaug 2000) to consumer behaviour, Martin and Schouten (2002, 2006) describe a phenomenon of hyperorganization, wherein people with shared or overlapping purposes organize for the purpose of achieving privileged outcomes. They create social interaction systems, construct new social boundaries and integrate and coordinate behaviours of consumption and production in the pursuit of common goals with economic impact.

As an example of hyperorganization, Martin and Schouten (2002) analyze the case of *Car Talk*, a call-in radio talk show on National Public Radio (in the US) dedicated explicitly to solving consumers' automotive problems, and implicitly to the purpose of producing humour and entertainment. They find that in all respects the *Car Talk* phenomenon meets McPhee and Zaug's (2000, 5) definition of an organization as:

> a social interaction system, influenced by prevailing economic and legal institutional practices, and including coordinated action and interaction within and across a socially constructed system boundary, manifestly directed toward a privileged set of outcomes.

Except that it isn't. What is organized around the radio show is something much larger and more fluid than the formal *Car Talk* organization, which is a group of fewer than a dozen people in Cambridge, Massachusetts. Most of the production of the program occurs in collaboration with callers from the listening audience. Without its extra-organizational partners, i.e., consumers engaging in co-production, *Car Talk* the phenomenon could not exist. There would be no product.

Communities of purpose are manifestations of hyperorganization. They are communicated into existence among people who may be quite diverse in their lifestyles, locations, occupations, personal ambitions and social backgrounds. They blur the boundaries between production and consumption, consuming productively (Firat and Dholakia 1998) or producing with emotional intensity and payoffs that rival the benefits of leisure consumption (Roberts, Scammon and Schouten 1987). Although they may be managed by formal non-profit or for-profit organizations, communities of purpose form across and largely outside the boundaries of a formal organization. Their total social impact is achieved by the efforts of organizational and extra-organizational members working together. And while members of the managing organization may receive financial compensation for their labour, members of the broader community of purpose receive no remuneration. Rather, they contribute philanthropically with financial and/or human capital in support of the community's goals.

We offer a working definition of a community of purpose as a social interaction system organized among people with shared or overlapping goals in order to pursue privileged outcomes. Other characteristics of communities of purpose are also worth noting. First, they tend to flourish through electronic and social media. Second, their boundaries are socially constructed and tend to be highly malleable; it's easy in and easy out. Third, they may draw from the intellectual, technological and artistic abilities of a very diverse body of people. And fourth, the payout for success tends to be non-financial in nature; it comes in the form of personal satisfaction and other positive emotional outcomes. In the next section we examine other communities of purpose and draw a few lessons from them.

CREATING CHANGE: COMMUNITIES IN ACTION

Thompson and Troester (2002) tap into communities of purpose organized around natural health as a value and a set of consumption goals. Their research highlights the diversity among the microcultures that make up a larger natural health marketplace; and although it doesn't emphasize the communicative organization of the market as a community of purpose, it does a nice job of articulating the shared physical, mental and spiritual consumption goals that unite the otherwise diverse players. The natural health movement has continued to grow to the point that an enormous constellation of businesses and consumers has organized around the acronym LOHAS, for lifestyles of health and sustainability, to create an estimated US$209 billion marketplace for goods and services focused on health, the environment, social justice, personal development and sustainable living (LOHAS 2009).

Thompson and Coskuner-Balli (2007), in their study of organic farming and community-supported agriculture (CSA), tell the history of countercultural groups striving for "sustainability and communal connectedness" (136), becoming co-opted by corporate leviathans and, then, re-emerging as countervailing market forces in the form of CSA. They report that in North America over fifteen hundred CSAs, which clearly are communities of purpose, link small-scale growers directly with consumers. Consumers pay at the beginning of a season for weekly "shares" of a farm's produce; they typically have opportunities to visit the farm and meet the growers; and some contribute occasional farm labour as part of their payment. The organization Local Harvest, which maintains a grass-roots database of CSAs, cites advantages of CSA for farmers, including cash flow and price advantages of early season payment and the opportunity to get to know their customers. Advantages for consumers include ultra-fresh and often organic foods, exposure to new vegetables and preparations, relationships with farmers and increased knowledge of growing practices (Local Harvest 2009).

A particularly interesting community of purpose, Carrotmob, uses social media such as Facebook and Twitter to mobilize consumers into "buycotts" (Carrotmob 2009). Playing against the idea of a boycott, a buycott organizes consumers to make purchases at a particular business during a specified time with the understanding that a pre-negotiated percentage of the revenues will be used by the business to invest in sustainability initiatives.

In our own research we've been impressed by the creativity and the effectiveness of communities of purpose in pursuing goals of environmental and social change objectives. For over two years we conducted research as participant observers in the nascent and developing sustainability efforts of

Wal-Mart (Martin and Schouten 2009). Wal-Mart has declared three ambitious goals: zero waste, purely renewable energy and sustainable products (Wal-Mart 2009). What they have achieved to date has been as a result of leveraging its Sustainable Value Networks (SVNs), a dozen communities of purpose with separate but complementary areas of concern. They are the:

- greenhouse gases network
- alternative fuels network
- sustainable buildings network
- logistics network
- waste network
- packaging network
- food, agriculture and seafood network
- wood and paper network
- jewellery network
- textiles network
- chemicals network
- electronics network

Managed from within the Wal-Mart organization by network captains with at least director status, the SVNs are comprised of Wal-Mart associates, members of supplier firms, members of non-governmental and governmental organizations and academics. Together, the members of an SVN identify and tackle problems of sustainability, and they produce innovative solutions that yield significant financial and environmental gains. The SVN system began in the US but has expanded rapidly throughout the company's global markets, including Latin America and China. What we learn from Wal-Mart's SVNs is that communities of purpose can be fostered and managed from anywhere in the value chain; that they can be valuable sources of innovation; and, where common goals can be identified, even former adversaries (e.g., Wal-Mart and various activist organizations) can work together effectively and with mutual satisfaction.

Finally, it may bear mentioning a community of purpose that resides closer to home for some contributors to this volume. Under the auspices of the Association for Consumer Research there has organized a community dedicated to what they call transformative consumer research (TCR). A community of scholars, TCR "seeks to encourage, support, and publicize research that benefits consumer welfare and quality of life for all beings affected by consumption across the world" (TCR 2009).

CIRCLING BACK

Return with us for a moment to the Isle of Man TTXGP road race and ask these questions: Why would motorcycle engineers with gasoline in their veins devote time and energy to designing electric motorcycles? And, given the electric bikes' anemia compared to their internal-combustion cousins, why would any self-respecting racer want to ride one? The answer: because they love motorcycles, they love racing and they have seen the future. It's a future where ear-splitting noise and fume-spewing exhausts have no resonance with cultural values. Motorcycle racing is the extreme fringe behaviour that sells motorcycles and accessories to mainstream riders. If the market turns to zero-carbon-emission machines, racing will need to lead the way in performance and innovation. In that spirit, the TTXGP is an organization upon which hyperorganization constructs a new community of purpose. The purpose: to secure a future for motorcycles and motorcycle racing in a changing world.

Communities of purpose are the most under-researched of all the various kinds of consumption communities. And yet, of all of them, communities of purpose are probably the most important. Their ability to mobilize and leverage resources such as time, money, courage and creativity is remarkable. Their willingness to do so for the greater good of humanity is unparalleled. They have the potential to create markets and industries or to bring them down. It may be that where culture and consumption are concerned, communities of purpose will be the change agents with the greatest overall impact.

FINANCIAL COLLAPSE: A POSTSCRIPT

If commercial America is any indication (and of course it is), then in the final years of the first decade of the twenty-first century a broader cultural shift is under way with an ethos of environmental and social sustainability building at its core. Hundreds of diverse communities of purpose, pockets of environmental and social consciousness in sectors ranging from industry and business to consumers to NGOs, have started to knit together into something larger.

The cultural forces at work are global, and include the intergovernmental influences that first surfaced to worldwide attention in the form of the Brundtland Commission Report (United Nations World Commission on Environment and Development 1987), which is credited with bringing the term *sustainable* into common usage. The cultural shift was further propelled by the growing scientific consensus about climate change. Pro-sustainability forces in industry became publicly visible through the works of visionaries like Paul Hawken with his influential book *The Ecology of Commerce* and Ray Anderson at the helm of the floor-covering giant, Interface. The shift in the private sector has continued to grow as the business case for sustainable practices has begun to clarify. Popular culture has added to the momentum through media events such as Al Gore's *An Inconvenient Truth*.

The last obstacle to a mass shift toward a culture of sustainability, in the United States at least, has probably been mainstream consumers, who for the most part have been locked into lifestyles of materialism and overconsumption since the beginning of the marketing era. Intellectually, consumers appear to understand that more stuff does not equate to more well-being, and yet we have continued act as if we believed it did. The tipping point, if there has been one, is the global recession of 2008 and 2009 (so far). Job losses, furloughs, salary reductions, plummeting retirement portfolios and general anxiety over money may have, in the context of a growing appreciation for concepts of sustainability, actually motivated large segments of the consumer society to begin to reassess core values around wants and needs. The recession has provided a global reality check. Not only is it suddenly more difficult and less desirable to consume with abandon, it may even be passing out of fashion.

REFERENCES

Archer, Margaret Scotwood. 1996. *Culture and Agency: The Place of Culture in Social Theory*. Rev. ed. Cambridge: Cambridge University Press.

Arnould, Eric J., and Craig J. Thompson. 2005. Consumer Culture Theory (CCT): Twenty Years of Research. *Journal of Consumer Research* 31(4): 868–882.

Belk, Russell W. 1988. Possessions and the Extended Self. *Journal of Consumer Research* 15 (September): 139–168.

Blair, Elizabeth M., and Mark N. Hatala. 1991. The Use of Rap Music in Children's Advertising. *Advances in Consumer Research* 19:719–724.

Carrotmob. 2009. http://carrotmob.org/about/ (accessed 4 October 2009).

Carson, Rachel. 1962. *Silent Spring*. Boston: Houghton Mifflin.

Côté, James E. 1996. Sociological Perspectives on Identity Formation: The Culture–Identity Link and Identity Capital. *Journal of Adolescence* 19 (5): 417–428.

Firat, A. Fuat, and Nikhilesh Dholakia. 1998. *Consuming People: From Political Economy to Theaters of Consumption*. London: Routledge.

Frank, Aaron. 2009. Rebooting Racing: The Zero-Emissions TTXGP Electrifies the Isle of Man. *Motorcyclist* (October): 73–75.

Hawken, Paul. 2007. *Blessed Unrest: How the Largest Movement in the World Came into Being and Why No One Saw It Coming*. New York: Viking.

Kates, Steven M. 2002. The Protean Quality of Subcultural Consumption: An Ethnographic Account of Gay Consumers. *Journal of Consumer Research* 29 (December): 383–399.

Klein, Naomi. 2002. *No Logo*. New York: Picador.

Lave, Jean, and Etienne Wenger. 1991. *Situated Learning: Legitimate Peripheral Participation*. Cambridge: Cambridge University Press.

Local Harvest. 2009. http://www.localharvest.org/csa/ (accessed 1 December 2009).

LOHAS. 2009. http://www.lohas.com/about.html (accessed 4 October 2009).

Martin, Diane M., and John W. Schouten. 2002. The Communicative Construction of Car Talk. In the Proceedings of the NCA Organizational Communication Division Pre-Convention Conference at the annual meeting of the National Communication Association, New Orleans.

———. 2006. Hyperorganizations: Communication and the Organizing Grammars of the Marketplace. Presented at the Asia Pacific Association for Consumer Research Conference in Sydney, Australia.

———. 2009. Engineering a Mainstream Market for Sustainability: Insights from Wal-Mart's Perfect Storm. In *Explorations in Consumer Culture Theory*, ed. John F. Sherry Jr. and Eileen Fisher, 150–167. London: Routledge.

Martin, Diane M., John W. Schouten and James H. McAlexander. 2006. Claiming the Throttle: Multiple Feminities in a Hyper-Masculine Subculture. *Consumption, Markets and Culture* 9 (3): 171–205.

McAlexander, James H., John W. Schouten and Harold J. Koenig. 2002. Building Brand Community. *Journal of Marketing* 66 (January): 38–54.

McCracken, Grant. 1986. Culture and Consumption: A Theoretical Account of the Structure and Movement of the Cultural Meaning of Consumer Goods. *Journal of Consumer Research* 13 (June): 71–84.

McPhee, Robert D., and Pamela Zaug. 2000. Organizational Theory, Organizational Communication, Organizational Knowledge, and Problematic Integration. *Journal of Communication* 51 (3): 574–591.

Muniz Jr., Albert M., and Thomas C. O'Guinn. 2001. Brand Community. *Journal of Consumer Research* 27 (4): 412–432.

Nelson, Senator Gaylord. 2009. How the First Earth Day Came About. *Envirolink*. http://earthday.envirolink.org/history.html (accessed 5 May 2009).

Riessman, Catherine K. 1993. *Narrative Analysis*. Newbury Park, CA: Sage.

Roberts, Scott D., Debra L. Scammon and John W. Schouten. 1987. The Fortunate Few: Production as Consumption. *Advances in Consumer Research* 15:430–435.

Schouten, John W., Diane M. Martin and James H. McAlexander. 2007. The Evolution of a Subculture of Consumption. In *Consumer Tribes: Theory, Practice, and Prospects*, ed. Bernard Cova, Robert V. Kozinets and Avi Shankar, 67–75. London: Elsevier/Betterworth-Heinemann.

Schouten, John W., and James McAlexander. 1995. Subcultures of Consumption: An Ethnography of the New Bikers. *Journal of Consumer Research* 22 (June): 43–61.

Seyfang, Gill. 2009. Growing Sustainable Consumption Communities: The Case of Local Organic Food Networks. In *The Politics and Pleasures of Consuming Differently*, ed. K. Soper, M. Ryle and L. Thomas, 188–208. New York: Palgrave MacMillan.

TCR. 2009. http://www.acrwebsite.org/fop/index.asp?itemID=325 (accessed 4 October 2009).

Thompson, Craig J., and Geckoes Coskuner-Balli. 2007. Countervailing Market Responses to Corporate Co-optation and the Ideological Recruitment of Consumption Communities. *Journal of Consumer Research* 34 (2): 135–152.

Thompson, Craig J., William B. Locander and Howard R. Pollio. 1989. Putting Consumer Experience Back into Consumer Research: The Philosophy and Method of Existential-Phenomenology. *Journal of Consumer Research* 16 (2): 133–146.

Thompson, Craig J., and Maura Troester. 2002. Consumer Value Systems in the Age of Postmodern Fragmentation: The Case of the Natural Health Microculture. *Journal of Consumer Research* 28 (4): 550–571.

United Nations World Commission on Environment and Development. 1987. Our Common Future, Center for a World in Balance. http://www.worldinbalance.net/agreements/1987-brundtland.html (accessed 18 May 2009).

Walley, Noah, and Bradley Whitehead. 1994. It's Not Easy Being Green. *Harvard Business Review* (May–June): 46–51.

Wal-Mart. 2009. Global Sustainability Report. http://walmartstores.com/sites/sustainabilityreport/2009/en_threeKeyGoals.html (accessed 4 October 2009).

Weick, Karl E. 1979. *The Social Psychology of Organizing*. Reading, MA: Addison-Wesley.

———. 1995. *Sensemaking in Organizations*. Thousand Oaks, CA: Sage.

10 Value Creation and the Visual Consumer

Jonathan E. Schroeder

A debate has emerged about the consumer today. On one hand, consumption researchers argue that consumers construct identity, express themselves and create meaning through their consumption. On the other hand, consumption critics maintain that consumers have been put to work for companies, as aesthetic labourers, working consumers and immaterial agents, building value for brands without proper compensation. Both positions shows an heightened awareness of the consumer's role in "co-creating" brand value, and "co-producing" products, services and brands via active engagement with brands in brand communities, on websites and in social interaction—acknowledging, celebrating, contesting, embracing, negotiating and sometimes protecting brands.

These recent concepts highlight the evolving understanding of the roles that consumption and production play in both the lives of consumers and in the wider market society. All acknowledge the active roles consumers play in producing value for themselves and, often, for companies and their brands (see Cova and Dalli 2009; Schroeder 2009; Wikström 1995; Zwick, Bonsu and Darmody 2008).

CONSUMPTION, EXPERIENCE AND VISION

Recent work in marketing and related fields embraces the concept of "experience"—firms market experiences, consumers crave experiences and the so-called experience economy warrants new frameworks for thinking about the consumer's roles in society. Additionally, new thinking in consumer research contests the basic conception of the consumer as passive recipient and target of market offerings. An emerging paradigm of *consumption as experience* assumes that consumers play active roles in creating meaning and value in their interactions with the market. In this way, a basic distinction between consumers and producers has changed—consumers no longer occupy the end of the marketing chain, having assumed prominent roles in value creation. Thus, an experiential perspective dislocates the subject of consumption, and refigures basic understandings of production and consumption (see Carù and Cova 2007; Ekström and Brembeck 2004).

In this chapter, I present a way of thinking about a key aspect of consumer experience, one that I have called *visual consumption* (Schroeder 2002) that provides an experiential way to think about consumer roles. Visual consumption places an emphasis on the acts of looking, observing and seeing as primary consumer experiences. Visual consumption encompasses critical ways that consumers construct, maintain and express their identities. What we see, what we notice, what we document in visual media are all important consumer processes.

In this discussion, visual consumption provides a way of discussing the complex interactions between consuming and producing images. Visual consumption, then, is a conceptual process of making sense and integration, and a consumer process of gazing, looking and categorizing visual experience. To begin with, we will revisit a key development in consumer behaviour in the twentieth century—the triumph of self-service retailing. Then we turn our gaze toward photography, as a consumer behaviour closely associated with memory and nostalgia, to illuminate how consumers often cling to warm visions of the past, particularly during difficult times, like the recent financial crisis.

LOST IN THE SUPERMARKET

Sainsbury's—a major UK grocery chain—has recently opened a museum in the Docklands area of London. The museum and its elaborate website, called the Sainsbury's Archive, celebrate Sainsbury's history and heritage. According to the site: "a unique collection of more than 16,000 documents, photographs and objects which illustrate the history of today's supermarket chain. It also shows how shopping and eating habits in the UK have changed since the first Sainsbury's shop opened in 1869". One of the website themes concerns "progress"—which includes a lengthy section of the introduction of self-service in the UK in 1950. Billed as a new way of shopping, self-service revolutionized shopping:

> Self-service stores moved the wrapping and weighing of goods from the front of the shop to the back rooms. At first, the staff and equipment required proved expensive, but soon manufacturers began to package their goods before sending them to Sainsbury's, reducing costs. Customers selected their goods from specially designed display shelving units known as "gondolas", put them in a wire basket, then paid for everything at once at the checkout. (Sainsbury's Archive website: http://www.museumindocklands.org.uk/)

Self-service became the basic retail routine at most UK supermarkets within twenty years. Sainsbury's museum—developed during the financial crisis—also serves to remind consumers of its past, before debt swaps, government bank bailouts and subprime loans.

Today, it may be difficult to comprehend the changes in consumer roles wrought by the introduction of self-service. Consumers began to take on more responsibility for selecting, weighing, comparing and recognizing products and brands. Among other imperatives, the look of brands and product packaging assumed central importance. Furthermore, consumers now needed to search for their own products, spot them on the shelves and visually inspect them for purchase. Visual consumption within supermarkets took on more importance, and, as we know, the self-service movement quickly spread to most areas of retailing.

In the midst of a revolution in customer service, where self-swipe, self-pack and self-pay augments self-service, the rise of Internet shopping and a general outsourcing of service provision to consumers, the shift toward self-service sixty years ago may seem a bit quaint. However, self-service remains a relatively unrecognized movement toward visual consumption. The self-serving consumer relied on visually recognizing products, brands and quality. This consumer emerged as a more active consumer—selecting and sorting products of their own choosing.

For contemporary consumers, the Internet provides a primary retail environment—one that relies on and structures the consumer's vision. The Internet mandates visualizing almost every aspect of corporate strategy, operations and communication. Moreover, the requirements and potentials of the Web have profoundly influenced the dissemination of financial analysis, corporate reports and consumer information. The Internet produced a visual revolution in retailing, in which competitive advantage depends on effectively presenting visual information—digital pictures of products, employees, happy customers, competent and caring managers and executive, clear balance sheets and financial data and visions of the good life. Thus, the Net remains a primarily visual experience for most users. What does this visual imperative mean for consumers? We can look at photography for some answers.

THE VISUAL IN BRAND CULTURE

In the latter half of the twentieth century, social and cultural sciences combed the world for seemingly mundane images in people's lives that spoke in powerful and subtle ways about the often hidden values and tacit assumptions woven into societies, joining efforts in many disciplines to democratize and appropriate popular, everyday objects for scholarly attention. Items such as advertising images, food labels and television shows became seen as untapped repositories of the tacit values, desires and roles in society (Campbell and Schroeder 2010).

From this way of thinking, meaning and value was not just something that was *found* or *discovered*, but *produced* through the objects people bought, sold, made, used and preserved, collected, discarded and, of course, *saw*. Photography emerged in the nineteenth century as one of the most powerful and omnipresent technologies of consumer production. This apparent paradox—production through consumption—characterizes consumer culture. Photography introduced a new activity to perform and a new way for people to experience the world. Cameras directed attention to the visual landscape as a vast reservoir of potential pictures and experiences to snap and share. Today, of course, cameras are everywhere—in mobile phones, computers, surveillance cameras, security systems, speed cameras, border crossings—and photographic image production has grown tremendously. Many consumers have assembled huge image archives, stored on mobile phones, computers and online photo sharing sites. The digital photograph has emerged as a central consumer object, providing raw material for self-promotional websites, posting possibilities for social media sites like Facebook and MySpace and commercial potential for consumer-generated brand campaigns for companies like American Apparel, Ray-Ban and Renault-Nissan.

For example, PetSmart, a leading US retailer of all things pets offers customers a chance to be featured on their "Pets of the Day" area of their website. It's easy—just upload a picture of your pooch or pony and he or she can be showcased and archived on the site. I find this area of the site the most enjoyable to look at—it is updated every day, and the pictures are generally appealing and attractive, if not professionally polished. It is this aspect of "co-production"—we can consider these PetSmart customers to be co-producing the website by providing free content—that makes photography such a powerful tool of co-creation. Customers need not report to the retail stores, corporate headquarters or advertising agency studios to provide compelling imagery for the company, and they seem to willingly provide photos for the site. Clearly, they benefit from this activity—it's fun to see one's pet featured on a popular, national forum, one with a much wider audience that most consumer's "I love my cat" blog.

In this way, photography offers an easy way for consumers to "participate" with a successful brand; it helps shape their experience with PetSmart, and structures a relationship that apparently offers benefits for both consumer and company. Of course, one might argue that PetSmart gains the most value from the Pets of the Day feature, as this helps bind customers to the site and builds value for the brand. In any case, consumers—this one included—seem to enjoy the feature, and it showcases a straightforward way to engage customers with a brand.

Photography shapes experience; it guides how people see, what they see, what they remember, what they consider worth seeing, how they imagine things look, how they think about their own identity and that of others and how they think of their ancestors. Photography surrounds consumption: it informs, it shows, it communicates, it structures choice, it dazzles—and it offers a creative way of thinking about consumer experiences. Yet photography itself remains relatively invisible—we take for granted that most of the information about the world comes to us via photography in the forms of film, still pictures, television, video and webpage design.

I consider photography as a way of experiencing life—picturing reality, making things visible, bringing images into our homes and offices from around the world, designating certain sights relevant for our attention and filling us with thousands of images each day. In many ways, consumers are like tourists, traveling the world for experiences, sights and sensations (see Schroeder 2002). Consumption is replete with images, visions and encounters; managers are told to build relationships with customers and to deliver experiences. Tourism is an apt metaphor for contemporary consumption, as consumers can be seen as tourist documenting, sharing and experiencing their lives through photography, posting photos on MySpace, uploading snapshots to websites like Flickr, fotolog and YouTube as well as sending photographic files over email, mobile phones and Facebook. In one way, we can see parallels to the self-service movement, as today's photographers need not depend on processing centres, printing and waiting around for their photos. *We* do the work now. Thus, photography embodies many changes in consumer roles today.

Photography made possible a way of "capturing" experience—a way to concretize lived existence in pictures. The camera lens selects and highlights. Taking a picture of something gives it presence, at least in the photograph. Photographers can make anything look good, or aesthetically pleasing. The snapshot, a straightforward, generally unposed photograph of everyday life, has emerged as an important style in contemporary strategic communication. Many recent corporate images portray models in classic snapshot poses—out of focus, eyes closed, poorly framed—in contrast to more traditional and historical patterns of formal studio shots or highly posed tableaux. "Intentional" snapshots are often characterized by "disruptions" in formal photographic traditions—off lighting, poor focus, blurred images, awkward poses or harsh shadows—that contribute to their strategic power by appearing authentic, casual and everyday. Snapshot aesthetics provide a *visual frame* for strategic images—a "here and now", contemporary look, by (appearing to be) capturing a moment, offering a fresh, unposed look to the image. Snapshots often appear rushed, carelessly composed, taken almost by chance, thus revealing subjects (relatively) unposed, "natural".

Contemporary strategic snapshots embody a paradox of consumer roles—spontaneous yet composed; authentic yet constructed; realistic yet sophisticated—that refers to a fundamental issue within photography. The snapshot aesthetic embodies the experience economy by showing people in the midst of seemingly real, sometimes exciting, but often mundane experiences. Snapshot aesthetics is an important visual aspect of documenting, glamorizing, promoting and understanding consumer experience (Schroeder 2008). Fun and leisure generally fills snapshots—we don't often take pictures of working, routine shopping or household chores. Furthermore, after decades of Kodak's marketing efforts, snapshots remain powerfully bound up with travel, memories and consumer experience.

WE'RE ALL GOING ON A SUMMER HOLIDAY

Every semester, my university asks, well, no, *requires*, me to fill out a form detailing the time I spend on various activities, such as teaching, research and service. The form covers two time periods, the "semester" and "vacation". I have complained over and over that the time period designated as "vacation" occurs during times that I, and most other faculty, am hard at work. The only response I have received is to remind me that our students are on vacation during this time, and that is the category on the form. Of course, in the UK, people go on *holiday*, not vacation, so that may contribute to my confusion as an American working in England. But in any case, the shifting distinctions between work and vacation, between job and leisure and between occupation and avocation, represent important discussion points in considering consumer roles. As these boundaries blur, with home computers, home networks and home offices on one hand, and office kitchens, employee recreation rooms and lifestyle choices on the job on the other, the realms of work and play, along with consumption and production, are shifting.

Photographs and travel have been inextricably linked since photography's emergence in the mid-1800s. Photography brought visions of distant places home to millions of people who might never travel far from home, giving them a first glimpse of places—sights previously available only from engravings, drawings or paintings. The effects were enormous, yet photography's present ubiquity makes it difficult to imagine how early photographed functioned: "faced as we are today with familiar images of exotic places beamed across the world in seconds, it is easy to forget the intense curiosity photographs of faraway lands excited at the time" (Ford 1989, 54). Photography supplanted earlier forms of travel images that played critical roles in geographic, anthropological and physical knowledge about the world. In the US, the burgeoning photographic enterprise supported the westward expansion: "photography went west with the railways, which hired photographers to depict their progress and assure the public it was safe and thrilling to tour this magnificent territory" (Goldberg 1996, 16). Travel and travel photography soon became prerequisites of modernity, a signal of affluence and a mark of the good life (Osborne 2000). The Internet also depends on photography for much of its appeal, and offers consumers a comprehensive catalogue of the world's sites.

Travel represents a key consumer experience as well as a powerful metaphor to understand consumer roles. Travel suspends some of the rules and habits that govern behaviour, and substitutes different norms and customs, in particular those that are appropriate to being in the company of strangers. Traveling can lead to new and exciting forms of sociability, play, inquisitiveness, extraversion and gregariousness that home or work lacks. However, there are rules and rituals for travel. How do we organize and make sense of what we see? Sociologist John Urry outlines several aspects of "consuming places" that shed light on the complex interconnections between travel, photography and consumption.

First, places are reinvented as sights of consumption, providing an arena for shopping, hanging out, using goods and photographing or videotaping friends and family. Second, places themselves are in a sense consumed visually. Third, places can be literally consumed; what people take to be significant about a place—industry, history, buildings, literature, environments—is over time depleted, devoured or exhausted by use. Fourth, it is possible for localities to consume one's identity so that such places become almost literally all-consuming places (Urry 1995). Industries such as arts, tourism and leisure are all important in the cultural transformations of places into consumption sites.

Consuming places represent a complex integration of consuming place and consuming goods and services. Furthermore, mobile phone cameras provide easy picturing possibilities of every site visited. Taking pictures overlays a structuring ritual—prescribing what to see and how to see it, and influencing how it will be remembered (Robinson and Picard 2009; Scarles 2009). Travelers often seek out so-called authentic products, such as local wines from France, Russian caviar, Cuban rum, Greek cheese. Photographs show you've been there and experienced that, and make perfect posts to your blog and Facebook page. Tourist sites can also be ordered on an authenticity scale; there is a growing business in off-the-beaten-path tours for consumers in search of non-tourist sights, eco-travel and adventure travel (Caruana and Crane 2008). Of course, one place that consumers consume via photographs is the cherished past.

Anthropologist Orvar Löfgren has produced insightful scholarly work on vacations. His work suggests that tourism—and how consumers experience vacations—is central to understanding consumer roles (Löfgren 1999). As Löfgren points out, "vacationlands may appear like territories of freedom, freedom from work, worries, rules, and regulations. But behind this carefree façade there are many unwritten rules. The skills of vacationing have a long history, and into each new vacationscape we bring expectations and anticipations as well as stable routines and habits" (1999, 5). This paradox—working at leisure—forms the heart of his analysis, both in terms of the vacationer and the tourist industry. It takes a great deal of effort to enjoy a vacation.

Löfgren views vacationing as a kind of cultural laboratory "where people are able to experiment with new aspects of their identities, their social relations, or their interaction with nature" (1999, 7). He contrasts the vacation with work to understand the wants and needs of the vacationer. Löfgren shows how the tourist phenomenon was created, and how tourists came to expect certain experiences. Thus, a "new mode of consumption was emerging, based on the idea of leaving home and work in search of new experiences, pleasures, and leisure" (Löfgren 1999, 5). The camera came to represent fun and adventure, an association that resonates today with the snapshot aesthetic in contemporary corporate communication (Schroeder 2008).

Within the tourism sector, experiences become commodities via marketing a more eventful life to tourists eager for change, diversion, escape or relaxation. Tourists often go in search of "peak experiences"—those events or feelings that take them away from their daily life. Often, vacationers are looking through a camera, more recently a digital camera. Photography formalizes looking, making it both more noticeable and more acceptable. The camera stares when it is not polite to look. Photographic practice distinguishes cosmopolitans from mere tourists (cf. Hannerz 1990).

PHOTOGRAPHY AND CONSUMER ROLES

Today consumers post these snapshots on travel websites such as Tripadvisor and Top Table as evidence of good—or bad—tourist experiences. The sites offer thousands of photographs, overwhelming at times, as looking through them becomes its own sort of escape, as we can marvel at beautiful visions, recoil at unkempt hotel rooms or laugh at cultural misunderstandings. These photos provide valuable information for consumers as well as for tourist businesses; as they build up an image archive of hotel rooms, restaurant décor, buffet food and tourist sites. Thus, what once was the province of consumption transforms into production—producing information, entertainment and value.

Travel is often purely visual consumption—visiting museums, historic sites, natural areas or paying for a hotel room's view. Photographing travel, aside from structuring the journey, helps travelers resolve dissatisfying aspects of any trip. It is difficult to guarantee positive holiday experiences. Photographs offer evidence of a trip well spent. Photographs can help dispel cognitive dissonance—they can "prove" that you had a good time. A classic travel photography guide wryly suggests that "the fun of seeing it all again is often more enjoyable than the original experience, for the second viewing is without the tensions that complicate the trip" (Wooley 1965, 132). Thus, photography assumes a prominent role in consumer experience—it helps us make sense of what we have experienced, what we value and what we want to remember.

Cameras seem to impart agency to the photographer—empowering us to document what interests us and create our own images and share our own stories. These sentiments resonate with many theories of postmodern perception and the hyperreal, but it is beneficial to document how these guides create consumer expectations, how they play a role in constructing the society of the spectacle (Debord 1994). The camera helps you see, notice, frame and experience. Photography enhances the ordinary—taking pictures influences social perception and interpersonal interaction and heightens perceptual experience. Photography transforms everyday life into ocular occasions—events that can be photographed, uploaded, posted and commented upon in an instant in the digital age. This *staged spontaneity*—photographs that appear like snapshots, but often aren't, or lose that quality when used in corporate sites—represents a key attribute of contemporary use of photography.

A crucial part of consumption, photography structures consumer experience, provides images of the good life and informs our understanding of the world. Consumer experience remains fundamental to consumer processes of fashion, identity formation and desire. Photography has become a major consumer experience, one that exemplifies the quest for images in contemporary life, and this activity offers a key tool of consumer co-creation, as "consumer generated" imagery has emerged as an important contributor to both consumer and producer website creation. Thus, what was once play and leisure—taking photos for fun—transforms into work and value production.

WORKING AT CONSUMPTION

Shopping at Sainsbury's grocery stores—a key ritual for many UK consumers—highlights conceptual tensions of contemporary consumer roles. On one hand, we have more "agency"—as we alone are in charge of picking out our choices, placing them in our shopping trolleys and paying for them at the till. Of course, Sainsbury's has structured our choices, strategically directed us through the store and tempted us with offers throughout, including those last-minute necessities at check-out. *That magazine looks interesting—is that really Britney Spears?* But in general, the experience feels empowering, as we can spend as much time as we want comparing and compromising.

Sainsbury's online offers even easier shopping—a retail environment devoted to visual recognition of brands and products. On the other hand, we have been put to work for Sainsbury's and other companies— toiling away to create value for them, outsourced to bag groceries, swipe barcodes and deliver selections of the goods ourselves. Online shopping mitigates some of this labour, but generally consumers are busy working for many firms. *Now what is my password again?* Perhaps in the aftermath of the recent financial crisis, it makes sense for firms to source this "free" labour. From posting photos on corporate websites, generating commercial campaigns in company contests and joining brand communities, consumers are participating in a co-creation, an economic phenomenon:

about experimenting with new possibilities for value creation that are based on the expropriation of free cultural, technological, social, and affective labor of the consumer masses. Based on the cooperation with and among consumers, co-creation represents a dialogical model that no longer privileges the company's vision of production and thus what constitutes, in the jargon of the marketing profession, "customer value". Therefore, rather than putting customers to work as more or less unskilled workers to further rationalize (Fordist) production processes and their focus on predictability, calculability, and efficiency, co-creation instead aspires to build ambiences that foster contingency, experimentation, and playfulness among consumers. From this perspective, customers are configured as uniquely skilled workers who, for the production of value-in-use to occur, must be given full rein to articulate their inimitable requirements and share their knowledge. (Zwick, Bonsu and Darmody 2008, 166)

Thus, consumer's "work"—all that co-creation, engagement and participation—can be viewed with a critical lens, a generally unpaid grab for consumer labour and value production, one that further frames people as consumers and emphasizes their roles in value creation.

From this point of view, posting fun photographs of Fido, celebrating heavenly hotel rooms or documenting disastrous dinners emerge as sites of value production for global firms, in an almost exploitative mode. This consumer-generated imagery, when utilized in company campaigns and websites, represents unpaid labour. Once again, from the consumer's perspective, this activity—or *work*—may seem fun and frivolous, but from the company's point of view, it may be at the heart of value creation.

Employees, too, participate in co-creation processes. For example, photographs of me on my university's website represent free "aesthetic labour" (Pettinger 2004). I am not paid specifically for my image—no lucrative model fee—nor have I signed a contract stipulating how my image can be used. I am generally happy to see myself represent the university in this way, but I do wish that more thought would go into how this works, and that I could have some say in how my own image might be used—after all, it's *my* image. These staged snapshots of me, after all, help promote the university. Of course, one might argue that this promotion helps me too, or adds value to my position within the university. But at the same time, I may see little or no "payoff" from this value, nor have much control over its dissemination and circulation. Given how readily images can be taken from websites, a dissatisfied student or angry colleague could easily use my Web photo for all sorts of negative uses—think about how celebrity shots end up in all kinds of websites, both positive and negative. I'm not complaining, having one's photo on a university website is a reasonable request, but I am just trying to point out the complexities of using pictures of "real" people in promotion, people who are not compensated for their images and have little control over how they are used. It seems clear that consumers must obtain some benefits from their co-creation behaviour. However, to be "drafted" into helping organizations produce value sounds unappealing.

So, academics are lining up on either side of this debate, some fascinated by the creative potential of consumer co-creation, heralding a new era of consumer empowerment (see Denegri-Knott, Zwick and Schroeder 2006), while others often insightful critiques on the potentially exploitative roles that consumers play in corporate value production (for example, Gabriel and Lang 2008). At one level, this debate reflects broad conceptual concerns over *agency*—how much one person can do in society—and *structure*—how society influences and structures individual behaviour—that cannot easily be resolved. Nevertheless, the debate offers important insights into the roles that consumers play today—roles that have certainly expanded in recent years to include co-producing and co-creating for companies. Whether or not consumers willingly engage in these roles and perhaps enjoy them is one issue, but the overall role of consumption in society cannot be fully understood by asking consumers what they do and what they like. In many ways, our experiences are commodified. Some willingly participate in this commodification, enjoying the role of the brand co-creator, building brand expertise and showing off brand knowledge. Others worry that consumption has become the only viable identity project. Thus, the conceptual debate will continue, hopefully helping us understand the complex roles consumers play in society.

REFERENCES

Campbell, Norah, and Jonathan E. Schroeder. 2010. Visual Culture. In *Encyclopedia of Consumer Culture*, ed. D. Southerton. Thousand Oaks, CA: CQ Press/Sage.

Carù, Antonella, and Bernard Cova, eds. 2007. *Consuming Experience*. London: Routledge.

Caruana, Robert, and Andrew Crane. 2008. Constructing Consumer Responsibility: Exploring the Role of Corporate Communications. *Organization Studies* 29:1495–1519.

Cova, Bernard, and Daniele Dalli. 2009. Working Consumers: The Next Step in Marketing Theory? *Marketing Theory* 9 (3): 315–339.

Debord, Guy. 1994. *The Society of the Spectacle*. Trans. D. Nicholson-Smith. New York: Zone Books.

Denegri-Knott, Janice, Detlev Zwick and Jonathan E. Schroeder. 2006. Mapping Consumer Power: An Integrative Framework for Marketing and Consumer Research. *European Journal of Marketing* 40 (9–10): 950–971.

Ekström, Karin, and Helene Brembeck, eds. 2004. *Elusive Consumption*. Oxford: Berg.

Ford, Colin. 1989. *The Story of Popular Photography*. North Pomfret, VT: Trafalgar Square.

Gabriel, Yiannis, and Tim Lang. 2008. New Faces and New Masks of Today's Consumer. *Journal of Consumer Culture* 8:321–340.

Goldberg, Vicki. 1996. Photographs in History's Shifting Gaze. *New York Times*, sec. 2.

Hannerz, Ulf. 1990. Cosmopolitans and Locals in a World Culture. *Theory, Culture and Society* 7 (June): 237–251.

Löfgren, Orvar. 1999. *On Holiday: A History of Vacationing.* Berkeley: University of California Press.

Osborne, Peter D. 2000. *Travelling Light: Photography, Travel and Visual Culture.* Manchester: Manchester University Press.

Pettinger, Lynne. 2004. Brand Culture and Branded Workers: Service Work and Aesthetic Labour in Fashion Retail. *Consumption, Markets and Culture* 7 (2): 165–184.

Robinson, Mike, and David Picard, eds. 2009. *The Framed World: Tourism, Tourists and Photography.* Aldershot: Ashgate.

Scarles, Caroline. 2009. Becoming Tourist: Renegotiating the Visual in the Tourist Experience. *Environment and Planning D: Society and Space* 27:465–488.

Schroeder, Jonathan E. 2002. *Visual Consumption.* London: Routledge.

———. 2008. Visual Analysis of Images in Brand Culture. In *Go Figure: New Directions in Advertising Rhetoric*, ed. E. McQuarrie and B. J. Phillips, 277–296. Armonk, NY: M. E. Sharpe.

———. 2009. The Cultural Codes of Branding. *Marketing Theory* 9:123–126.

Urry, John. 1995. *Consuming Places.* London: Routledge.

Wikström, Solveig. 1996. The Customer as Co-Producer. *European Journal of Marketing* 30 (4): 6–19.

Wooley, A. E. 1965. *Traveling with Your Camera.* New York: A. S. Barnes and Co.

Zwick, Detlev, Samuel K. Bonsu and Aron Darmody. 2008. Putting Consumers to Work: "Co-Creation" and New Marketing Govern-Mentality. *Journal of Consumer Culture* 8 (2): 163–196.

11 "Keeping Up with the Children"
Changing Consumer Roles in Families

Karin M. Ekström

INTRODUCTION

In today's society, family members negotiate identities, lifestyles and relations to each other and people outside the family through consumption. This is a fundamental change from the pre-industrial society, where interaction between family members mainly occurred through production. However, it should be pointed out that consumer culture is not a new phenomenon. Slater (1997) discusses that it originated in the eighteenth century and was part of creating a modern world. Nonetheless, consumption has come to play a much larger, even major, role in people's lives during the later half of the twentieth century, in particular during recent decades. This is also noticeable in family life today: many discussions and family activities are centred around consumption.[1] Bauman (1998) even argues that consumption has replaced work as a status indicator. The symbolic nature of consumption has also become more noticeable. Having the "right brands" is important in order to conform to groups, but also as a tool for distinction. Everybody participates in "the catwalk of consumption" regardless of whether they enjoy consumption or have a more restrictive attitude towards it (Ekström 2007a). This holds true also for family life. Social bonds between family members and others are often negotiated through consumption, and deviating by not consuming in the same way as other families brings with it psychological and social risks (Ekström and Hjort 2009).

Consumer roles in families have changed and are changing in a continuously shifting consumer culture, which involves fast technological changes. Family members of all ages face new demands and challenges as consumers. Yet it is particularly the role of children as consumers that has changed during recent years, above all through exposure to new media and commercial activities in public as well as in private spheres.

CHILDREN AS CONSUMERS

Children are becoming consumers and establishing relations to brands at a very young age compared to earlier in history. They are exposed to product placement in TV shows and on websites such as MySpace and Facebook. They see brands at the shopping centre, at home and at school. Birthday parties are celebrated at McDonald's. At school, they are confronted with the sponsoring of school material.

Furthermore, the borders between the private and the public are blurred and tend to merge. The commercial activities in the market have historically been described as endangering children, whereas homes and schools have been viewed as places where children are protected from pressures to consume. Yet, the worlds are in fact interpenetrated. Cook (2004) questions whether a separation between market and household is worthwhile any longer. Separations between culture and commerce can also be questioned, since the activities often are connected. For example, a visit to the museum often involves a visit to the museum shop. Furthermore, children are not merely consumers of media; their media consumption patterns are part of their social network. Multitask activities such as listening to the radio in the MP3 player, surfing on the Internet and receiving and sending SMS-messages on the mobile phone are an integrated part of their social bonding.

Marketers have also recognized the importance of children as current and prospective consumers. Children have purchasing power and the brands children favour are often likely to be preferred also in their adult life. Several managerial-oriented publications emphasize the importance of children as brand loyal consumers. Marketers know that children are not only consumers of products for themselves and products for the family, but also influence decisions concerning products aimed at parents and other family members.

The prevalent view throughout history has been that children as consumers are more vulnerable than adults. Has today's consumer culture made children even more vulnerable, since they face more commercial messages and experience consumption practices in private as well as public spheres? The discussion of children as consumers has often been restricted by a dualistic discourse. Their consumption experiences are either depicted as a stressful exposition to the dilemma of handling an abundance of choices and unexpected events, or as joyful discovery of opportunities in the marketplace. Discussions on children as consumers in public policy and academic debates have often centred around whether they are being victimized (e.g., Schor 2004) or whether they should be regarded as competent consumers (e.g., Rönnberg 2003). Some argue that marketing is corrupting innocent children, giving them the tools to pester their parents and therefore emphasize a need for protection. Others view children as sufficiently knowledgeable, or at least as gradually developing competence to critically evaluate advertising and media messages. Cook (2004) does not advocate either of these positions. I believe that children are vulnerable since they lack the consumption experience that adults may have, but do not necessarily have in fact. Children sometimes have consumption experiences that adults may lack. It is a misperception to see children in general as passive and incompetent, since they sometimes are actively involved and quicker to learn novelties than their parents. Children differ as individuals and their roles as consumers need to be investigated in different contexts and media.

TV ADVERTISING AND CHILDREN'S ROLE AS CONSUMERS

The discussion about children as consumers has up till now focused on TV advertising and it has been intensive especially when the effects of TV advertising in general have been on the agenda. In the United States, this was the case in particular during the 1970s, when the effects of TV advertising directed to children were discussed by consumer organizations and governmental agencies (Cross 2002). This trend was also noticeable in research (e.g., Goldberg and Gorn 1978). The debate regarding the effects of TV advertising has continued throughout the years in the United States (e.g., Armstrong and Brucks 1988; Macklin and Carlson 1999), but has not reached the same intensity as earlier. In other countries, discussions have been vivid in particular when TV advertising has been introduced, for example, in Sweden in the beginning of the 1990s (e.g., Bjurström 1994; Jarlbro 2001).

In discussions on the effects of TV advertising, some argue that children learn to be consumers while others emphasize a need for protection. The debate concerns whether children understand advertising or if they lack the cognitive ability or life experience to deal with it (Armstrong and Brucks 1988). Another issue is whether TV advertising fosters non-rational and impulsive product choices or provides information and help children to make decisions (Armstrong and Brucks 1988). Furthermore, some emphasize that TV advertising increases parent–child conflicts, while others point out that it is not only ads on TV that make children want products, but suggestions from peers and seeing products in the store (Armstrong and Brucks 1988). Another question over the years has been whether TV advertising contributes to undesirable socialization, teaching children materialism and immediate gratification, or whether advertising helps them to learn to cope with consumer society and teaches them values such as fairness, individualism, etcetera (Armstrong and Brucks 1988).

All these arguments can be applied not only to TV advertising, but to marketing activities in general. The debate is still going on and no consensus is in sight. Schor (2004) argues that companies' marketing efforts create commercialized children. According to her, an effect of merging worlds of adults and children is a growth of materialist attitudes, which is harming children. She proposes to decommercialize and reconstruct childhood, for example, by government regulation of advertising and marketing and by actions taken in the household, the community, schools and media. More specifically, she proposes that the United States Congress should pass a federal act mandating disclosure for all sponsored product placements in television, movies, videos, books, radio and the Internet. She also suggests that Congress should commission a series of independent studies trying to assess the age at which children can identify ads, the comprehension of ads among children at various ages and when children become able to understand and resist persuasion.

In general, discussions on children's exposure and experience of TV advertising as well as advertising are often based on the notion that children are passive rather than critical agents. However, children as well as adults sometimes ignore messages, make their own interpretation and reinterpret messages in their own way. Ekström and Brembeck (2003, 4) write: "We need to understand ads not as some evil intoxicating determining discourse that hypnotizes children or view the children as some crusader for some abstract form of resistance being a carrier of some new millennium discourse that will liberate us all." Children are not passive towards television; they are discussing it, arguing about it, criticizing it, both at home and with friends (Seiter 1993). Research should focus on what consumers do with advertising rather than what advertising does to them (O'Donohoe 1994).

Parents and educators can also help children to critically evaluate advertisements. However, an old study indicates that most of children's television time is not spent with adults, and parental instruction is rare also during shared viewing times (Roberts 1983). Debates on the effects of television advertising tend to forget that children view advertising at other times than during children's programs. Children are watching programs aimed at the family or the parents, but regulation of TV advertising considers children's TV programs exclusively. Often both advertisements for family products and products for the parents include children. This is a way to create attention both among adults and children, particularly in countries where TV advertising to children is forbidden for child products.

Another circumstance which adds to the complexity is that some media channels are regulated and others not. For example, TV advertising directed to children below the age of twelve is forbidden on Swedish TV channels, but those TV channels which broadcast by satellite from other countries are not covered by Swedish law. In other words, children can watch advertising also on Swedish television. Finally, we should be aware of the fact that the effects of TV advertising may change over time and differ between countries where TV advertising was relatively recently introduced, such as Sweden in the 1990s, and countries where it has been available for a long time, such as the United States. Research needs to consider cohort effects in that different generations can have different experiences of exposure to TV advertising.

CONSUMER CULTURE CONTEXTS

To understand children as consumers, it is not enough to study TV advertising. We have to investigate other media also. Children are, for example, exposed to advertising on the Internet and social media. It is also necessary to differentiate between how children act in private and public contexts in order to understand how they develop competence as consumers. In which situations should children be protected from commercial interests and who should be responsible for protection?

Advertising in schools is a controversial topic. Schor (2004) argues that this violates a fundamental principle of consumer sovereignty, namely, the right to escape ads and marketing. Again, a divergent view finds it pointless that children should be isolated from the marketplace in schools, when they in fact are confronted with it at home, at friends' houses, etcetera. As discussed earlier, the home and the market, the private and the public, are not separated as they were before. Technology has played a major role in blurring the borders. The market is present at home through the computer and the home is present in the market through the mobile phone. Since complete protection is impossible, a different strategy might be to discuss the effects of advertising and marketing explicitly in school in order for children to learn to become more critical consumers. Sponsring is another issue. It can give schools opportunities to acquire computers and books that otherwise would not have been available. However, it needs to be discussed explicitly with both parents and children. In my opinion, there are no clear-cut answers as regards sponsring, but it needs to be discussed from case to case.

Opinions regarding protection of children as consumers differ across families, cultures and political parties, and the dividing line is often whether children are seen as competent or not. For many years, it has been mainly the family and different educators who have been expected to take responsibility for developing consumer skills among children. Today, there are many agents of social change, such as retailers, media and advertising agencies, who also need to take responsibility regarding consumers' competence.

The views on children as consumers, including the protection of children as consumers, can also be expected to change as society changes. Increased deregulation, new technology and a global media world with exposure to advertising on the Internet have become parts of everyday life and require constantly new learning among old as well as young consumers. In a changing society, *all* consumers have to continuously learn new consumer roles. All consumers need to learn to be critical consumers. It is my firm opinion that children should learn this from early ages.

RELATIONS BETWEEN CHILDREN AND PARENTS

Parents who do not see their children as capable of evaluating product offers are likely to be more protective than parents who think their children have the skills or could and should develop them. A range of child-rearing practices exist, covering the spectrum from a laissez-faire view to parents who shield their children from consumption. The parents' involvement of course also depends on how much time they have at their disposal. The term "curling parents" was coined by a Danish psychologist Bent Hougaard (2004) for parents who, as a result of lack of time and bad conscience, do everything to make their children's childhood as smooth as possible. They may, for instance, drive the children to leisure activities rather than asking them to use public transportation. He argues that this behaviour will result in a lack of respect from children, affecting the relations between children and adults negatively both at home and at school. Opinions differ across families and cultures whether a friendship or an authoritarian relation between parents and children is preferable. Is children's influence perceived as participation, contribution or interference (Ekström 2007b)? In China, a spoilt child is sometimes referred to as "little emperor".

The parent's involvement in their children's consumption experiences can also reflect upon the parents themselves. Belk (1988) observes that possessions can become part of the owner's extended self when an individual appropriates the object. This can also be applied to human relations. For example, a child who succeeds as a consumer making good deals can reflect on the parent(s) as being good parent(s) training consumer competence.

A recent media phrase, "helicopter parents", has been coined for parents who are highly involved, for example, in their children's homework and sports activities to make sure that they succeed. This concerns not only young children. An article in a Norwegian newspaper (Kaspersen 2005) discusses the tendency that more parents in Norway, Denmark and the United States are getting involved in their children's university studies, for example, by asking for the syllabus in order to control that the classes paid for are attended by the child. The expression "helicopter parents" implies that youth is prolonged in today's society. The European Parliament and the Council adopted in 2006 a Youth in Action program for the period 2007–2013 in which youth is defined as fifteen to twenty-eight years old (in some cases thirteen to thirty; see http://ec.europa.eu/youth/youth-in-action-programme/doc74_en.htm). In some countries (e.g., Sweden), it has become more common during the last decades for young adults in their twenties to live with their parents due to housing shortages. In other countries (e.g., Spain and Italy), this has historically long been the case. Adult children living at home are likely to interact with their parents and therefore they also have more opportunities to influence each other. The family has historically been considered the most important reference group (people you identify with and get influenced by), in particular during childhood. However, interaction with family members continues often throughout life as they give each other information and advice and influence consumption decisions and patterns.

Parents and children are, therefore, not necessarily separated in the process of consumption. Children's consumption is related to their parents' consumption, since children are a reason for parents to spend (Cross 2002; Martens, Southerton and Scott 2004). Consumption often starts before the child is born, for example, by arranging baby showers. Cross (2002, 444) provides a historian's perspective and claims that parents spending on children enter a fantasy world: "By giving to children, parents restored their own long-lost pleasure and temporarily freed themselves from the boredom or fixation that most consumers regularly experience". Research on consumption in families has not sufficiently recognized the dynamics of interactions and negotiations. Decision-making has been in focus and is often viewed as either individual or joint. However, joint decisions are also influenced by individual family members and vary in degree from sitting around the dinner table trying to reach an agreement to discussing purchases on the mobile telephone. Individual decisions are also influenced by joint decisions, for example, a family decision to go on a holiday may influence family members to postpone certain individual purchases. A major change in consumer culture during the last decades is that family consumption has become more individualized. For example, it is not uncommon for each family member to have his/her own TV, computer, mobile phone, digital camera, MP3 player.

In general, children's influence on their parents has often been described as more negative than positive, even though this differs if it concerns a product for the child, the parent(s) or the family. A common expression in marketing is "pester power", i.e., children's ability to continuously influence their parents. Parents are victimized and portrayed as slot machines that children continuously pull in order to acquire more things (Tufte 1999). Parents pressed for time may feel guilty about not spending enough time with their children and therefore allow them more influence. Children can become dream children or trophy children (Tufte 1999). At the same time, children may have the interest, knowledge, experience or time to get involved in purchases that other family members lack. Children are observant of new trends and can contribute to making decisions in families, and parents can learn from their children about consumption (Ekström 1995, 2007b).

Children of today experience technological change at a rate different from their parents when they were children. Ekström (1995, 2007b) found that parents learnt from their children, who provided information before purchases, but also afterwards helped them to install or use the products purchased. Society has developed into a prefigurative culture, a culture in which adults learn not only from adults, but also from their children (Mead 1970). In an old study by Mueller (1958), the desire for innovation was found to be higher among couples with children than among those with no children. The fact that children make parents aware of new trends, new technology, environmental issues, etcetera, and also influence their consumption patterns can result in a behaviour we might call "keeping up with the children" (Ekström 2007b), similar to "keeping up with the Joneses".

In today's society, it is not uncommon that grandparents ask their children and grandchildren for advice, in particular regarding consumer decisions involving technology. It would also be interesting to know to what extent "keeping up with the grandchildren" (Ekström 2007a) exists.

If we want to overcome the rather unhelpful dichotomy between children as victims and as competent consumers, we need to consider negotiations regarding consumption between parents and children more in-depth. Studies on children's consumption have neglected practices through which children and their parents consume (Martens, Southerton and Scott 2004). DeVault (1991) discusses the importance of considering repeated activities such as routines and rituals in family life. Parents and children sometimes form alliances and influence and learn from each other (Ekström 1995, 2007b). Consumption overall can create bonds between family members. Children are introduced to brands that their parents use and vice versa. Furthermore, reversals of traditional roles are visible in today's consumer culture in that parents wear clothes with child motifs and children wear clothes originally designed for adults.

NEGOTIATIONS AND THE SURROUNDING SOCIETY

Negotiations between parents and children do not occur in isolation, but in relation to the surrounding society such as peers, teachers, retailers and media. Martens, Southerton and Scott (2004) emphasize that studies of children's consumption experiences need to take into account their parents' consumption orientations as well as influence from other adults and children in the networks of daily life. Also, children learn things in school that they sometimes later teach their parents, for example, cooking recipes (Ekström 1995). Moschis (1976) found a positive relationship between the number of consumer-related courses taken at school and the adolescent's propensity to discuss consumption with his/her parents. Marketing and sponsoring of school materials influence not only children, but are also likely to have an impact on parents. Children can be seen as channels for reaching out to parents. For example, anti-smoking campaigns in schools can have as a result that children attempt to influence their parents to stop smoking (Ekström 1995). This could be a coincidence or an explicit or implicit strategy. A women's magazine from the 1920s in Sweden (*Husmodern* 1927) mentions that Norwegian children who were sent on holiday camps learned how to clean and to keep things orderly and then taught the parents and elderly siblings to do the same when they had returned home. Is it appropriate to use children as channels for reaching out to parents, and if so, under which circumstances?

Living in consumer culture involves pressure for children and parents to conform to consumption among others such as peers. Martens, Southerton and Scott (2004, 169) write:

Consumption might be a source of anxiety in terms of making the right choices on behalf of children, but a competent grasp of the norms that govern parents' and children's consumption is the means to both alleviating that anxiety and to achieving the desired ends—which is that parents and children gain a sense of acceptance and belonging within their desired social group.

It happens that parents sacrifice their own consumption for their children. For example, Hjort (2004) found examples of low-income parents who neglected their own consumption in order to be able to allow their children to consume and take part in consumer culture. We need to know more about negotiations regarding consumption in families in general and in families with scarce resources in particular, since consumption is an important social marker. How do children's development of competence and critical consumerism vary in different families? How is status constructed in different families? Which factors determine if it is status to have an environmentally built house or the biggest house in town? Finally, children that have grown up during prosperous economic times lack experience and may not even have heard of economic recessions. Their consumer roles as well as their interpretation of the meanings of consumption, involving spending and saving, are likely to differ compared to children living under economic scarcity.

SOCIAL CONSTRUCTION OF CHILDHOOD

Children's role as consumers and their influence on their own and their family's consumption decisions are determined not only by children's competence, but by society's view on childhood. As mentioned earlier, the prevalent view of childhood throughout history and even today is that children are more vulnerable than adults. Children should be protected from marketing activities. This view has been reinforced by cognitive developmental theories such as Piaget's (1970) theory in consumer socialization research. Piaget's theory indicates that a person is developed through interaction of biological/genetic factors and environment, and four stages of cognitive growth are identified. A child has to reach a certain age to understand and evaluate advertising. The highest stage of growth appears during adolescence, according to Piaget. Johansson (2003) argues that developmental theory and early socialization theories look upon childhood as a transportation distance from the incomplete to the complete. Children have to wait till adulthood to become full-fledged consumers.

The interpretive development in childhood studies in Europe (e.g., Lee 2001; Tufte, Kampmann and Hassel 2003) presents a different view on childhood. Childhood is viewed as a social construction which is heavily influenced by cultural aspects. Children are beginning to be seen as equals to adults as reflected in the United Nations' convention of children's rights from 1989. Also, social sciences refer nowadays to children as actors, humanities refers to children as creators and political sciences refers to children as citizens with democratic rights (Tufte, Kampmann and Hassel 2003). The interpretive turn in childhood studies accentuate that childhood is not universal: there are childhoods instead of childhood since each childhood is unique (James and Prout 1997). The interpretive-based theories view an understanding of childhood from the participant child as opposed to the observer. Subjective knowledge is generated in a subjectively constructed social world. The lack of a universal childhood is one reason why the interpretive researchers' do not think clear-cut causative models work. We need to develop theories that differentiate childhood. Bartholomew and O'Donohoe (2003) argue that age/stage theories of child development should be monitored and modified if in fact children are maturing at a younger age in today's society. Also, James and James (2004) state that children's agency should be incorporated into theories of childhood by considering their experiences of childhood and the way they shape their childhood. Overall, the complexity of children's roles as consumers needs more attention in future research.

CHILD ORIENTATION

A greater child orientation has been noticeable during the last century in many Western countries. Ellen Key (1909) argued early for children's self-determining rights. Cook discusses how the child's perspective became institutionalized in the context of commercial enterprise from the 1920s and onwards. He writes: "In the process, children have come to acquire the status of persons—of socially adjudicated subjects—in and through the mechanisms of market exchange" (2003, 121). Also, Seiter (1993) finds this tendency in popular, middle-class-directed parenting literature of the 1920s. However, it is in particular during the last decades that a greater child orientation has been noticeable in many Western countries, for example, in Sweden. Children are expected to have their democratic rights to participate in consumption decisions. They are beginning to be seen as more equal to adults.

Qvortrup (1994) distinguishes between human being and human becoming. A child who is given respect and considered competent is looked upon as human being. A child who is a growing, incomplete human being is considered human becoming. Lee (2001) does not consider becoming as having less status, but argues that it represents the continuous changes we face in life. He thinks that both children and adults are continuously confronted with new situations, facing challenges and novelties. Hence, we are all becomings, both adults and children. He (2001, 43) writes: "To be accurate in our studies of children, and fair in our treatment of them, we must abandon our stereotype of them, and try to recognize them for what they are—persons in their own right". Future research needs to allow children's voices to be heard.

In a continuously changing society, it is necessary to ask what it means to be a consumer and how competence is developed for all consumers, even though it is particularly pertinent for children who are learning for the first time to become consumers. The development of competence for functioning in society is studied though the construct of socialization in sociology. In marketing, research on consumer socialization deals with how to function in the market place. Ward (1974, 2) defines consumer socialization as: "the process by which young people acquire skills, knowledge, and attitudes relevant to their functioning as consumers in the marketplace." A majority of research has focused on children or adolescents learning to become consumers. In economic psychology, research on economic socialization focuses explicitly on understanding of the economic world and focuses also on young consumers. Again, in a continuously changing society, we must recognize that consumer socialization is lifelong (Ekström 2006). Family members such as parents, children and grandparents interact and learn from each other, often in a reciprocal process and often throughout life.

CONCLUSION

The prevailing dualistic view of seeing children as either competent or victimized presents a too simplistic picture of children's situation today. We need to understand in which situations competence exists and how competence is acquired. Also, we must recognize that all consumers regardless of age learn to be consumers in a continuously changing society. This chapter has focused in particular on children who learn to be consumers at an early age, but I have also pointed out that parents and grandparents learn from children. Children have different consumption experiences and interact in social spheres that sometimes differ from those of other family members. It is noticeable among immigrant families that children bring new consumption patterns from the "new" country into the home.

There are societal changes in how we view children on the one hand and adult consumers on the other that coincide. For both, there has been a shift during the last decades from conceptualizing them as passive and reactive to seeing them as critical agents actively interpreting and negotiating the meaning of consumption. Still, neither adults nor children are competent consumers in all areas of life. It differs depending on which context we are studying. Consumers and marketing activities exist in interrelated contexts where individual as well as socio-cultural perspectives need to be considered. There are different childhoods but also different parenthoods (Ekström 2007a), and both involve different experiences. By avoiding dualisms such as market–home, private–public, we can concentrate on situations and practices used by consumers for developing competence in different commercial culture contexts. Social media needs to be considered. It is not sufficient to study how children navigate in traditional media. Symbolic consumption with strong visual elements is highly prevalent in today's consumer culture and critical for social comparison. Group pressure among young consumers seems to be more related to consumption than earlier. More research is needed on how consumers in general and young consumers in particular can develop competence to become critical consumers.

A sharper picture of what it means to be a child consumer, developing competence in a continuously changing society, must originate from the young consumers themselves. It is through the eyes of the children that we can reach a better understanding of how children's competence as consumers can be developed. The voice of the child needs to be taken into account both in the choice of theories and the research methods used. We must also develop theories that differentiate childhood, and in order to understand the practices used by children in-depth, more ethnographic studies are necessary. They will allow us to listen to the voice of the child consumer in a less crude way than questionnaires do and allow for more subtle nuances to be noticed.

Parents and educators have for a long time been seen as having the main responsibility for developing children's competence. In today's consumer culture, there are also other agents of social change (e.g., retailers, media, advertising agencies) that should take responsibility for developing children's competence. It is also important to understand how children interpret the practices used by different agents of change. Finally, to view children as active consumers acquiring their own consumer skills communicates sovereignty, but are children always prepared for this consumer role? Can it sometimes be experienced as too burdensome, involving too much responsibility at a too young age? We need more academic research considering child consumers in different socio-cultural contexts, understanding the continuously changing consumer roles through the eyes of children.

NOTES

1. However, let us not overlook that families today negotiate relations not only through consumption, but also through production. For example, family members can together produce a family home page on the computer.

REFERENCES

Armstrong, Gary M., and Merrie Brucks. 1988. Dealing with Children's Advertising: Public Policy Issues and Alternatives. *Journal of Public Policy and Marketing* 7:98–113.

Bartholomew, Alice, and Stephanie O'Donohoe. 2003. Everything under Control: A Child's Eye View of Advertising. *Journal of Marketing Management* 19:433–457.

Bauman, Zygmunt. 1998. *Work, Consumerism and the New Poor.* Buckingham: Open University Press.

Belk, Russell W. 1988. Possessions and the Extended Self. *Journal of Consumer Research* 15 (September): 139–168.

Bjurström, Erling. 1994. Children and Television Advertising. A Critical Study of International Research Concerning the Effects of TV-Commercials on Children. Swedish Consumer Agency: Report 1994/95:8.

Cook, Daniel T. 2003. Agency, Children's Consumer Culture and the Fetal Subject: Historical Trajectories, Contemporary Connections. *Consumption, Markets and Culture* 6 (2): 115–132.

———. 2004. Beyond Either/Or. *Journal of Consumer Culture* 4 (2): 147–153.

Cross, Gary. 2002. Valves of Desire: A Historian's Perspective on Parents, Children, and Marketing. *Journal of Consumer Research* 29 (December): 441–447.

DeVault, Marjorie L. 1991. *Feeding the Family, The Social Organization of Caring as Gendered Work.* Chicago: University of Chicago Press.

Ekström, Karin M. 1995. *Children's Influence in Family Decision Making: A Study of Yielding, Consumer Learning and Consumer Socialization.* Göteborg: Bas ek.för.

———. 2006. Consumer Socialization Revisited. In *Research in Consumer Behavior, Vol. 10*, ed. Russell W. Belk. Oxford: Elsevier Science Ltd.

———. 2007a. Participating in the Catwalk of Consumption. In *Children, Media and Consumption: On the Front Edge. Yearbook at the International Clearinghouse on Children, Youth and Media*, ed. Karin M. Ekström and Birgitte Tufte. Göteborg: Nordicom.

———. 2007b. Parental Consumer Learning or "Keeping Up with the Children". *Journal of Consumer Behavior* 6:203–217.

Ekström, Karin M., and Helene Brembeck. 2003. New Perspectives on Advertising to Children. Paper presented at the 32nd European Academy of Marketing Conference.

Ekström, Karin M., and Torbjörn Hjort. 2009. Hidden Consumers in Marketing—The Neglect of Consumers with Scarce Recourses in Affluent Societies. *Journal of Marketing Management* 25 (7–8): 697–712.

Goldberg, Marvin E., and Gerald J. Gorn. 1978. Some Unintended Consequences of TV Advertising to Children. *Journal of Consumer Research* 5 (June): 22–29.

Hjort, Torbjörn. 2004. *Nödvändighetens pris; Konsumtion och knapphet bland barnfamiljer.* Lund: Lund Dissertations in Social Work.

Hougaard, Bent. 2004. *Curlingföräldrar.* Stockholm: Pan.

Husmodern. 1927. Barn som skapa om sina föräldrar; Norska slummens främsta ger små livsbilder ur sin verksamhet. Husmodern, Stockholm: Åhlén och Åkerlund, 20–21.

James, Allison, and Adrian L. James. 2004. *Constructing Childhood: Theory, Policy and Social Practice.* New York: Palgrave Macmillan.

James, Allison, and Alan Prout, eds. 1997. *Constructing and Reconstructing Childhood: Contemporary Issues in the Sociological Study of Childhood.* London: Falmer Press.

Jarlbro, Gunilla. 2001. *Children and Television Advertising. The Players, the Arguments and the Research during the Period 1994–2000.* Swedish Consumer Agency.

Johansson, Barbro. 2003. Barn som aktörer i konsumtionssamhället. In *Mediebarndommen: Artikkelsamling basert på en konferense i Trondheim, 27–28 mars*, ed. I. Selmer-Olsen and S. Sando. Trondheim: Dronning Mauds Minne.

Kaspersen, Line. 2005. Foreldre til besvaer. *Dagens Naeringsliv* (September): 15, 64.

Key, Ellen. 1909. *The Century of the Child.* New York: G. P. Putnam's Sons.

Lee, Nick. 2001. *Childhood and Society: Growing Up in an Age of Uncertainty.* Buckingham: Open University Press.

Macklin, M. Carole, and Les Carlson. 1999. *Advertising to Children: Concepts and Controversies.* Thousand Oaks, CA: Sage.

Martens, Lydia, Dale Southerton and Sue Scott. 2004. Bringing Children (and Parents) into the Sociology of Consumption. *Journal of Consumer Culture* 4 (2): 155–182.

Mead, Margaret. 1970. *Culture and Commitment: A Study of the Generation Gap*. New York: Natural History Press/Doubleday and Co. Inc.

Moschis, George P. 1976. Acquisition of the Consumer Role by Adolescents. PhD diss., Madison Graduate School of Business, University of Wisconsin.

Mueller, Eva. 1958. The Desire for Innovations in Household Goods. In *Consumer Behavior: Research on Consumer Reactions*, ed. H. Clark Lincoln, 13–37. New York: Harper and Brothers Publishers.

O'Donohoe, Stephanie. 1994. Advertising Uses and Gratifications. *European Journal of Marketing* 28 (8–9): 52–75.

Piaget, Jean. 1970. The Stages of Intellectual Development of the Child and Piaget's Theory. In *Readings of Child Development and Personality*, ed. Paul H. Mussen, John J. Conger and Jerome Kagan. New York: Harper and Row.

Qvortrup, Jens. 1994. *Childhood Matters. Social Theory, Practice and Politics*. Avebury: Aldeshot.

Roberts, Donald F. 1983. Children and Commercials: Issues, Evidence, Interventions. In *Rx Television: Enhancing the Preventive Impact of TV*, eds. Joyce Sprafkin, Carolyn Swift, and Robert Hess. New York: Hawthorne Press.

Rönnberg, Margareta. 2003. *TV-reklamen—vår tids myter; Men könsrollskonserverande och konsumtionsfrämjande för barn?* Uppsala: Filmförlaget.

Schor, Juliet B. 2004. *Born to Buy: The Commercialized Child and the New Consumer Culture*. New York: Scribner.

Seiter, Ellen. 1993. *Sold Separately, Parents and Children in Consumer Culture*. New Brunswick, NJ: Rutgers University Press.

Slater, Don. 1997. *Consumer Culture and Modernity*. Cambridge: Polity Press.

Tufte, Birgitte. 1999. Genom tjat har barnen tagit makten bland storkonsumenterna. *Sydsvenskan*, 6 February.

Tufte, Birgitte, Jan Kampmann and Monica Hassel. 2003. *Bornekultur, et begreb i bevaegelse*. Copenhagen: Akademisk forlag.

Ward, Scott. 1974. Consumer Socialization. *Journal of Consumer Research* 1:1–16. http://ec.europa.eu/youth/youth-in-action-programme/doc74_en.htm.

Part IV

The Consumption Bubble and Beyond?

12 Relative Deprivation, Inequality and Consumer Spending in the United States

Robert H. Frank

The American personal savings rate, which stood at nearly 10 per cent in the mid-1980s, has declined steadily in the years since (see Figure 12.1). For the first time since the Great Depression, this key rate actually became negative during 2005 and 2006, when many consumers were using home equity loans and expanded credit card debt to spend more than they earned.

Traditional economic models have difficulty explaining this trajectory. The reigning model of consumption and savings remains Milton Friedman's permanent income hypothesis (Friedman 1957), which says that families consume a constant fraction of their permanent income each year. Roughly speaking, a family's permanent income is the annualized present value of all its current and future income. According to the permanent income hypothesis, aggregate consumption over time should remain a constant fraction of aggregate permanent income. Yet consumption now is a substantially higher fraction of permanent income than it used to be.

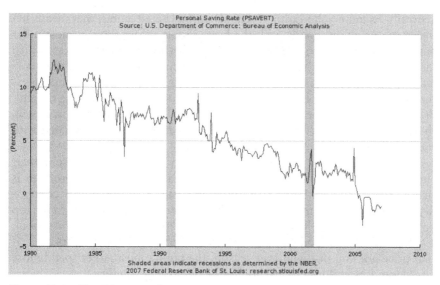

Figure 12.1   The US personal savings rate.

The failure of the permanent income hypothesis to track experience is rooted in its failure to account for the role of context in consumption decisions. As all available evidence suggests, spending decisions are driven not by income alone, but also by the spending of others. As the economist Richard Layard famously wrote: "In a poor country, a man proves to his wife that he loves her by giving her a rose, but in a rich country, he must give a dozen roses" (1980, 741). Expenditure patterns have changed dramatically because the context that shapes individual spending decisions has also changed dramatically.

HOW CONTEXT AFFECTS INDIVIDUAL
SPENDING DECISIONS

Job applicants are advised to dress well for their interviews because they'll get only one chance to make a good first impression. Dressing well, however, is a relative concept. It means looking better than other candidates for the same job. To know how much someone will choose to spend on an interview suit, then, it is necessary to know how much others are spending.

Context also shapes what kinds of houses people consider necessary or desirable. When I was a young man just out of college, I served as a Peace Corps math and science teacher in rural Nepal. I lived in a two-room house with no electricity or running water. This house never seemed unsatisfactory to me in any way. It was in fact a much nicer house than those of most other teachers in my village school. In an American city, however, most teachers would be embarrassed to live in such a house.

As in the case of clothing, context influences housing demand for instrumental as well as psychological reasons. An important goal for most families is to send their children to the best possible schools, and because students generally attend neighbourhood schools in the United States, that means living in the neighbourhoods with the best schools. More than in most other nations, American school budgets are funded by local property taxes, which means that schools in neighbourhoods with more expensive homes are normally better funded than schools in poorer neighbourhoods. Beyond that is the link between school quality and average student quality. Because the children of high-income parents generally perform better than others in school, there is a perceived advantage to being enrolled in a school populated with these children.

The problem is that no matter how fervently parents desire to send their children to a good school, not all of them can succeed. The problem is that a "good school", like a good interview suit, is an inherently context-dependent concept. Only half of all schools at any moment can be in the top half of the school quality distribution. To send its children to a good school, a family must thus spend at least the median price for homes in its area. If that price goes up, for whatever reason, the family must either spend more or else send its children to a school of below-average quality.

Context affects demand in similar ways across a host of different expenditure categories. When context changes, expenditure patterns change. In recent decades, context has been changing in ways that have substantially increased the pressure for middle-income families to increase their spending faster than their incomes.

THE POST-1970S INCREASE IN INCOME INEQUALITY

During the three decades following World War II, incomes in the United States grew at almost 3 per cent per year for families up and down the income ladder. That pattern began to change, however, sometime during the 1970s. Since then, the bottom 80 per cent of the income distribution has experienced little or no growth in real income. On average, those in the top 20 per cent experienced post-1970s income growth comparable to the immediate post-WWII era.

Within the top 20 per cent, the post-1970s growth pattern was similar to the pattern observed for the population as a whole. The top 1 percent of earners, for example, now earn three times as much as they did during 1979, while those higher up on the earnings ladder have seen even more rapid earnings growth.

Detailed data for those at the very top of the earnings distribution are sparse. One reliable source is the annual *BusinessWeek* survey of executive compensation. According to this survey, CEOs of large American companies have seen their total compensation rise more than tenfold since 1980. Earnings growth among investment managers has been even more spectacular. According to Institutional Investor's *Alpha Magazine*, for example, the hedge fund manager James Simons earned US$1.7 billion in 2006. Two other managers earned more than US$1 billion that year, and the combined income of the top twenty-five managers exceeded US$14 billion. In contrast, the median hourly wage for men in the United States, adjusted for inflation, is actually lower now than it was in 1980. What little growth there has been in median family earnings in recent decades has resulted from increased labour force participation and longer hours of work for married women (Frank 2007).

These shifts in relative income have altered spending patterns in dramatic ways.

DUELING THEORIES OF CONSUMPTION

According to traditional economic models, consumer satisfaction is an increasing function of absolute consumption. These models thus assume, preposterously, that an investment banker will remain equally satisfied with his twin-engine Cessna, even after discovering that his new summer neighbour commutes to Nantucket in an intercontinental Gulfstream jet. If the context in which consumption occurs plays no role in individual spending decisions, each family's consumption will depend only on its income and not at all on what others spend.

Given the changes in income that have taken place since the late 1970s, Milton Friedman's permanent income hypothesis implies that spending by the wealthy should have increased substantially, while spending by middle-income families should have remained largely stagnant. The permanent income hypothesis also asserts that a family's savings rate is completely independent of its permanent income. To the objection that wealthy families appear to save at higher rates than poor ones, Friedman responded that this pattern was a mere statistical artifact.

In any given year, he argued, some families enjoy windfall gains while others suffer windfall losses. So among those with high current incomes in any year, there will be a disproportionate number who enjoyed windfall gains. By the same token, among those with low current incomes, we will see a disproportionate number who suffered windfall losses. Friedman's central claim was that families save windfall gains and dip into savings to maintain consumption when they suffer windfall losses. This, he observed, means that even if all families save the same proportion of their *permanent* income, the proportion of *current* income saved will be larger for families with high current income than for families with low current income.

It's an ingenious theory, but it doesn't fit the facts. As study after careful study has demonstrated, individuals with high permanent incomes save at sharply higher rates than those with low permanent incomes.

In science, the traditional pattern is for a theory to be discarded when a competing theory does a better job of tracking the data. With respect to consumption theory, we see a curious reversal of that pattern in economics. Before Friedman published his permanent income hypothesis in 1957, the reigning theory of consumer spending was the relative income hypothesis, first described by James Duesenberry (1949). According to Mr. Duesenberry, consumer spending is driven by two principal frames of reference— one moulded by the consumer's own past experience, the other by spending patterns in the surrounding community. To this day, the relative income hypothesis continues to explain the data better than the permanent income hypothesis.

When the permanent and relative incomes hypotheses were battling it out in the 1950s, both had to accommodate three basic fact patterns: the rich save at higher rates than the poor; national savings rates remain roughly constant as income grows; and national consumption is more stable than national income over short periods. The first two patterns appear contradictory: if the rich save at higher rates, savings rates should rise over time as everyone becomes richer. Yet this does not happen.

Mr. Duesenberry's explanation of the discrepancy is that poverty is relative. The poor save at lower rates, he argued, because the higher spending of others kindles aspirations they find difficult to satisfy. This difficulty persists no matter how much national income grows, and hence the failure of national savings rates to rise over time. To explain the short-run rigidity of consumption, Mr. Duesenberry argued that families look not only to the living standards of others, but also to their own past experience. The high standard enjoyed by a formerly prosperous family thus constitutes a frame of reference that makes cutbacks difficult, which helps explain why consumption levels change little during recessions.

Despite Mr. Duesenberry's apparent success, many economists felt uncomfortable with his relative income hypothesis. To them, it seemed more like sociology or psychology than economics. The profession was therefore immediately receptive to alternative theories that sidestepped those disciplines. Milton Friedman's permanent income hypothesis was such a theory. Over time, it completely displaced the relative income hypothesis in leading economics textbooks, and it continues to dominate research on spending. Yet Duesenberry's relative income hypothesis provides a much better explanation for recent changes in spending patterns.

EXPENDITURE CASCADES

When people earn more money they spend more. The poor follow this pattern and so do the middle class. The rich are no different. But unlike others, the rich now have a lot more money than they used to. And so it is no surprise that their spending has risen accordingly.

There is little evidence that middle-income Americans envy the spending of the rich. On the contrary, when Robin Leach's *Lifestyles of the Rich and Famous* was still on television, a large audience eagerly tuned in each week to see footage of their yachts and mansions. Nor is there any evidence that middle-income families have any illusions about being able to emulate the spending of the rich. These families may hope they'll become wealthy themselves some day, but in the meantime they're well aware that Ferraris and fifty-thousand-square-foot houses are beyond their reach.

For those just below the top of the earnings ladder, however, the spending of top earners matters very much. As social scientists have long emphasized, the most important comparisons are always local. When the rich build larger mansions, they inevitably shift the frame of reference that defines what the near rich consider necessary or desirable. Perhaps the larger mansions of the rich have made it now the custom to hold their daughters' wedding receptions at home, rather than in hotels or country clubs. Or perhaps they now regularly host dinner parties for twenty-four rather than eighteen guests. When that happens, the near rich, whose social circles intersect those of the rich, often feel a need to build bigger houses as well. Or perhaps some of the near rich wanted to build larger houses all along but feared it would be unseemly to do so. For these people, the larger mansions of top earners provided cover for doing something they wanted to do anyway.

Once the near rich build bigger, the frame of reference that defines acceptable housing for those just below them shifts as well, so they too build bigger, and so on. The end result is a wave of additional spending that cascades all the way down the income ladder. The median new single-family detached house built in the United States, which stood at sixteen hundred square feet in 1980, reached more than twenty-three hundred square feet by 2007.

Why is the median new house so much larger? Traditional economic models, in which context plays no role in consumption spending, offer no answer. Because median earnings are not significantly higher now than in 1980, these models say that median house size shouldn't have grown significantly. The relative income hypothesis explains the shift by noting that higher spending by top earners launched an expenditure cascade that changed the context that shapes housing expenditure for everyone.

Similar cascades have taken place across a broad swath of spending categories. Because they have a lot more money than before, the rich now buy larger and heavier vehicles, more expensive clothes and costlier gifts. Others don't have more money than before, but they, too, now spend more on these things. Because the rich have a lot more money now, they stage more elaborate coming-of-age parties for their children. In 2007, for example, David H. Brooks, a corporate CEO, spent more than US$10 million for his daughter's birthday extravaganza held at the Rainbow Room atop Rockefeller Center. The celebration included private performances by 50 Cent and Aerosmith, and the three hundred guests were given iPod videos as party favours. Middle-income families have no illusions about being able to host parties on that scale. But higher spending at the top has launched a cascade that has raised the bar that defines special occasions for middle-class families. Now, many of these families know their children will be disappointed if they don't hire a clown or a magician to perform at parties.

How can middle-income families spend more in all these ways if their incomes haven't risen? The answer is that they are exploiting every available margin. As noted at the outset, for example, savings rates have fallen to historic lows. Credit card debt is at record high levels. Some have taken additional jobs, while others have logged additional overtime. And many people have moved farther from the centre of local economic activity, enduring longer commutes in exchange for lower housing prices.

If rising inequality spawns expenditure cascades that make it more difficult for middle-income families to make ends meet, we should see increased incidence of financial distress among such families during times and in places where inequality is rising. Adam Seth Levine and I found evidence of such links. Using Census data for the one hundred largest US counties, we found the greatest increases in bankruptcy filings and the greatest increases in long commute times in counties that had the largest increases in income inequality between 1990 and 2000 (Frank and Levine 2005).

Social workers report that financial difficulties often head the list of factors associated with troubled marriages. In line with this observation, Levine and I found that the same counties with the largest increases in income inequality also experienced the largest increases in divorce rates between 1990 and 2000 (Frank and Levine 2005).

Other studies have also reported indirect evidence of a link between income inequality and financial distress. In a 2003 study using OECD data, for example, Sam Bowles and Yongjin Park found a positive association between hours worked and income inequality, both across countries at any moment in time and within countries over time (Bowles and Park 2005).

FURTHER EVIDENCE FOR THE RELATIVE INCOME HYPOTHESIS

The relative income hypothesis is also consistent with observed patterns in international savings rates that are not predicted by traditional consumption theories. The aggregate savings rate, for example, was lower in the United States than in Europe in 1980, and the gap has grown larger during the ensuing years. One could invoke cultural differences to explain the initial gap. But the prevailing view is that cultures around the world have grown more similar to each other with globalization, which leaves the growth in the savings gap unexplained.

The relative income hypothesis suggests, more parsimoniously, that the observed patterns in the savings data should mirror the corresponding patterns in the inequality data. It thus suggests that Americans saved less than the Europeans in 1980 because inequality was much higher in the United States than it was in Europe. And it suggests that the savings gap has grown wider because income inequality has been growing faster in the United States than in Europe in the years since then.

Finally, the relative income hypothesis suggests a plausible answer to the question of why aggregate savings rates have fallen even though income gains have been largely concentrated in the hands of consumers with the highest incomes. The permanent income hypothesis, which assumes that individual savings rates do not vary systematically with income, predicts no link between aggregate savings rates and differential rates of income growth across income classes. As a practical matter, however, even the staunchest defenders of the permanent income hypothesis have been forced to concede that rich people save more than others. If we take that fact as given, the observed pattern of income growth in recent decades would seem to imply a secular upward trend in aggregate savings rates. After all, the lion's share of all recent income gains has accrued to prosperous families with the highest savings rates. And yet, as noted, aggregate savings rates have fallen sharply.

The key to resolving the apparent paradox may be that although the rich may be saving more than ever, their absolute spending levels are also at record highs. This spending appears to have launched expenditure cascades all the way down the earnings distribution. And since the non-rich are far more numerous than the rich, the resulting decline in the savings rate of the non-rich could easily have offset the additional savings of the rich.

Reinforcing this interpretation is the fact that the patterns of income change within wealthy groups have mimicked those we observe for the population as a whole. As noted earlier, available evidence suggests that no matter how we partition the population, income gains are highly concentrated among top earners within each group. So even though more income is now flowing to members of prosperous groups, most members of such groups have been losing ground relative to their most prosperous peers. If local context is what really matters, the observed decline in aggregate savings rates is not anomalous.

CONCLUDING REMARKS

The long-standing decline in the personal savings rate in the United States bodes ill for the nation's future standard of living. If this trend is to be reversed, policymakers must first understand the forces that have produced it.

Because traditional economic models have not offered a satisfactory account of these forces, some commentators have focused on changing cultural norms. But even if we grant that American culture no longer celebrates thrift to the extent it once did, this change itself requires explanation. My own view is that cultural norms have been shaped by the same forces that have changed the economic environment within which individuals decide how much to spend and save. Among these forces, by far the most important have been those that govern how incomes are distributed. Unlike the balanced pattern of income growth we saw in the decades following World War II, income growth in recent decades has accrued almost entirely to those in the upper reaches of the earnings distribution. That change and the resulting increase in spending by top earners caused a cascade of changes in the frames of reference that guide spending decisions for consumers of all income levels.

As Philip Cook and I argued in our 1995 book, *The Winner-Take-All Society*, the increasing dispersion of pre-tax incomes in the US has been largely a consequence of market forces. When market forces cause income inequality to rise, policymakers in most countries employ tax policy to lean in the opposite direction. In contrast, US policymakers have been enacting tax cuts focused on high-income households, changes that have reinforced market trends in pre-tax inequality.

To reverse the decline in the US personal savings rate will require a reversal of the dramatic increase in income inequality that has occurred in recent decades. In the short run, the financial crisis will undoubtedly cause inequality in pre-tax incomes to contract. But once economic activity resumes, market forces will continue to concentrate income gains in the hands of top earners. All indications are that US policymakers will be more willing than in the recent past to limit inequality with tax policy.

REFERENCES

Bowles, Samuel, and Yongjin Park. 2005. Emulation, Inequality, and Work Hours: Was Thorstein Veblen Right? *Economic Journal* 115 (507): 397–412.

Duesenberry, James. 1949. *Income, Saving, and the Theory of Consumer Behavior.* Cambridge, MA: Harvard University Press.

Frank, Robert H. 2007. *Falling Behind. How Rising Inequality Harms the Middle Class.* Berkeley: University of California Press.

Frank, Robert H., and Philip Cook. 1995. *The Winner-Take-All Society.* New York: Free Press.

Frank, Robert H., and Adam Seth Levine. 2005. Expenditure Cascades. Cornell University mimeograph.

Friedman, Milton. 1957. *A Theory of the Consumption Function.* Princeton, NJ: Princeton University Press.

Layard, Richard. 1980. Human Satisfaction and Public Policy. *Economic Journal* 90:737–750.

13 (Un)sustainable Consumption and the New Political Economy of Growth

Maurie J. Cohen

INTRODUCTION: CONSUMPTION AND THE INTERNATIONAL FINANCIAL COLLAPSE

The cataclysm that began to sweep through international financial markets during the summer of 2007 placed the weaknesses of neoliberal economic globalization in bold relief. Venerated over the past thirty years, so-called Anglo-American capitalism was revealed to be little more than a combustible house of cards built on a foundation of unsecured credit, rampant consumerism and fervent deregulation. In a paroxysm of fiscal turpitude, central banks surrendered control of the money supply to pernicious financial managers who proved more than glad to grant themselves exorbitant salaries as compensation for indulging consumers' spendthrift proclivities.

The United States led the headlong rush, but it was by no means alone. Two conjoined measures of this rampage were the plunging propensity of households to save and the stratospheric rise in private indebtedness. After tracking along at approximately 10 per cent during most of the post–World War II era, the saving rate in the United States turned negative in 2005 and personal debt climbed from a modest 55 per cent of gross domestic product (GDP) in 1960 to an astounding 133 per cent in 2007.[1] An ancillary effect of the spiral of residential upsizing during the period was consumers' penchant to augment their purchasing power with home equity loans and other forms of credit. It is through such means that American consumers came to be extolled as the indefatigable engine of the global economy.

As a tenet of its foreign policy, this strategy paid off in spades for the United States. Countries like Canada, Mexico, Japan and Germany, ever alert for profitable ways to dispose of surplus domestic production, were induced to subvert other political interests in exchange for access to the seemingly infinite appetite of American consumers. To be sure, this "sticky power" strategy contributed to a ballooning trade deficit, but the trend was not generally viewed at the time as overly problematic (Cohen 2010; see also Mead 2004). Throughout this profligate era, consumption assumed an increasingly prominent role in the life of the nation, growing from 62 per cent of GDP in 1960 to its current level of 70 per cent.

It was, of course, not only American consumers that went on a spending binge. The federal government's budget deficit had earlier swelled during the 1970s, reaching its post–World War II nadir at 6 per cent of GDP in 1982.[2] An often underappreciated achievement of the Clinton administration was its ability not only to staunch the flow of red ink, but to return the budget to surplus by the late 1990s. A cornerstone of the early years of the second Bush presidency (beginning in 2001) was the passage of a series of tax cuts with benefits that flowed predominantly to the wealthiest households in the country. In the absence of corresponding expenditure reductions, and the fiscal demands of two wars (in Iraq and Afghanistan), the annual federal budget deficit skyrocketed and by 2009 stood at 12.3 per cent of GDP.

Financing this cumulating shortfall has become a major political preoccupation and it has thrust both the Department of the Treasury and the Federal Reserve into unusually prominent public roles. At the heart of the problem is that to remain financially solvent, the United States has come to rely on the People's Bank of China to purchase its treasury bonds and the outstanding value of American debt held by Beijing has soared in recent years to more than US$800 billion.[3] These circumstances have fostered a peculiar relationship between the two countries (dubbed Chimerica by Niall Ferguson). On one hand, even in the wake of the financial crisis, China continues to provide the cash that enables American consumers to maintain their accustomed lifestyles. In the absence of these funds, taxes in the United States would need to be much higher than they are at present. On the other hand, as a leading banker to the United States, China needs to exercise considerable care in how it manages its assets because any large-scale sell-off (or even rumours of such activity) would precipitate a decline in bond prices and a reduction in the value of remaining Chinese holdings. At the same time, financial authorities in Beijing need to be mindful of inflation in the United States as even modest reductions in the realizable value of its investment portfolio would be economically disastrous. Moreover, the colossal size of its current budget deficit (US$1.85 trillion according to the most recent assessments of the Congressional Budget Office) could encourage Washington to embark on a dangerous path of strategically inflating its debt by vigorously printing new currency. Ferguson (2005) has instructively observed that the United States is in the historically curious and politically delicate position of being a "debtor empire" and the financial situation of the country is tantamount to that of a nation fighting a world war without the war.

It is furthermore not unreasonable to expect that over the next few years new rounds of deficit-financed stimulus will be necessary to drive unemployment levels down to a politically acceptable level. A further consideration is the likelihood of subsequent recessionary dips that create the need for more bank bailouts. In fact, while popular attention has focused on institutions that are "too big to fail", financial regulators in the United States have had to rescue hundreds of smaller institutions and insurers themselves have been forced to solicit supplementary sources of capitalization. And this picture represents just the tip of a vast iceberg. The American treasury has yet to feel the crashing wave of claims that will come due as the generation of approximately seventy-seven million "baby boomers" becomes eligible for public health insurance and other expensive entitlements. Federal actuaries, including the former director of the Government Accountability Office, have valued these implicit liabilities at upwards of US$50 trillion.

In the face of these circumstances, little serious attention has been devoted to the macroeconomics of unsustainable consumption (cf. Czech 2000; Schor 2005; Daly 2007; Victor 2008). To be sure, ecological economists and industrial ecologists dutifully have cranked out ever more exacting studies on the heavy toll of prevailing patterns of resource utilization, but this work on biophysical throughput was rarely connected to the world of finance. At the same time, resultant policy prescriptions remained decidedly incremental because of a palpable fear of appearing too extreme or rankling diffident politicians (Tukker et al. 2010). It is thus difficult to avoid the charge that scholarship on sustainable consumption has failed to adequately recognize the outright unsustainability of the financial system and to acknowledge the role that so much easy money has had in propelling resource flows at all levels of the global economy.

WEAK VERSUS STRONG SUSTAINABLE CONSUMPTION

Consideration of the sustainability dimensions of prevailing consumption practices has tended to heavily favour conceptions of "weak sustainable consumption" founded on notions of atomized consumer behaviour advanced by social psychologists and behavioural economists. These approaches have given rise to policy recommendations built up around green consumerism, eco-labeling and household investments in energy efficiency. Other prominent strategies have come out of the realm of *sustainable production* and encourage complementary initiatives grounded in product policy, lifecycle engineering, waste and material minimization and eco-efficiency (see, e.g., United Nations Environment Program 2001; UK Department of Environment, Food and Rural Affairs 2003, 2005; Finnish Ministry of the Environment 2005; UK Sustainable Consumption Roundtable 2006; European Environment Agency 2005; German Federal Environment Agency 2007).

More heterodox social scientists have challenged these mainstream policy programs and charged that standard models of consumption ignore the social dimensions of household provisioning and the likelihood of perverse rebound effects. Another basis for criticism has been that the meager gains likely to result from such modest measures are incompatible with the ambitious targets that scientific experts maintain are essential if we are to avoid transgressing critical ecological thresholds (see Rockström 2009; Walker et al. 2009 for recent overviews). This mismatch appears to be especially prominent with respect to global climate change where influential analyses like the Fourth Assessment Report of the Intergovernmental Panel on Climate Change (IPCC) (2007) and *The Stern Review* (2007) assert a need to reduce greenhouse gas emissions by more than 80 per cent. There is moreover the problem that by emphasizing consumer rationality and narrow technical tactics, policymakers are marginalizing the essential politics of any meaningful program to elicit fundamental changes in consumption. Under such circumstances, the "sustainable" option becomes just another product on a supermarket shelf. Shoppers can conveniently procure full fat yogurt, low-fat yogurt or "sustainable" yogurt depending on their inclinations on a specific day and producers can claim that they are doing their bit by making such alternatives available. Viewed through this lens, weak sustainable consumption is just pretense and increasing throughput remains the foremost economic objective.

By contrast, proponents of "strong sustainable consumption" seek to foster transformational changes in both the quantity and the quality of resource use. Instead of consumer rationality and engineering redesign, this insurgent set of perspectives embraces a broad conception of moral responsibility. Some scholars situate household provisioning within the everyday social practices of consumers (Hobson 2002; Spaargaren 2003; Quitzau and Røpke 2008; Hargreaves, Nye and Burgess 2008) and others attempt to develop sustainable consumption as a means through which to encourage ecological citizenship, democratic engagement, innovative governance and alternative systems of economic organization (Fuchs and Lorek 2005; Cohen 2006; New Economics Foundation [NEF] 2008). There is additionally an effort to understand the complex dynamics of global supply chains and international trading regimes with an eye toward identifying leverage points where pressure for change can be maximally applied (O'Rourke 2005) and where household provisioning can effectively be relocalized (Seyfang 2006).

This work is frequently animated by spirited appraisals of consumption (and consumerism) and is clearly distinguished from the more established metabolic analyses that largely disregard the political dynamics behind material and energy flows. Some of this scholarship has drawn on the burgeoning body of literature on "happiness" and sought to uncover linkages between material abundance and lifestyle satisfaction (Jackson 2005, 2008; NEF 2006; Offer 2007). The underlying contention is that beyond a certain threshold level of consumption (and income) there is little improvement in subjective well-being. Equally paradoxical is the finding that the proportion of people in affluent countries that claims to be "very happy" has not changed over the last few decades despite manifold growth in the volumes of energy and materials appropriated for human use. These findings suggest that contentment is more a function of interpersonal comparison than a matter of absolute levels of accumulation. If happiness is indeed based on relative standing, consumers could presumably reduce their expenditures and curtail proportionately the amount of time they devote to paid employment without experiencing any diminution in perceived quality of life.

Some social entrepreneurs have sought to test these claims by, for example, modifying their lifestyles in accordance with the principles of voluntary simplicity (Elgin 1993; James 2007), while others have drastically reduced their personal environmental impacts as part of experiments in self-improvement (Levine 2007; Beavan 2009). More collective efforts like the formation of carbon reduction action groups (CRAGs) and the establishment of "transition towns" have also gained in popularity (Hopkins and Heinberg 2008).

Strong sustainable consumption takes as its point of departure the need to strive for multifactor improvements—ranging from factor 4 to factor 20—in the efficiency of materials and energy use (von Weizsäcker, Lovins and Lovins 1997; Hinterberger and Schmidt-Bleek 1999). These ambitious targets derive from recognition that it will be necessary to accommodate a worldwide population of nine billion people by 2050 (along with corresponding growth in resource utilization) and simultaneously control the most dangerous effects of global climate change. Such circumstances call for large-scale reductions in the volume of resources appropriated by wealthy countries and for endowing less affluent nations with "leap-frogging" capacity (Tukker et al. 2008; cf. Perrels 2008). This awareness has led to consideration of so-called transition pathways and the radical transformation of entire socio-technical systems (Rohracher 2001; Elzen, Geels and Green 2004).

TOWARD A MORE RADICAL VIEW OF (UN)SUSTAINABLE CONSUMPTION

An unarguable feature of weak sustainable consumption is that it has displayed a steadfast commitment to fitting itself around the strictures set by neoliberal economics. More pointedly, strategies have been formulated to encourage consumers to embrace a range of voluntary actions—from reducing automobile use to buying recycled paper to applying less toxic cleaning solutions. Interestingly, most proponents of strong sustainable consumption, despite attempts to shift the debate toward more fundamental reshaping of purchasing practices, have also remained tethered to the extant economic system.

The international financial collapse, however, has reverberated powerfully across the field and reconfigured its intellectual underpinnings with the force of a powerful earthquake. In the first instance, discussions about the future of consumption have widened considerably with a number of new voices joining the conversation.[4] In addition, several leading researchers have thrown short-term political pragmatism to the wind and begun to formulate thoroughgoing indictments of the contemporary allegiance to continuous economic growth.

While it is too early to know whether this trend will be a sustained, there is considerable newfound interest in revisiting, in light of unfolding economic events, past debates on limits to growth and the plausibility of moving toward a steady economic state. Three recently published documents—all released during spring 2009—are useful touchstones for gauging this apparent shift. The first report, a pamphlet authored by British environmental campaigner Jonathon Porritt (2009) is entitled *Living within Our Means*. The second example of this move to reframe sustainable consumption is a compendium called *Socially Sustainable Economic Degrowth* (Rijnhout and Schauer 2009) that comprises the proceedings of a workshop on degrowth (*décroissance*) held at the European Parliament. Finally, we review a report written by Tim Jackson and released under the auspices of the UK Sustainable Development Commission entitled *Prosperity without Growth*.[5]

Living within Our Means

Jonathon Porritt, the author of *Living within Our Means*, is a venerable figure within the ranks of UK environmentalism. After involvement with the Green Party (formerly the UK Ecology Party) and several years as director of Friends of the Earth, he co-founded Forum for the Future in 1996. The organization quickly became a fixture in both domestic and international policy discussions and Porritt serves as a prominent sustainability champion through a welter of interlocking positions on governmental and quasi-governmental bodies. In 2007, he published a book entitled *Capitalism as if the World Matters* that presaged his more recent treatise.

The report aims to draw a clear connection between the "credit crisis" and the "ecological crisis" and contends that the recent rash of bank failures is a harbinger of a more serious collapse yet to come—"the ultimate recession"—induced by global climate change. Porritt demonstrates for a mainstream audience the often neglected relationship between economic and biophysical unsustainability. Our propensity to accumulate untenable financial debt is inseparable from our proclivities to generate ecological debt. He contrasts the incongruity between urgent governmental efforts to inject aid into disabled banks with the lackluster public response to reduce greenhouse gas emissions. Porritt forcefully argues that this paradox is attributable to a steadfast commitment to economic growth, a tenacity that today rests largely on "articles of faith". This resolve persists despite demonstrable evidence that continual expansion of GDP does not contribute meaningfully to improvements in well-being in already affluent countries.

Living within Our Means reviews the financial and ecological consequences of unwavering devotion to economic growth in both the United States and the UK over the past four decades and highlights how it has been fostered by an ideological pursuit of deregulation, an enthusiastic and permissive regard for debt, a pronounced tendency to externalize costs, a systemic undervaluation of risk, a relentless commitment to short-term pay-offs and a diminishment in democratic engagement. Porritt also shrewdly inquires about the efficacy of calls for greater corporate social responsibility and persuasively claims that these appeals are little more than smoke-screens that enable managers to deflect calls for transformational change.

This appraisal is part of a larger critique of contemporary environmentalism that he accuses of focusing on "the symptoms of today's converging crises" rather than working to formulate system-level understandings of problems. This is an important point and it underscores the failure to make clear the political economy of unsustainable consumption. There is in affluent countries a chronic mismatch between productive and consumptive capacities and this imbalance creates a need to continually stoke consumer demand through the use of readily accessible credit, the deployment of blanket advertising and the encouragement of insidious forms of status consciousness.

Recommendations centre on realigning economic growth with biophysical constraints and embracing a robust public policy program centred on a "Green New Deal". First advanced by the London-based NEF (2008), this idea has elicited considerable popular interest as a way to lend coherence to efforts to promote investments in both energy efficiency and renewables, to create "green-collar" jobs, to renew natural capital and (in some cases) to encourage ecological tax reform. Porritt is appropriately skeptical about the benefits of parts of this package, particularly the win-win claims put forward by "green jobs" proponents, but he is indecisive about what to do once the drawbacks of this strategy start to become apparent. The tacit goal here, after all, is not just to boost the number of solar panel fabricators and "smart grid" contractors, but to concurrently thin the ranks of oil field roustabouts and other increasingly obsolescent workers. He does note though that a more accurate description of a Green New Deal would entail consideration of the downside of creative destruction, but political realities hamper such honesty. Further evidence of Porritt's ambivalence is present when he asks whether a generation of more environmentally prudent investments will "provide substantial, lasting sustainability benefits? Or will it simply increase levels of consumption, albeit on a slightly less unsustainable basis?" He concomitantly questions the potential of "decoupling", or the delinking of economic growth from energy and materials utilization. This objective has over the past two decades become the modern-day equivalent of the medieval philosopher's stone. There is, to be sure, no shortage of examples of *relative* decoupling (a measure of energy and materials use per unit of production), but evidence of far more important *absolute* decoupling (a measure of economy-wide energy and materials use) remains elusive. The latter mode of decoupling has been difficult to achieve because efficiency gains are ultimately overwhelmed by rebound effects and relentless increases in overall consumption.

The report comprehensively describes the deep structural flaws inherent in the dominant variety of capitalism. When viewed through Porritt's lens, it is evident that economic growth perversely undermines the well-being of a majority of the world's population while simultaneously perpetuating financial risks and ecological harms. In the end, though, he diverges from his severe diagnosis and recommends a series of incremental prescriptions (e.g., reregulation of capital flows, a Tobin Tax, salary caps, elimination of tax havens). He observes that there is a need "to reconnect the financial and the real economies", but retains confidence in capitalist-driven expansion, along as it is comes with better accounting and the "right kind" of growth. It is difficult to reconcile Porritt's indictment of the prior (and ongoing) pattern of debt accumulation with his call for large-scale "green" investment or to understand where the money for a "radically different kind of recapitalization programme" will come from. The era in which China has bankrolled the United States is ending and it will be necessary to adjust to a new set of expectations. Similarly, substantial deficit spending is not on the cards for the UK and Porritt encourages instead a "dramatic *redirection* of public spending as well as increased spending in some areas" (italics in original) and calls for a reevaluation of the country's budgetary priorities (i.e., elimination of an expensive identity card program, cancelation of controversial defence projects).

Living within Our Means is a sharp appraisal of the travails inherent in the current economic system, but it is written by an author who is ultimately unable to jettison an attachment to modest reforms. This dissonance stems in large part from Porritt's relief that President Bush has surrendered control of the White House. However, like numerous other foreign observers, he allows his adulation for Barack Obama to overwhelm sober assessment of the obdurate realities that plague domestic American politics. Porritt's hopeful expectations are unfortunately bound to clash with intransigent efforts to preserve the status quo. Despite its occasional inconsistencies, and unwarranted optimism, this treatise offers a useful framework for beginning to understand the political economy of (un)sustainable consumption.

Socially Sustainable Economic Degrowth

The second report comprises the proceedings of a workshop that the Greens and the European Free Alliance convened at the European Parliament in 2009. Proper review of this document needs to be situated in a wider framework that sketches out the social and political context of the expanding degrowth movement. Centred in France under the appellation *décroissance*, interest over the last few years has radiated across Europe, as well as to Canada, Australia, the UK, the United States and elsewhere. With intellectual roots in the eighteenth century, the contemporary tenets of degrowth philosophy flow from the work of Nicholas Georgescu-Roegen and several of his protégés including Herman Daly, Joan Martinez Alier and Serge Latouche (see Sippel 2009).[6]

The current wave of interest in degrowth began to build in France and neighbouring countries during the 1990s, largely as part of wider discussions on "post-development", but did not attract much public notice. The alternative economic agenda at the time was driven by voluble personalities like Jose Bové and others associated with the *Association pour la taxation des transactions pour l'aide aux citoyens* (ATTAC) who endorsed a strident politics of anti-globalization. About a decade ago, French Green Party candidates in local elections started to draw on the work of Latouche and to give political visibility to incipient degrowthist ideas. During the 2007 French presidential election, nearly all of the candidates were compelled to address the basic degrowth argument, even if their intent was to disavow it (Fournier 2008).

The spirit of common purpose that initially inspired a heterogeneous group of environmentalists during this period did not last long. As Baykan (2007) describes, cleavages developed between degrowthists, greens and deep ecologists. Nonetheless, political clashes in France over "peak oil" and the possible cresting of other forms of nonrenewable energy enhanced the popular appeal of degrowth ideas and led to formation of the Degrowth Party (DP).[7]

Placement of the DP on the conventional political spectrum has been a matter of considerable debate, in part because the Leftist parties in France retain resolve for productivism that is at least as strong as that projected by their counterparts on the Right. Further complicating any simple determination is that degrowthist commitment to economic localism finds favour among ardent French nationalists. Regardless of where the DP is politically situated, the global financial collapse that began in 2007 prompted new interest in alternative economic paradigms and this shift elevated the degrowth movement to its current level of prominence.[8] In particular, coordinated economic downsizing (or "rightsizing") has attracted the attention of analysts who are cognizant of the risks of global climate change or harbour doubts about the merit of continuing to premise improvements in societal well-being on increasing flows of energy and materials.

The root political-economic problem with which degrowthists engage is the disparity between legitimate consumer demand and productive capacity. Dominant neoliberal strategies for addressing this dilemma have been to reduce tax rates, to deregulate the banking sector and to tolerate unfettered advertising. In contrast, the standard Keynesian prescription is to rely on government to invigorate demand to maintain employment. Common to both schools is devotion to exports to expand markets for excess production and to grow the overall size of the economy.

Governments have long been large consumers in their own right, but since World War II the level of this activity has increased substantially. In particular, governments procure massive amounts of military equipment, agricultural commodities and health care services and products. In the United States, public spending (for all levels of government combined and including interest on outstanding debt) constitutes approximately 36 per cent of GDP. While the proportion of government expenditures tends to be larger among European countries, Continental governments have also sought to balance production and consumption by regulating working hours and playing a more active role in mandating compensation for annual vacations, prolonged illnesses and parental leave. Regardless of these differences, GDP growth has been for more than a half century an overriding and non-negotiable political imperative on both sides of the Atlantic.

Indeed, current commitments to economic growth remain so deeply entrenched across the political spectrum that the incipient efforts of degrowthists have a certain quixotic quality. This move to raise questions about the ultimate efficacy of economic growth is best understood as less of a coherent economic policy program and more as an inchoate assemblage of loosely defined precepts. Given the pervasiveness of the growth mindset, it has thus far been difficult, except under exigent circumstances, to gain practical knowledge of how a policy program of degrowth might be implemented. This dilemma stems in part from the fact that degrowthist concepts are not principally derived from mathematical models and scientific experimentation, but rather are grounded in insights developed by a group of dissident authors and disseminated through academic books, journal articles, newspaper commentaries, NGO reports and Internet blogs. Fournier (2008) echoes this interpretation when she describes the movement as "a rather loose and open network including a variety of forums for circulating, sharing and debating ideas and experiences" (532).[9] Accordingly, degrowth is at present not a discourse that is capable of galvanizing large numbers of people or swaying the decisions of governments to any significant degree. Nonetheless, it has begun to make an impression on political debate, especially in France, and to tap into public sensibilities at a moment when people are beginning to actively seek out new alternatives.

The report *Socially Sustainable Economic Degrowth* includes concise contributions by a half-dozen authors, including Joan Martinez-Alier and François Schneider, and a careful reading of them suggests that degrowth can be disaggregated into three major stylized principles. First, degrowthists emphasize the problems inherent in standardized modes of national accounting (in particular, the defects in GDP calculations). This critique has become familiar in recent years and centres on the observation that GDP, among other flaws, overlooks non-monetized labour (i.e., voluntary activity, housework) and perversely treats the liquidation of natural capital as income. A related claim is that beyond a relatively low income threshold (approximately US$5,000) further increments of per capita GDP engender little notable improvement in subjective well-being. The extension of this argument, as noted earlier, is that individual happiness in affluent countries could be achieved at substantially lower levels of income.

Second, the degrowth policy discourse diverges from orthodox conceptions of sustainability that to date have been heavily predicated on efficiency improvements. Over the past twenty years, singular emphasis on "doing more with less" has contributed in certain instances to a relative decoupling of economic growth and resource utilization, but that absolute decoupling in a world moving toward a global population of nine billion people will remain an elusive goal. The point here is that we will over the next fifty years be unable to achieve the requisite efficiency gains necessary to offset growth in aggregate consumption. Greater global social equity will therefore require a redistribution of planetary growth capacity from affluent to poor countries so that the latter can pursue their morally warranted aspirations.

Finally, degrowthists disapprove of the general pale of economism and productivism that pervades contemporary life. They seek less reductionistic ways to conceptualize human motivations and contend that it is necessary to formulate public policies that give credence to a more integrated set of impulses to guide appropriate conduct.

Several prescriptive interventions flow from the degrowthist diagnosis. Central to this agenda is the use of ecological taxation, the introduction of incentives to discourage overwork (and to allocate work more equitably), the relocalization of consumption and production, the provision of a citizen's income, the imposition of restrictions on advertising and the design of more durable and readily repairable consumer products. This is no doubt an ambitious call to arms and it remains unclear how many people will enlist in the movement. Nonetheless, it is has been more than thirty years since the last public debate on limits to growth and the recent surge in curiosity about degrowth suggests that we may be about to enjoin this discussion once again.

Prosperity without Growth

The UK Sustainable Development Commission has been a leading voice on a variety of sustainability issues over the last few years and its report, *Prosperity without Growth*, has in a short time created a resounding tumult with the field of sustainable consumption and beyond. The document (written by Tim Jackson and subsequently released as a book) elaborates upon many of the same issues—most notably the common roots between the financial and ecological crises—described in both *Living within Our Means* and *Socially Sustainable Economic Degrowth*. Of the three reports considered in this chapter, *Prosperity without Growth* provides the more insightful and intellectually rigorous treatment.

Jackson begins the discussion with a review of how the affluent nations (he most directly focuses on the United States and the UK) have come to define well-being in exclusively economistic terms, and more specifically in accordance with increases in GDP. At the same time, he argues that we have lost sight of the need to comport human ambitions with biophysical constraints, an observation that clearly puts this work in the stream of modern thought established by Dennis and Donella Meadows on limits to growth. Building on the observations of both Porritt and the degrowth movement, Jackson views ecological and financial sustainability as different sides of the same coin, or as he says, "the economic crisis presents a unique opportunity to address financial and ecological sustainability together" (2009, 18). Such an approach entails recognizing that the banking crisis was not simply due to the ineptness of regulatory authorities to police rogue trading activity or the licentiousness of homebuyers, but rather it was an epiphenomenon of the breakdown of the economic-growth-at-all-costs model of capitalist development. Borrowed money sits at the heart of the paradigm and these pools of funds enabled (and continue to enable) large swaths of the public to appropriate resources far beyond their actual ability to pay for them.

As highlighted earlier, sustainability policy-making to date has largely centred on improving energy and materials efficiencies and Jackson takes readers through yet another discussion of the important difference between relative and absolute decoupling. He also emphasizes that a singular focus on efficiency is perilously imprudent because increasing population and inevitable rebound effects in aggregate consumption will quickly wipe out any improvements. At the same time, when one actually does the arithmetic on lowering greenhouse gas emissions, it becomes obvious that the required reductions are massively in excess of anything we could achieve with current (or even anticipated) technologies. In one scenario based on the IPCC's mid-range target, it would be necessary to annually reduce carbon intensity by 9 per cent for the better portion of the next fifty years (from 770 to 14 grams of carbon dioxide per US dollar). This is quite evidently unrealistic. Jackson's clear-eyed analysis challenges the generally sanguine assessment of *The Stern Review* (Stern 2007) with respect to timely implementation of carbon abatement.[10]

In what is perhaps the most innovative aspect of *Prosperity without Growth*, Jackson knits together a compelling discussion relating the economic pressure that motivates businesses to endlessly pursue novelty in the production sphere with a symbiotic quest by consumers to seek out new goods with which to demonstrate and enhance their social status. To reconcile these interlocking dilemmas, and to rise to the ambitious challenges of making meaningful progress on global climate change, Jackson considers a variety of alternatives that have lately been garnering attention including a Green New Deal, a new ecological macroeconomics, an emphasis on alternative hedonism, a shorter work week, a renewed effort to reduce social inequality (so as to constrain consumption-fueled status competition) and a shift in investment priorities from private to public goods.

Constructive progress implementing these measures certainly holds critical challenges for government and on this score Jackson delivers an incisive appraisal of the incapacity of current governing institutions. He sketches out how evolutionary processes have created a societal need to strike a balance between selfishness (individualism) and altruism (cooperation) and then delineates how in recent decades the line has shifted (especially in the United States and the UK) to strongly favour the former. The prevailing situation is moreover not a political accident, but rather an ineluctable reflection of the structural requirements of economic growth and the need to continually foster novelty. Drawing on the work of economic historian Avner Offer (2007) and psychologist Shalom Schwartz (1999), Jackson asserts a need to endorse public policies that reverse preferences for short-term pleasure by creating incentives that privilege commitments to the future. In response to anticipated claims that governments should not be seeking to influence the values of its constituents, he contends that wage policies, product standards and social programs are just some of the ways that the state is already deeply complicit in swaying individual aspirations.

Jackson concludes by trying to trace out a pragmatic transitional program for realizing the ambitious objectives set forth in his manifesto and he reiterates many of the policy proposals outlined by both Porritt and the degrowthists. He agilely sidesteps some of the obvious obstacles that adherents of economic growth at all costs will invariably direct at his ideas, but the report is less vocal in identifying who will carry the banner for prosperity without growth. While Jackson's report has received enthusiastic support from like-minded constituencies in the UK, he himself makes clear that policy elites have greeted it with incredulity. In North America, nascent organizations working toward similar ends have encountered similar blank stares. The situation on the European continent will continue to be more accommodating, but it is debatable whether these are the audiences that most need to reflect upon this report. We are then left with a visionary and imaginative intellectual formulation of the core problem that awaits a historic moment with sufficient impetus to impel it forward.

CONCLUSION

Interest in sustainable consumption for more than a decade has been largely confined to a relatively small group of interdisciplinary scholars working out of the fields of ecological economics, industrial ecology, environmental sociology and environmental psychology. The public agenda has been carried forward mostly by a contingent of NGOs and a supportive cadre of mid-level staffers at national and supranational agencies. These proponents of sustainable consumption have been primarily focused on assessing the magnitude of various energy and materials flows and encouraging consumers to embark on primarily voluntary efforts to mitigate the impacts of their materialist lifestyles.

During the past year, a jolt has coursed through this community and given rise to several vigorous critiques of how incessant emphasis on economic growth shapes prevailing commitments to consumerism and—despite efficiency improvements—drives ever larger volumes of resource throughput. A notable reorientation is occurring from merely accounting for the impacts of consumption to the formulation of policy programs that connect up with more politically robust concerns about public health.[11] These developments suggest that the issue is coming to be viewed in more socially problematic terms and that a new, more publicly visible phase in the discursive career of sustainable consumption is about to commence.

NOTES

1. The GDP for the United States in 2008 was US$14.33 trillion, approximately 23 per cent of a gross world product of approximately US$61 trillion.
2. In 1943, at the height of World War II, the federal budget deficit in the US was 30.3 per cent of GDP.
3. Valuation based on data from the Department of the Treasury and calculated for May 2009. Current bond holdings represent more than a tenfold increase since 2000. The rate of growth of new bond purchases has slowed over the past year, but still remains positive.
4. See, for example, Roach (2008), Stiglitz, Sen and Fitoussi (2009), Speth (2008), Auerswald and Acs (2009), Etzioni (2009) and Foster and Magdoff (2009). Even prominent media commentators like David Brooks (2009) talk about the need to "[find] ways to tamp down consumption."
5. See also the websites for the following organizations/projects: Center for the Advancement of a Sustainable State Economy (http://www.steadystate.org), Growth in Transition (http://www.growthintransition.eu), Research and Degrowth (http://www.degrowth.net), Sustainable Consumption Research and Action Initiative (http://www.scorai.org) and recent reports by NEF (2009) and Commission of the European Communities (2009).
6. In addition to its general compatibility with certain schools of thought within ecological economics, degrowth economics shares several common features with the emergent field of "biophysical economics" (Day et al. 2009; Mayumi 2009).
7. For details on the Italian Degrowth Network see http://www.decrescita.it/modules/article/view.article.php?a45.
8. Refer to Fournier (2008); Kallis, Martinez-Alier and Norgaard (2009); van Griethuysen (2010); Spangenberg (2010); Hall (2009); Huppes and Ishikawa (2009).
9. Paul Krugman's (2009) observation on a related point also merits consideration. He writes that "elections aren't necessarily won by the candidate with the most rational argument." Put another way, it is relatively inconsequential whether the claims of degrowth proponents pass muster under the microscope of rigorous economic analysis any more than the political viability of neoliberal economics rests on an ability to do so.
10. This section of *Prosperity without Growth* draws heavily on Helm (2009).
11. Refer to, for example, Dowler (2008) and McCartney and Hanlon (2009).

REFERENCES

Auerswald, Philip, and Zoltan Acs. 2009. Defining Prosperity. *The American Interest* 6 (5): 13.

Beavan, Colin. 2009. *No Impact Man*. New York: Farrar, Straus and Giroux.

Brooks, David. 2009. The Nation of Futurity. *New York Times*, 17 November, A33.

Cohen, Maurie. 2006. Sustainable consumption research as democratic expertise. *Journal of Consumer Policy* 29(1):67–77.

———. 2010. The Political Economy of (Un)sustainable Consumption. *Environmental Politics* 19 (1): 108–127.

Commission of the European Communities. 2009. *GDP and Beyond: Measuring Progress in a Changing World*. Brussels: CEC.

Czech, Brian. 2000. *Shoveling Fuel for a Runaway Train: Errant Economists, Shameful Spenders, and a Plan to Stop Them All*. Berkeley: University of California Press.

Daly, Herman. 2007. *Ecological Economics: Selected Essays of Herman Daly*. Northampton, MA: Edward Elgar.

Day, John, Charles Hall, Alejandro Yañez-Arancibia, David Pimentel, Carles Martí and William Mitsch. 2009. Ecology in Times of Scarcity. *BioScience* 59 (4): 321–331.

Dowler, Elizabeth. 2008. Food and Health Inequalities: The Challenge for Sustaining Just Consumption. *Local Environment* 13 (8): 759–772.

Elgin, Duane. 1993. *Voluntary Simplicity: Towards a Way of Life that Is Outwardly Simple and Inwardly Rich*. New York: William Morrow.

Elzen, Boelie, Frank Geels and Ken Green, eds. 2004. *System Innovation and the Transition to Sustainability: Theory, Evidence, and Policy*. Northampton, MA: Edward Elgar.

Etzioni, Amitai. 2009. Spent: America after Consumerism. *New Republic*.

European Environment Agency. 2005. *Household Consumption and the Environment*. Copenhagen: EEA.

Ferguson, Niall. 2005. *Colossus: The Rise and Fall of the American Empire*. New York: Penguin.

Finnish Ministry of the Environment. 2005. *Getting More for Less: Proposals for Finland's National Programme to Promote Sustainable Consumptionand Production*. Helsinki: Finnish Ministry of the Environment.

Foster, John, and Fred Magdoff. 2009. *The Great Financial Crisis: Causes and Consequences*. New York: Monthly Review Press.

Fuchs, Doris, and Sylvia Lorek. 2005. Sustainable Consumption Governance: A History of Promises and Failures. *Journal of Consumer Policy* 28 (3): 261–288.

German Federal Environment Agency. 2007. *Sustainable Consumption: Securing the Future*. Berlin: German Federal Environment Agency.

Hall, C. Michael. 2009. Degrowing Tourism: Décroissance, Sustainable Consumption, and Steady-State Tourism. *Anatolia* 20 (1): 46–92.

Hargreaves, Tom, Michael Nye and Jacquie Burgess. 2008. Social Experiments in Sustainable Consumption: An Evidence-Based Approach with Potential for Engaging Low-Income Communities. *Local Environment* 13 (8): 743–758.

Helm, Dieter. 2009. *The Economics and Politics of Climate Change*. New York: Oxford University Press.

Hobson, Kersty. 2002. Competing Discourses of Sustainable Consumption: Does the "Rationalisation of Lifestyles" Make Sense? *Environmental Politics* 11 (2): 95–120.

Hopkins, Rob, and Richard Heinberg. 2008. *The Transition Handbook: From Oil Dependency to Local Resilience*. White River Junction, VT: Chelsea Green.

Huppes, Gjalt, and Masanobu Ishikawa. 2009. Eco-Efficiency Guiding Micro-Level Actions towards Sustainability: Ten Basic Steps for Analysis. *Ecological Economics* 68 (6): 1687–1700.

Intergovernmental Panel on Climate Change. 2007. *Climate Change 2007: Synthesis Report*. Geneva: World Meteorological Association and United Nations Environment Program.

Jackson, Tim. 2005. Live Better by Consuming Less? Is There a "Double Dividend" in Sustainable Consumption? *Journal of Industrial Ecology* 9 (1–2): 19–36.

———. 2008. Where Is the "Wellbeing Dividend"? Nature, Structure, and Consumption Inequalities. *Local Environment* 13 (8): 703–723.

———. 2009. *Prosperity without Growth: Economics for a Finite Planet*. London: Earthscan.

James, Oliver. 2007. *Affluenza*. London: Vermillion.

Kallis, Giorgos, Joan Martinez-Alier and Richard Norgaard. 2009. Paper Assets, Real Debts: An Ecological–Economic Exploration of the Global Economic Crisis. *Critical Perspectives on International Business* 5 (1–2): 14–25.

Krugman, Paul. 2003. *The Great Unraveling: Losing Our Way in the New Century*. New York: Norton.

———. 2009. Paranoia Strikes Deep. *New York Times*, 9 November, A23.

Levine, Judith. 2007. *Not Buying It: My Year without Shopping*. New York: Free Press.

Mayumi, Kozo. 2009. Nicholas Georgescu-Roegen: His Bioeconomics Approach to Development and Change. *Development and Change* 40 (6): 1235–1254.

McCartney, Gerry, and Phil Hanlon. 2009. What Can Health Professionals Contribute to the Challenge of Sustainability? *Public Health* 123 (12): 761–764.

Mead, Walter. 2004. America's Sticky Power. *Foreign Policy* 141 (March): 46–53.

New Economics Foundation. 2006. *The Happy Planet Index: An Index of Human Well-Being and Environmental Impact*. London: NEF.

———. 2008. *A Green New Deal*. London: NEF.

———. 2009. *The Great Transition*. London: NEF.

Offer, Avner. 2007. *The Challenge of Affluence: Self-Control and Well-Being in the United States and Britain Since 1950*. New York: Oxford University Press.

O'Rourke, Dara. 2005. Market Movements: Nongovernmental Organization Strategies to Influence Global Production and Consumption. *Journal of Industrial Ecology* 9 (1–2): 115–128.

Perrels, Adriaan. 2008. Wavering between Radical and Realistic Sustainable Consumption Policies: In Search for the Best Feasible Trajectories. *Journal of Cleaner Production* 16 (11): 1203–1217.

Porritt, Jonathon. 2009. *Living within Our Means: Avoiding the Ultimate Recession*. London: Forum for the Future.

Quitzau, Maj-Britt, and Inge Røpke. 2008. The Construction of Normal Expectations: Consumption Drivers of the Danish Bathroom Boom. *Journal of Industrial Ecology* 12 (2): 186–206.

Rijnhout, Leida, and Thomas Schauer, eds. 2009. *Socially Sustainable Economic Degrowth*. Vienna: The Club of Rome–European Support Centre.

Roach, Stephen. 2008. Dying of Consumption. *The New York Times*, 28 November, 43.

Rockström, Johan. 2009. A Safe Operating System for Humanity. *Nature* 461:472–475.

Rohracher, Harald. 2001. Managing the Technological Transition to Sustainable Construction of Buildings: A Socio-Technical Perspective. *Technology Analysis and Strategic Management* 13 (1): 147–150.

Schor, Juliet. 2005. Prices and Quantities: Unsustainable Consumption and the Global Economy. *Ecological Economics* 55 (3): 309–320.

Schwartz, Shalom 1999. A Theory of Cultural Values and Some Implications for Work. *Applied Psychology* 48 (1): 23–47.

Seyfang, Gill. 2006. Ecological Citizenship and Sustainable Consumption: Examining Local Organic Food Networks. *Journal of Rural Studies* 22 (4): 383–395.

Sippel, Alexandra. 2009. Back to the Future: Today's and Tomorrow's Politics of Degrowth Economics *(décroissance)* in Light of the Debate over Luxury among Eighteenth- and Early Nineteenth-Century Utopists. *International Labor and Working-Class History* 75 (1): 13–29.

Spaargaren, Gert. 2003. Sustainable Consumption: A Theoretical and Environmental Policy Perspective. *Society and Natural Resources* 16 (8): 687–701.

Spangenberg, Joachim. 2010. The Growth Discourse, Growth Policy, and Sustainable Development: Two Thought Experiments. *Journal of Cleaner Production* 18 (6): 561–566.

Speth, James Gustave. 2008. *The Bridge at the Edge of the World: Capitalism, the Environment, and Crossing from Crisis to Sustainability.* New Haven, CT: Yale University Press.

Stern, Nicholas. 2007. *The Economics of Climate Change: The Stern Review.* New York: Cambridge University Press.

Stiglitz, Joseph, Amartya Sen and Jean-Paul Fitoussi. 2009. *Commission on the Measurement of Economic Performance and Social Progress.* Paris: The Commission.

Tukker, Arnold, Martin Charter, Carlo Vezzoli, Eivind Stø and Maj Munch Andersen, eds. 2008. *System Innovation for Sustainability: Perspectives on Radical Changes to Sustainable Consumption and Production.* Sheffield: Greenleaf.

Tukker, Arnold, Maurie Cohen, Klaus Hubaeck and Oksana Mont. 2010. Impacts of Household Consumption and Options for Change. *Journal of Industrial Ecology* 14 (1): 13–30.

UK Department of Environment, Food, and Rural Affairs. 2003. *Changing Patterns: UK Government Framework for Sustainable Consumption and Production.* London: DEFRA.

———. 2005. *Securing the Future: The UK Sustainable Development Strategy.* London: HMSO.

UK Sustainable Consumption Roundtable. 2006. *I Will If You Will: Towards Sustainable Consumption.* London: UK Sustainable Development Commission and National Consumer Council.

United Nations Environment Program. 2001. *Sustainable Consumption Opportunities: Strategies for Change.* Geneva: UNEP.

Walker, Brian, Scott Barrett, Stephen Polasky, Victor Galaz, Carl Folke, Gustav Engström, Frank Ackerman, Ken Arrow, Stephen Carpenter, Kanchan Chopra, Gretchen Daily, Paul Ehrlich, Terry Hughes, Nils Kautsky, Simon Levin, Kal-Göran Mäler, Jason Shogren, Jeff Vincent, Tasos Xepapadeas and Aart de Zeeuw. 2009. Looming Global-Scale Failures and Missing Institutions. *Science* 325:1345–1346.

van Griethuysen, Pascal. 2010. Why Are We Growth-Addicted? The Hard Way towards Degrowth in the Involuntary Western Development Path. *Journal of Cleaner Production* 18 (6): 590–595.

Victor, Peter. 2008. *Managing without Growth: Slower by Design, Not Disaster.* Northampton, MA: Edward Elgar.

von Weizsäcker, Ernst Amory Lovins and L. Hunter Lovins. 1997. *Factor Four: Doubling Wealth, Halving Resource Use.* London: Earthscan.

14 If US Consumption Declines Will the Global Economy Collapse?[1]

Neva Goodwin

We are at a moment in history when it is necessary to move as quickly as possible away from dependence on fossil fuels as energy sources—especially coal and petroleum. While there are other pressures, such as peak oil and the pollution and environmental degradation associated with fossil fuel use, it is the threat of global climate change that makes this move so urgent.

Some other contemporary human systems, aside from energy, are also not sustainable. These include many aspects of use of natural resources (soil, water, biota), as well as the economic-cultural system employed to keep raising output and consumption—the activities generally used to define economic growth. This system was seen as so essential that Alan Greenspan felt it necessary to lower interest rates nearly to zero in order to sustain the consumption bubble of the 1990s and the early twenty-first century. Consumers were encouraged to borrow money on the basis of inflated house values, so as to be able to spend beyond their incomes.

It became evident that the consumption bubble was unsustainable when it turned out that the value of many capital assets was to a considerable extent fictional. These capital assets included home values as well as many far less tangible "values" (derivatives and other sorts of bundled, etiolated or overleveraged assets) that were bought and sold on stock exchanges.

Standard economics texts say that the basic economic questions are *what to produce, how, and for whom*. Industrial economies are structured so that firm survival depends on profits, while profitability is only loosely related to social and environmental needs. It is most profitable to sell to those who already have a lot, because those are the people with the most purchasing power; as inequality grows, so does the lop-sidedness of the answer to the *for whom* question.[2] Profitability also ignores externalized costs, so that the answers to the *how* question have resulted in huge environmental destruction, as well as socially destructive forces. As for *what* is produced: growing labour productivity, followed by ever-expanding output, creates enormous economic and cultural pressure to sell, and to buy, unnecessary things.

The motivation for firms to sell what they produce has become a—perhaps *the*—great driver of modern culture. Corporations determine most of what reaches us through the media. They create the work settings in which most of us will live for approximately half our waking hours for at least half of the years of our lives. Increasingly they control government, including lawmakers, and the agencies that are supposed to control corporate activity. And we exist in a situation where there is considerable dissonance between the goals of firms *versus* the health of society and its members.

Mass consumerism seems, on the face of it, fairer than a society that is top-heavy with elite consumption. Neither variant is sustainable in the forms we know today. Given the kinds of things that are desired in wealthy contemporary societies, and given the way these things are produced, transported, used and disposed of, it is physically impossible for all of the world's people to emulate the lifestyles held up as desirable in the fifty or so wealthiest countries. Severe food and water shortages would most likely be the first disasters to arrive, followed shortly by disease and massive armed conflicts, within and among countries, desperate to hold or get vanishing natural resources. We cannot continue, let alone extend, the consumption and lifestyle patterns of the richest 15 per cent of the world's peoples. How do we ramp down without falling into the precipice we want to avoid?

Some aspects of the existing global economic situation make it especially difficult to envision a reasonable path to overall reduction, fairer distribution and more sustainable composition of production and consumption. They include the following:

> *Global trade*: wages and prices, demand and supply, have been globalized.[3] Reduced demand in the high-import countries (especially the US) leaves producers elsewhere with shrunken markets to sell into.

> *Global capitalism*: a system that cannot, in its current form, give primacy to needs over wants; it has no way to recognize populations (infants and children, elderly, disabled) who lack market power to fulfill their needs. There is nothing in what George Soros calls the "fundamentalist" version of market ideology that encourages business people to place social or ecological sustainability on a par with, let alone ahead of, individual gain.

> *Global financial system*: a huge proportion of the money flowing through the system is financial wealth, often only distantly related to real things. As recently discovered, while financial wealth is commonly imagined to represent claims on real things, some of the real things never existed (e.g., what were assumed to be viable mortgages were not viable), and some are simultaneously claimed by a number of owners, beyond any real value (e.g., highly leveraged assets).

Global inequality and wealth concentration: some five hundred corporations control a large proportion of the world's financial wealth, which is being used in almost every nation to influence public debate and policy-making on the issues outlined earlier. At the same time, the price of grain faced by the world's poor is elevated by the feed-grain demands of the wealthy of the world, whose diets often include meat twice a day.

Global culture: images of the good life of the wealthy are spread throughout the world, creating dissatisfaction and desires among those who don't yet have it all, and habituation (without significantly increased well-being) among those who do.

Economists often say—and the rest of the world believes them—that the only alternative to economic growth is economic collapse. This chapter is written by an economist who believes that in a contest between finite nature and human expansion, humanity will inevitably be the loser. Therefore, we have no alternative but to find out how to climb back down from our excessive consumption patterns.

The place where many people both start and end their thinking on this subject is that, when US consumers reduce their consumption levels, many other parts of the world lose the demand they had counted on to support their exports. "Export-led growth" has been the mantra of World Bank economists and other economic advisors to poor (and some rich) countries for nearly half a century—and it was a trick that had previously been discovered several times by different countries (Chang 2007). This approach contains a fallacy of composition: obviously, not everyone can sell more than they buy. The US has for decades made this strategy possible for others by being the consumer of last resort.[4] Since about 1980 the world became so used to this state of affairs that any alternative became frighteningly unimaginable. And the recent economic collapse has seemed to justify the fear: US purchasing declined, and many around the world have suffered.

The recent economic hardship may prove to be an early symptom of the collapse of the old paradigm. Along with the hardships we may see the opening of new possibilities, and an escape from the mindset described in the previous section.

Consider China—the country that seemed to epitomize dependence on the US appetite for imported goods. It has quietly begun to do what a minority of economists have urged since at least 1990: to create its own internal demand, so that Chinese factories will be able to sell into their own country, without being as dependent as they are now on foreign demand.[5] When this is securely in place, China will no longer need to prop up its main trading partner by purchasing US government bonds.

The challenge for China, and the other major dollar hoarders, is to let the value of the dollar sink slowly enough not to cause another global crisis (while also not losing all the value of their dollar holdings), yet to allow it to sink to a level that will reflect real international values (including, one would hope, the values of externalities).[6] The likelihood of another round of global financial turmoil depends, more than anything else, on how skillfully the Asian powers can manage this transition.

We will simply assume two things: the dollar will decline against other currencies, creating sharp downward pressure on imports into the US; and US consumption will, sooner or later, shift in the direction of more sustainable patterns, including reduced long-distance trade. Given these assumptions, this section will move toward a list of ways in which developing countries may be able to benefit from such a changing world.

Human resources: a downsizing in US wealth relative to the rest of the world will reduce the draw that is summarized as "brain drain". All of the looming crises of the twenty-first century—demographic shifts, resource shortages and climate change, and the disease, armed conflicts and forced migrations that are liable to accompany these—will require good thinkers, planners and leaders everywhere in the world.[7] Developing countries will be much better off if their wisest and best-educated citizens have less reason to spend their lives abroad.

Technology: environmental realities create the necessity for massive technological innovation and progress. Among the most critical requirements for a bearable future is that the less-wealthy countries be given easy access to all of the best systems and ideas for leap-frogging the situation of the present overconsumers, in order to attain a positive fourth Industrial Revolution while there are still enough natural resources available to smooth this transition.

Pollution reduction: as the US and other wealthy countries adapt their systems of production, distribution, consumption and waste treatment to environmental realities, there will be reductions in pollution of all kinds, including many kinds of pollution that are having adverse effects throughout the world on human and ecological health. As one example, recession causes carbon emissions to decline in the US; this was seen in the 1991 and 2000 recessions, and has been even more pronounced in 2008.[8]

Realignment of trade: in the same way that China is finally awakening to the reality that its domestic market is potentially all the demand it needs for a flourishing economy, other regions may also find that they can conceive regional economic units that are large enough to greatly lessen dependence on more distant customers. The emergence of more localized trade systems will be easier under a regime of reduced potency of the US dollar and lessened US control of the WTO, World

Bank and IMF, and when smaller countries are no longer cowed by the threat of reduced US trade.

Reassessing scale: realignment of trading relationships could be a step toward a broader movement to economies of smaller scale, away from long-distance-trade-based systems that require massive use of fossil fuel. The latter have historically been responsible for displacement of small farmers and conversion of forests to export-oriented agriculture. There are environmental advantages, as well as some advantages of financial and resource security, in moving to more local production and consumption, based on regional strengths and natural capital.

Response to local demand: the demand to which local producers respond will be generated relatively more from local consumers, instead of coming from the US. The composition of local demand will depend importantly on the relative weights of elite versus mass-consumption. This depends importantly on the distribution of wealth and income. In places with a relatively even distribution the demand for basic goods will be a larger component of demand than in situations of greater inequality, where there will be greater demand for luxury goods. A tilt toward basic goods is desirable from many points of view, including environmental sustainability and the greater well-being that results from their satisfaction than from accumulation of status goods (see Frank, this volume).

Reduced impact of US cultural/ideological exports: the American Dream is a dream of bigness and excess: big houses and cars, huge salaries for the corporate or media stars in a "winner-take-all society". It in some way relates to what may be called a monoculture mentality, in which it is assumed that single, big solutions may be found for all problems; examples are massive "slum clearance" as a way of achieving urban renewal, or single-species systems of agriculture and animal husbandry that require massive doses of antibiotics or pesticides to counteract the unnatural uniformity. Other US cultural or ideological exports have included the economic ideologies of free markets, growth and "only selfishness is rational". With the end of US superpower status it will be easier for other cultures to pick and choose what US models are worth importing, and which are not.

US consumption in competition with world needs: US consumers will face requirements to adjust not only the quantity but also the composition of what is consumed. If they feel less affluent they may begin to take seriously the growing stream of information about how to achieve better nutrition on less money. Any reduction in American consumption of grain-fed animals and poultry will put more grain onto global markets, at least counteracting the upward pressure on grain prices from biofuels and from an increasingly import-hungry China. Another possible and desirable outcome is that the combination of rising resource prices with other (e.g., regulatory) pressures for conservation will result in reduced US demand for other increasingly scarce resources, such as fish, timber and fossil fuel—again making it easier for the rest of the world to meet their needs.

It may be hoped that within fifteen to twenty years the post-carbon era will be well established, moving toward a time (perhaps after 2050) when energy may become plentiful again. Until then it will continue to be critical to minimize the use of energy as well as of materials—especially water and toxic materials. Everywhere in the world this will advantage closed loop systems, green design and labour-intensive services. Such shifts will require tax incentives and the elimination of subsidies to industries that cannot adapt to these new realities, or to dinosaurs within essential industries— such as coal and petroleum within the energy industry, or mechanized, high-input monocultures within agriculture. It will also require many kinds of planning at every scale of social organization

Who will do that planning? If it is believed that it must be done at the highest government level, in the US it is necessary to look back as far as the Second World War to find examples of the sort of planning that is needed. We have seen a relatively clumsy effort at this approach in the erratic decisions made by the White House economic team in the twelve months following the fall of 2008: let this company go bankrupt, prop up that one with loans, strengthen one government agency, change the mandate of another, stimulate this sector, coax or coerce that—etcetera. Out of this rather messy, ad hoc effort one can discern, as a guiding principle or goal, the question: *what is best for the whole economy/society?* In some situations governments (at various levels) are in the best position to ask and answer such a question, but it is worth reviewing the other actors in society who might also take it on.

The economic actors to whom this role has been effectively given for the last half century are the large corporations, including banks and other financial entities. When people choose to let the market decide what to do, on the grounds that it is always more efficient, they are in fact leaving the decisions to the large corporations. Trust in these entities has been much reduced, as it has become clear that *what is best for the whole economy/society* is not their concern. If the corporation of the future is to have a say in the direction of the economy, it will need to be a significantly revised institution, operating by different rules, within a different corporate culture, both internal and external. There are good efforts under way to envision such new corporate organization.[9] In response to the common belief that it is essential to leave as much as possible to "the market" because of the superior efficiency of this mode, it is important to remember that efficiency is not a virtue when it is harnessed to the wrong goals, such as short-term profits at the expense of long-term contribution to a healthy society.

What other groups might we consider to take responsibility for the question *what is best for the whole economy/society?* A partial answer, especially important until or unless radical reform can make corporations responsive to this goal, looks to the so-called universal investors. These are investors who are so large that they cannot afford *not* to be invested in virtually the entire economy. Including most notably pension funds and insurance companies, these also happen to be organizations that have a strong stake in the future: their missions require them to generate earnings that will at least not decline for a long time. These two facts mean that universal investors have strong reasons to object if any company's actions are polluting the social or ecological environment on which the viability of all commercial enterprises depends.[10]

The diffuse and diverse world of non-profit organizations includes some that already play important watchdog roles, monitoring the environmental and other impacts of corporations, reporting on the honesty and responsibility of government or international agencies, etc. There is a role of "ombudsman for future generations" that has been discussed at various times, but too rarely put in place or given the broad resources and powers it would require.

Another aspect of the American ideology may be designated "corporate and consumer culture". The two pieces of this are mirror images of each other. Corporate culture, until now, has tended increasingly in the direction of accepting the tenet of economic theory that only selfishness is rational. That translates into managers enriching themselves at the expense of all stakeholders, increasingly including the stockholders, who are the owners of the company. The mirror image is the consumerist culture, as whipped up by the corporate need to sell ever more products. A culture of consumerism is one in which individual identity, self-respect and social position are strongly tied to the purchase of marketed goods; spending money is seen as a pleasurable and desirable end in itself; and there is encouragement for the belief that the purchase and use of high-end goods, in particular, will bring happiness.

To stand up to these pernicious cultural beliefs and assumptions different forces need to be brought into play. One is the force of morality. Religions, parents, schools and ethically oriented organizations can and do offer a variety of alternative moral beliefs to "only selfishness is rational". To be sure, at any time and place in human history it would be possible to find sociopaths guiding their lives exclusively by this cynical belief, and there have probably been societies other than our own wherein it became dominant; but the survival of the human species has required many contrary impulses to be built into our genetic as well as our cultural makeup.[11]

If we are to look towards such a cultural shift, we must also consider aggregation issues: many people are prevented from taking action by the fear that "I'll look like a sucker if I make sacrifices and no one else does." In addressing the onrushing global crises assumed in this chapter there are, fortunately, people of conviction who act for the greater good even when they seem to be stepping out alone. The critical question is what cultural, cognitive and spiritual support can assist others to join in.

The word *sacrifice* was used in the preceding paragraph. Without previously using that word, this chapter has asked the question of how the global economy could survive reduced consumption by the currently high-consuming populations. The question of how those populations would feel about reducing their consumption has not been addressed here—although the economic crisis of 2008–2009 (2010? and . . .?) has forced significant reductions. An important point here is that, if a whole society sets out to consume less it is possible that much can be done without feeling like cut-to-the-bone sacrifice. There is some encouragement in the young field that calls itself hedonic psychology (other people know it as happiness studies), which has established strong evidence for a set of propositions[12] that to some may sound like simple common sense, but that are directly opposed to basic assumptions in standard economics:

- Individual increases in material wealth do not raise the happiness of the whole society; indeed, evidence from Japan and the US, where the standard of living has risen greatly since the 1950s, shows no increase—if anything a decline—in the happiness of the population as a whole.
- Wealth very much beyond basic needs, when it belongs to and is spent on behalf of individuals, operates within a zero-sum game wherein success by a few creates, among the rest, hopeless wishes for emulation and overall well-being is not increased. By contrast, wealth that belongs to, and is spent on behalf of, a whole society can be used to promote public goods such as environmental protection and restoration, to protect the well-being of future generations. More equal societies are better able to cope with emergencies; moreover, if a cultural norm of equality promotes the more use of resources for public goods, less for private status consumption, they will be happier.
- Human well-being—the ultimate purpose of any economy—is not only tied to what people *have*, but also to how they feel about it and what they do with it. Leisure to enjoy the riches that advanced economies have accumulated in the last centuries is becoming one of the most significant scarce resources; for many, well-being will be better served by more *time* than by more *products*. This gives credibility to a scenario in which some systems of production and consumption could be modified to produce less output (thereby mitigating climate change) but more well-being.

Change in what we produce and consume is one aspect of the necessary future; the other aspect will probably entail revision in how, and how much, we work. The kinds of work that are most essential for human survival and well-being include: raising children; producing food; providing education to assist people to develop, exercise and explore their mental, physical and spiritual potentials; providing home environments that are pleasant, comfortable and sanitary, and that support self-actualization; supporting and maintaining physical and mental health in children and adults; providing care for those who are sick, old or otherwise unable to care for themselves; and maintaining, and where possible, restoring the health of the earth's ecosystems.

There are (at least) two striking characteristics of the foregoing list: women have been the predominant workers in most of the activities named here; and these activities have generally been among the least well-paid (or even unpaid) categories of work.

This outcome can be traced back through the history of the industrial revolutions that have given us the economies we know today. Two trends allowed mass-consumption to come into being and to grow as the force supporting ever-increasing production. One was the trend for the price of human labour to rise, relative to the prices of energy and raw materials—hence spreading purchasing power. The second was the trend for a growing proportion of the average household budget to be liberated from purchasing necessities, and made available for "extras"—starting with pottery dishes and machine-loomed fabrics; moving on to bicycles and oil lamps; through Keyfitz's "standard package" (Keyfitz 1998) of electric lighting, refrigerators, televisions and automobiles; to computer gadgets, cell phones, jet skis and US$5,000 barbecue grills.

There was some tension between these two trends: while labour in general became better paid, labour associated with the provision of basic necessities had to remain cheap or free in order to allow the household budget to shift toward the exciting new products of the consumer society. This tension was resolved by populating the labour force committed to the essential work largely with those members of society with least economic power: minorities, migrants and women.

The increasing productivity that has so dramatically characterized the industrial revolutions was, it should be recalled, specifically the productivity of labour; in many cases the productivity of energy and materials, with their costs declining, was allowed to stagnate or decline. Much of this "progress" must be rethought, with economic production and expenditure better reflecting both the priority of the activities that most contribute to human well-being, and also the true costs of production, including all externalities. Overall *the requirements of both nature and society will force the economy to respond with significant shifts in relative prices*. While the transition to the post-carbon future is under way, energy prices will rise. The products of the natural world—the food, fuel, minerals, etcetera, whose prices, as "commodities", plummeted throughout the twentieth century—will be revalued at levels representing the full, long-range cost of their extraction, processing and reinsertion into nature, or else their recycling within the production process. Thus materials and, at least in the medium run, energy will be more expensive than they have been, relative to wages.

What does this mean about economic growth, in GDP terms? The same amount of money might flow through the economy, but it would represent less purchasing power, with respect to goods. The pressure of rising material and energy costs will induce energy- and materials-saving technological change—similar to the way the last two centuries of relatively rising labour costs induced labour-saving technological change.

Can technological change be energy and materials saving and at the same time continue to employ ever less labour? It is hard to imagine how this could be, in spite of two—now, apparently, three—recent "jobless recoveries" from recessions, and comments such as this: "There appears to be a new tendency to substitute against labor. It's permanent, as long as there are alternatives like outsourcing and robotics."[13] The old tendency to substitute against labour is unrelated to outsourcing (where labour is still employed, just in a different location), and given the energy- and materials-intensity of robots, they will have to be many times more productive than human beings in order to compete.

Another critical question is: how can the "relative" prices of three major inputs—materials, energy and labour—rise simultaneously? This is only possible if there is a fourth input whose price is sinking in relation to the others—and which is significant enough so that the combination of the four prices does not simply produce inflation. Can this fourth input be technology? To consider this possibility we need to conceptually break down "technology" into two portions: that which requires the addition of significant quantities of materials and/or energy (as was the case, for example, with Green Revolution technology, or with robotics); and that which is information-intensive ("ii tech"; see Goodwin 1991). The latter can be embodied in human beings, in the form of knowledge and skills, as well as in material things, such as computer chips. Only a very significant rise in the proportion of ii tech among all productive inputs will make it possible for the prices of materials and energy to rise while the price of labour at least does not decline, relative to consumer goods.

This is a stiff requirement. It may hold true in some industries, whose workers will be made so much more productive through ii tech that they will be able to command relatively high wages—on the standard economic assumption of a positive relationship between the wage and the marginal value of the worker's output.[14] However, it seems unlikely that this will maintain, for most workers, wages high enough to allow the average household consumption bundle to contain a quantity of goods that does not shrink in the foreseeable future. The net effect of the trends that are predictable on environmental grounds is, overall, incomes that have less purchasing power, at least in relation to goods with a relatively high content of materials and energy.

To add to this effect I would like to raise the—admittedly idealistic— possibility that a sane society might find ways of raising the relative compensation for the kinds of work that are most essential for human survival and well-being. Three examples will suggest how this could, conceivably, come about.

The first is food production. Sustainably managed farms will replace some of the physical inputs of agribusiness (chemical weed and pest killers, heavy machinery) with human inputs of time, intelligence and smart technology. Food production will be more labour-intensive than the factory farms of the United States today, where less than 3 per cent of the labour force is enough to feed our entire population. The people who do such farmwork will require more education than has been assumed for farm labourers of the past. For educated people the choice of farming as a profession will compete with other possibilities; it will not be chosen if it is a back-breaking, no-time-off, low-paid activity. With food production requiring more workers than were needed in the American monoculture model, while these future farmworkers are relatively better paid, food will then become relatively more expensive, requiring Americans to pay somewhat (but, it turns out, not a great deal) more than the 13 per cent of household income that is normal in the US today (a proportion that is very low by the standards of the rest of the world).[15]

The second example is education. Education appears, among industries that now exist, to be the one where there is the most room for expanded employment. It can be a positive benefit at all stages of life—especially if the concept of education is expanded to include a greater component of arts, crafts, skills and even games, for those who do not enjoy the book-learning component that is now so heavily emphasized. It is both a means to other ends (e.g., income-enhancing skills) and also, importantly, an end in itself. While education can be enhanced by technology, such enhancements have not yet been successful in greatly reducing the need for labour inputs. It can function with a low ratio of materials and energy to labour.[16] For this reason, if labour costs do stagnate or decline relative to other inputs, and given that education is a labour-intensive industry, we can at least anticipate that the trend toward rising education costs will be moderated.

The third example—raising children—may be the most difficult because this takes place for the most part in homes, where there is no market through which the primary caregivers—the parents—can be paid. Where there is a market for parent substitutes (babysitters, day-care providers), these have traditionally been regarded as unskilled workers and paid accordingly. The old assumption was that parents raised their children purely as an act of love, making a choice that would not have been affected if it had been subject to a price. This assumption has been staggering under the weight of some facts. First, women who achieve education, a means to earn income outside of their homes, and access to contraceptives, show a very strong preference for having fewer children. Second, the sharp drop in fertility that accompanies migration from rural to urban settings is best explained by the fact that children are an economic asset in farm families and an economic liability in urban life. Indeed, the cost of raising children in urban settings is often cited as the reason for fertility declining below replacement rates in one industrialized nation after another.[17] It is this last fact that may, in the end, force a rethinking of the economic costs and benefits of child raising. A possible approach would be a "basic income" policy that allocates funds to every household based on the number of people who are there to be taken care of, with much higher allocations for those who cannot take care of themselves: infants and infirm elderly would probably count for the most, followed by older children.

Some different lessons may be drawn out of these three examples. They suggest that, in a Fourth Revolution model society, more resources may go toward child raising and food production than is now the case. The relative cost of a unit of education (such as a year in college) may go down, but the total amount of educational activity in a society could greatly increase. The examples agree, however, in supporting the preceding argument, which sums up to an image of a society in which the service component of the average household market basket is increased, while the goods component is markedly reduced.

While human ingenuity will continue to find ways to "do more with less" (to quote the twentieth-century visionary, Buckminster Fuller), the bottom line will be that everyone will need to accept lifestyles that require reduced throughput of materials, and also of energy, until the transition to the post-carbon era results in a great sufficiency of cheaply and sustainably available renewable energy. Given population aging, for the rest of this century it also seems likely that each active worker will be supplying goods and services for a larger number of non-workers than is now the case. Within the "goods" category, household consumption will revert to a higher proportion of necessities, more like the consumption baskets of a hundred years ago or more. Aspirations to live in the style of Americans at the beginning of the twenty-first century are off the table for virtually everyone—including Americans.

NOTES

1. The author is grateful to Kevin Gallagher, Jonathan Harris, Brian Roach and Tim Wise for very helpful comments and suggestions.
2. As of 2004 the richest 1 per cent of US households owned 33 per cent of all household wealth—up from 22 per cent eighteen years earlier (Kennickel 2007).
3. There are signs that the world is steadily approaching, though it has not yet reached, the once-ridiculed ideal of factor price equalization—a good thing when it means wages in poor countries rise toward those in the rich; not so popular when it is the reverse.
4. Between 1960 and 2008 US imports as a percentage of gross world product went from about 1.5 per cent to a little over 5 per cent (World Development Indicators database; US Bureau of Economic Analysis, International Economic Accounts).

5. Exports as a percentage of GDP for China grew from around 20 per cent in the early 1990s to 43 per cent in 2007, then dropped to 35 per cent in 2008 (World Development Indicators database). China's efforts to build up new markets for exports in developing countries are not incompatible with a continuing reduction in the country's export orientation.

6. It should be noted that this, like other "hopes" scattered throughout this chapter, is not something that is likely to occur spontaneously, e.g., through unregulated market forces. Imposition of a price on carbon, such as a cap and trade or carbon tax regime, will be necessary to internalize that particular externality.

7. See Homer-Dixon (2001) for a forceful argument for the need to maintain and increase human capital in response to the challenges of the twenty-first century; and the danger that these challenges could have the effect of reducing expenditures on education while encouraging the replacement of science with superstition—an effect that is already evident in significant portions of the US population.

8. US Department of Energy, Annual Energy Outlook 2009; http://www.eia. doe.gov/oiaf/aeo/index.html (accessed 9 November).

9. See, for example, http://www.corporation2020.org/.

10. Some religious groups, especially religious pension funds, have been leaders in this movement. One might expect that foundations and universities would take a similarly broad view of the impact of their endowments' management. This in fact has been slow to happen; however, such a movement now seems to be building. The author of this chapter is working with others to promote it in the US.

11. There is no longer much debate between "the selfish gene" and "group survival" among those who follow science. Both are understood to be relevant drivers of human, animal and even plant behaviour.

12. See, for example, Cobb, Halstead and Rowe (1995); Deaton (2008); Diener, Diener and Diener (1995); Diener and Oishi (2000); Frank (1999, and in this volume); Kahneman, Diener and Schwarz (1999); and Lane (1991, 2005).

13. Allan Sinai (*New York Times* 2009), chief global economist at the research firm Decision Economics.

14. This relation often appears less tight than that between the wage and the worker's ability to appropriate more of the profit than others who have helped to produce it: recent decades have provided numerous examples of top corporate managers receiving annual compensation such that, if it had been reduced to just one or a few millions, would have left enough in the profit kitty to double the incomes of all the non-managerial employees.

15. For an analysis of the impacts of rising food prices on poor consumers, and some factors that can mitigate these impacts, see Goodwin (1991).

16. By comparison, health care—an industry whose human importance rivals education—has become highly materials- and energy-intensive. It is possible, however, to imagine a movement toward a form of health care that has a much greater human component, along with massive inputs of information-intensive technology. This form is more likely to emerge in places where the emphasis shifts more toward health maintenance rather than remediation.

17. Germany, Italy and Japan are examples of countries whose population is already in actual decline, while many other wealthy nations are headed in that direction. Russia is not such an obvious case, as its population decline has coincided with both economic and psychological depression, rather than the situation of advanced commercialization of the first three. China, also, cannot be cited in support of this hypothesis, since in that country political diktat is the overriding reason for reduced fertility.

REFERENCES

Chang, Ha-Joon. 2007. *Bad Samaritans: The Myth of Free Trade and the Secret History of Capitalism*. Random House Business Books.

Cobb, Clifford, Ted Halstead and Jonathan Rowe. 1995. If the GDP Is Up Why Is America Down? *Atlantic Monthly* 276 (4): 59.

Daly, Herman. 1991. From Empty-World to Full-World Economics: Recognizing an Historical Turning Point in Economic Development. In *Environmentally Sustainable Development: Building on Brundtland; Environment Working Paper No. 46 of the World Bank Sector Policy and Research Staff*.

Deaton, Angus. 2008. Worldwide, Residents of Richer Nations More Satisfied. http://www.gallup.com/poll/104608/Worldwide-Residents-Richer-Nations-More-Satisfied.aspx.

Diener, Ed, Marissa Diener and Carol Diener. 1995. Factors Predicting the Subjective Well-Being of Nations. *Journal of Personality and Social Psychology* 69:851–864.

Diener, Ed, and Shigehiro Oishi. 2000. Money and Happiness: Income and Subjective Well-Being across Nations. In *Subjective Well-Being across Cultures*, ed. E. Diener and E. M. Suh. Cambridge, MA: MIT Press.

Frank, Robert. 1999. *Luxury Fever: Money and Happiness in an Era of Excess*. Princeton, NJ: Princeton University Press.

Goodwin, Neva. 1991. Lessons for the World from US Agriculture: Unbundling Technology. *World Development* 19 (1): 85–102.

Homer-Dixon, Thomas. 2001. *Environment, Scarcity, and Violence*. Princeton, NJ: Princeton University Press.

Kahneman, Daniel, Ed Diener and Norbert Schwarz, eds. 1999. *Well-Being: The Foundations of Hedonic Psychology*. New York: Russell Sage Foundation.

Kennickel, Arthur B. 2007. *Currents and Undercurrents: Changes in the Distribution of Wealth, 1989–2004, Survey of Consumer Finances, Federal Reserve Board*.

Keyfitz, Nathan. 1998. Consumption and Population. In *Ethics of Consumption: The Good Life, Justice, and Global Stewardship*. Lanham, MD: Rowman and Littlefield.

Lane, Robert E. 1991. *The Market Experience*. Cambridge: Cambridge University Press.

———. 2005. *After the End of History: The Curious Fate of American Materialism*. Ann Arbor: University of Michigan Press.

New York Times. 2009. The Recession's Over, but Not the Layoffs, 8 November, 3.

15 Philosophies for Less Consuming Societies

Russell Belk

MORE CONSUMING SOCIETIES

Although current concern about overconsumption is not the first in the history of humankind, it does appear to be more global, sustained and serious than many prior outcries that too much is more than enough. The indictments of overconsumption are many, including the excessive impact of heavy users on diminishing resources, global warming, growing gaps between rich and poor, widespread and increasing poverty, unequal and unjust distribution of wealth, declining feelings of community and the failure of the excesses of consumption to bring happiness. As if such negative traits as greed, materialism, envy and acquisitiveness were not enough, we seek to underscore them by adding adjectives: rapacious greed, destructive materialism, malicious envy, mindless acquisitiveness. Numbers and statistics are added to further emphasize the scope of our problems with consumption:

- Every day each person in the affluent world consumes 120 pounds of stuff; most of it is superfluous and has a deleterious effect on the environment (Ryan 1998).
- The global consumer class, led by Americans, is responsible for 96 per cent of the world's radioactive waste and 90 per cent of the ozone-destroying chlorofluorocarbons (Durning 1992).
- Between 1979 and 1997, the richest 20 per cent of Americans' income grew from being nine times that of the poorest 20 per cent to fifteen times more (Cohen 2003).
- In 2003 China added eleven thousand more cars to its roads every day (Halweil and Mastney 2004). If China's per capita energy use were to match that of the United States, world oil consumption would double.
- The US spends more for trash bags that ninety of the world's countries spend in total and has two times as many shopping malls as high schools (de Graaf, Wann and Naylor 2001).

The list could go on, but the point is clear. We consume obscene amounts of stuff and in so doing we endanger planetary survival, nourish global resentment and exploit the bulk of the world's people and material resources for the benefit of the few who are part of global consumer culture. The resource impact and global injustice of our consumption mania are bad enough, but Chua (2004) warns that class and ethnic warfare may also result if the gap between indigenous poor and non-indigenous rich continues to grow. In light of these problems, the assumption that economic growth and prosperity are vital national and global goals is increasingly being questioned.

All of these indicants that our consumption has become excessive, burdensome and in many ways problematic are external and aggregate. At a more internal and personal level there are further, and perhaps more deeply felt, reasons to consider consumption as a problem rather than a solution. Consumers who buy using credit cards spend more than those using cash (Hirschman 1979). By 2001, Americans were spending 14 per cent of their disposable income paying interest on debt they had accumulated from purchases made on credit (Updegrave 2003). Many Americans had learned to pay off one credit card with another, make durables purchases on plans that promised no initial interest charges but that soon led to exorbitant charges and to draw money from their home equity to pay for extravagant lifestyles and risky investments (Manning 2000). The mortgage meltdown from subprime bad risk mortgages that resulted when the housing price bubble burst in 2006 was a wakeup call for most everyone and a financial disaster for many. Underlying this crisis for many was a problem with compulsive consumption (Faber and O'Guinn 1988). Compulsive consumers spend far more than they can afford, not for the benefits of ownership or consumption, but in an attempt to fill deep psychological needs like the need for love. Like compulsive hand-washing, gambling or eating, compulsive buying is not an instrumental behaviour as much as an addiction. Often compulsive consumers' purchases are never used at all and the attention received from the sales clerk is a major reinforcer of their compulsive behaviour. Television shopping channels also cater to compulsive buyers (Lee, Lennon and Rudd 2000) and Internet shopping can be a problem for these buyers as well (Norum 2008).

But compulsive consumption is an abnormality affecting no more than 10 per cent of buyers. Credit card abuse and problems of excessive debt are more common, but these too are not yet problems that affect the majority of the world's consumers. The focus of most personal indictments of consumption is the average consumer in affluent countries. For example, in 1950 the average American home size was 983 square feet. By 2004 it had grown 140 per cent to 2,349 square feet (Adler 2006). The size of so-called McMansions can be five or even ten times greater. But even this is not enough to house our growing inventory of possessions, which Schor (1991) reports have also more than doubled over this period. Arnould and Lang (2007) found that eighteen of twenty-four middle-class southern California homes studied had given up all of their garage space (consisting of either two- or three-car garages) in order to house their stuff. And Clayton (2003) documents that there is currently a boom in the market for rented warehouse storage for our excess possessions. While many of those who lost their homes in the recent recession sought to save their stuff in self-storage units, many others just can't give up their souvenirs, old furniture, old clothes and collections. The US currently has 2.3 billion square feet of self-storage space and seven times as many storage facilities as Starbucks (Mooallem 2009). This is enough to accommodate the entire population of the US, albeit with standing room only.

It is not just adults who are caught up in such frenzies of consumption. Children in traditional societies learn the names of plants and animals and how they should be regarded. Children in consumer societies instead learn the names of brands and stores and how they should be regarded. By the time children enter school, they have a repertoire of hundreds and even thousands of brand name and logo matches (Belk, Bahn and Mayer 1982; Belk, Mayer and Driscoll 1984). Those who are lacking an intimate familiarity with advertising jingles, music and knowledge of the latest brands may fail to fit in with their peers (Ritson and Elliott 1999). Knowledge of what brands are cool and uncool is a significant form of cultural capital among teens and preteen consumers (Belk 2006; Frank 1997; Heath and Potter 2004). And for marketers and advertisers, an array of increasingly sophisticated and often invisible marketing techniques like anti-advertising, under-the-radar marketing, stealth marketing, product placement, viral marketing and product seeding are used to try to influence teen and tween consumers (e.g., Boyd and Kirschenbaum 1997; Cross 2004; Goodman 2003; Quart 2003; Schor 2004; Shrum 2004).

The resulting escalation of consumer desires is not limited to the West. From fast foods (Watson 1997) and Coca-Cola (Varman and Belk 2009) to cellular phones (Mazzarella 2003) and luxury goods (Lu 2008; Wang 2008), growing Eastern economies, highlighted by China and India, are beginning to move in the same rampant consumerist directions as the West. The sudden increase in affluence in China since 1979 coupled with an influx of Western products and media have resulted in an increase in individualism and materialism (Chan, Zhang and Wang 2006; Leung 2008; Lu 2008; Wang 2008). With China's one-child policy China's "little emperors" are being indulged materially as they never have been before (e.g., Jing 2000). The more collective Chinese also display a tendency to pool incomes within extended families and sacrifice necessities like food in order to buy luxuries like televisions (e.g., Belk 1999). Such trends suggest that Asia is catching up with Western consumption patterns at a much greater rate than might be expected from per capita income figures.

All of this explosion of consumption (e.g., Croll 2006; Davis 2000) has prompted a considerable amount of thought and writing about how we might reduce consumption and live simpler lives (e.g., see Schudson 1998; Shi 2001). This chapter explores two of the main, but different, philosophies that have been offered for accomplishing this: Voluntary Simplicity and Buddhist Economics.

LESS CONSUMING SOCIETIES

The idea that people would be better off if they lived more simply is not a new one. There are ancient ascetic traditions like those of the Shramanas in India and Epicureans, Stoics and Spartans of ancient Greece. For Aristotle, the Greek ideal of the Golden Mean, or moderation in consumption offered a more viable consumption style than asceticism (Van Hook 1923). The Eastern philosophies of Taoism, Buddhism, Zoroastrianism, Shinto and Confucianism all emphasise simple living and reverence for nature and each has had some influence on Western Judeo-Christian philosophies and practices including the aesthetic and communal traditions of early Christianity (Shi 2001). Various simple living Western religious groups have emerged and many followers continue to live in enclaved communities that eschew modern gadgets and conveniences. They include the Mennonites, Amish, Shakers, Quakers, Amana Colony and Harmony Society. All of the world religions, including Judaism, Hinduism, Christianity and Islam condemn excessive desire, wealth, materialism, envy and greed (Belk 1983), although in their modern forms, many of the same religions have made accommodations to (and even championed) materialism (e.g., Coleman 2000; Lyon 2000; Miller 2000; O'Guinn and Belk 1989).

Prominent among the more secular philosophies for less consuming societies is the American Transcendentalist movement, with Henry David Thoreau's (1854/1997) *Walden* as its most famous example. Although Thoreau's cabin was not far from the city and the home of his friend and mentor Ralph Waldo Emerson, and although he received a number of visitors during his two-year stay in the woods, *Walden* is frequently cited as an attempt to escape the ways of the city (Concord, Massachusetts). The experiment was part of Thoreau's reaction against the Industrial Revolution going on around him and also led him to practice and advocate vegetarianism, carpentry and agrarianism. He was largely self-sufficient during his stay at Walden Pond, building his own cabin and selling the beans he grew to buy supplies. He relished reading and the life of leisure that he was able to enjoy at Walden. There are parts of his writings there that are echoed in Marshall Sahlins's (1972) account of the Bushmen of the Kalahari, whom he called "the original affluent society"— hunter-gatherer people who worked considerably less than contemporary city dwellers and used their free time for leisure. *Walden* remains a frequently read and influential source of inspiration for would-be simplifiers in the West.

A contemporary of Thoreau's, Karl Marx, offered a different vision of simple living wisdom. In his early writings Marx (1844/1975) maintained that private property should be abandoned, even though the "crude communism" of communal ownership would need to involve societally owned property during the first stages of communism. This would remove unjust capitalist profits from the appropriated labour of workers as well as keep greed in check. In later writings, Marx (1867/1978) softened his view on property and insisted that only the means of production needed to be removed from private ownership. By removing the means of production from private hands, Marx envisioned a society in which the extremes of both wealth and poverty were largely leveled (Gorin 1980). But despite the grand ideas of Marx, it is generally conceded that since the demise of communism in Europe and the development of "market socialism" in Asia, that the Marxist vision has been overcome by the more greed-based capitalism. As Sulak Sivaraksa (1992, 102) summarises:

> At one time people thought the Marxist approach would be the answer. Unfortunately Marxism failed, because instead of using the socialist approach of equality, fraternity, and liberty, the second world used state capitalism, totalitarianism, and centralism.

Although many contemporary Marxists would endorse this view, in other analyses it was the lures of consumer society as much as the failings of communist states that ultimately brought down or marketised such economies (see Belk 1998). If so, communism was unable to overcome the problems of commodity fetishism or the worship of anthropomorphised consumer goods that concerned Marx (1867/1978).

Since Thoreau there have been a number of advocates and practitioners of simple living. They include Mahatma Gandhi (1930/1961), Richard Gregg (1936), Scott Nearing (1954), Erich Fromm (1961), E. F. Schumacher (1973), Duane Elgin (Elgin 1977, 1981; Elgin and Mitchell 1977), C. R. Ashbee (Maccarthy 1981), Peter Gould (1988), Juliet Schor (Schor 1998; Schor and Taylor 2003), Kalle Lasn (1999), Alan Badiner (2002), Stephanie Kaza (2005) and David Wann (2007). There are a number of common themes throughout these writings, as well as some significant differences. I have chosen to emphasise two such streams of philosophical thought concerning living more simply (Voluntary Simplicity [VS] and Buddhist Economics) in what follows because they differ in their primary visions of less consuming societies. I recognise that I oversimplify to a degree, both due to space constraints and due to the numerous variants of each vision and the degree to which they cross-fertilise each other in contemporary writings. I also recognise that Buddhist practice and Buddhist writing, especially Western writing on Buddhism and consumption, often differ. This is something on which I shall say more near the end of this review.

VOLUNTARY SIMPLICITY

Although Duane Elgin's (1977, 1981) writings are the most well known and currently influential work explicating and advocating VS, the term dates back to Richard Gregg's book twenty-five years earlier. Gregg, a Quaker, had gone to India in the 1920s and was greatly impressed with Gandhi's non-violent philosophy of resistance as well as his *Swadeshi* practices emphasizing the preference for home-grown products over global products, even when the global products are functionally superior (Sarkar 1973). One of the distinctions that Elgin (1981) makes is between VS and involuntary poverty (see also Rudmin and Kilbourne 1996). Poverty is involuntary and debilitating in Elgin's view, but voluntary simplicity is enabling as well as ennobling of the human spirit. Whereas poverty is seen to lead to feelings of helplessness, despair and passivity, VS is personally empowering, uplifting and a freely chosen way to move toward a way of life that is sustainable and uses appropriate technology that adapts to nature rather than high technology that opposes nature.

Others have emphasised that VS is helpful to the environment because it is a lifestyle that uses less energy and has a smaller environmental footprint (e.g., Leonard-Barton 1981; Valaskakis 1979). It has been regarded by some in marketing as a radical idea because instead of reinforcing the norm of using more, it advocates material simplification of lifestyles (e.g., Ensley 1983). Others who acknowledge the negative link between materialism and well-being instead welcome VS as a promising antidote to materialism (e.g., Grønhaug and Ogaard 1982). Elgin and Mitchell (1977) and others during the late 1970s and early 1980s (e.g., Sharma 1981) were optimistic that the VS of the time would continue to grow in popularity and become the dominant Western lifestyle. But despite the rise of green politics (Gould 1988), VS practitioners remain a minority of the population rather than the majority that Elgin and Mitchell (1977) predicted would have been achieved by now. Subsequent work identified particular characteristics of voluntary simplifiers such as their upscale demographics, liberal views and innovative character (e.g., Craig-Lees and Hill 2002; Etzioni 1998; Miller and Gregon-Paxton 2006; Shaw and Newholm 2002; Zavetovski 2002).

More recent treatments of VS regard it as more of a subculture or counter-culture lifestyle that is not likely to be adopted by the masses (e.g., Cherrier and Murray 2005). On the other hand, thanks to Juliet Schor (1998) and the Center for a New American Dream (http://www.newdream.org/) that she co-founded, the vocabulary of VS has changed to "downshifting"—a less radical sounding way to live a simpler life without dropping out of participation in mainstream society (e.g., Cherrier and Murray 2007). The idea of downshifting is to work less, eat more locally, drive less and enjoy a moderately different lifestyle with a lesser environmental footprint. As might be expected, the VS movement has also embraced related movements like Kalle Lasn's (1999) "Buy Nothing Day" (the day after American Thanksgiving when the Christmas shopping season begins, aided by merchants' "door buster" sales held on that day. Earth Day (on the vernal equinox), global warming (e.g., Gore and West 2006), the green movement, carbon neutrality, the so-called "anti-globalization" movement, sustainable consumption, ethical consumerism and fair trade are among the other movements that contemporary VS advocates tend to endorse. The tone of VS seems to have shifted in the adoption of the concept of downshifting and the rationale has become more aggregate and is less framed in terms of emphasizing psychological well-being (the "outwardly simple, inwardly rich" emphasis of Elgin [1981]). Notions of sacrifice are still present, but there is also a more positive spin on some of the suggested actions, making them sound almost fun.

BUDDHIST ECONOMICS

Even though contemporary Western writings on Buddhism also sometimes invoke aggregate societal issues like globalization, commoditization and rampant consumer culture, the focus of Buddhism is more inward than outward. Greed, desire and materialism are held to be the source of our suffering, according to Buddhism (Payutto 2002). Our attachment to material things is also a part of this suffering (Pryor 1990, 1991), the solution to which is to overcome greed through generosity and compassion (Batchelor 2002; Goldstein 2005). Another part of the Buddhist recommendation is that of caring for and sharing with others, and in so doing creating a caring community (Chödrön 2005; Watts and Loy 2002). By practicing generosity (*dana*), sharing, compassion and caring, the focus of the person on the self is turned around and focused on others. This produces joy (rather than the more fleeting feeling of material pleasure) and is consistent with the Buddhist concept of non-self (Batchelor 2002; Kolm 1985; Watts and Loy 2002). A further concept from Buddhism that ties these acts and orientations together is that of mindfulness. Goldstein (2005, 18) explains:

> By mindfulness I mean the quality of paying full attention to the moment, opening to the truth of change and impermanence. . . . The more deeply we see the impermanent nature of reality, the less seduced we are by impermanent phenomena such as consumer goods.

Watts and Loy (2002, 100) recognise the same qualities of mindfulness, but also add a dimension of community mindfulness:

> Mindfulness takes form in religious communities as group prayer or meditation or ritual, traditional and powerful forms for maintaining community connections. . . . Theoretically, mindfulness involves developing concentration into unity or one-pointedness. Thus, practically, in terms of community, it means bringing individuals together in united awareness and feeling through the sharing of time, energy, and information.

This communal aspect of Buddhism and the focus on non-self is something that is absent in VS approaches to reducing consumption. Also missing in VS are Buddhism's emphases on generosity and caring for others as antidotes for selfishness, the emphasis on non-attachment and the focus on greed, desire and materialism as the sources of suffering. With this perspective, Buddhism may involve renunciation of the things previously thought to bring pleasure, but it does not involve sacrifice of the things that really do bring pleasure. A further difference is that whereas VS emphasises that less is more and that the simpler the life you can lead the better, Buddhism is less about extremes and instead advocates the middle way, without the excesses of either too much or too little. Having tried both extremes, Buddha himself was an advocate of neither indulgence nor austerity, but rather something in between (Goldstein 2005; Inoue 2002). The same call for moderation applies in Buddhism when it comes to making money (Williams 2002). Making money is fine, but like the ancient Greek concept of the Golden Mean, it should not become obsessive or excessive.

Another difference between Buddhism and VS is found in their views of poverty. As noted earlier, VS condemns involuntary poverty and lauds the voluntary poverty of living simply. This seems to privilege reducing consumption once someone has reached a certain level of wealth, but sees it as impossible for those who have not first enjoyed some level of wealth to strive for continuing their modest levels of consumption. Buddhism, on the other hand, suggests that we pay too much attention to the problems of poverty and not enough attention to the problems of wealth. Although one interpretation of karma is that those who are reborn into poverty or as lower life forms are reaping the just rewards of their earlier lives, Buddhism is concerned with being compassionate toward those who are suffering. Where it differs is in its attitude toward "development", especially the type that may simply be a code word for exploitation of the less affluent world by the more affluent world (Ger and Belk 1996; Loy 2002). Those of us living in affluence have made a secular religion of development in order to justify our own standard of living. In Loy's (2002, 149) view:

> Unless there are losers, we cannot feel like winners. If the "undeveloped" are not unhappy with their lot, we may come to doubt our own happiness with what we have, unable to rationalise the things we have had to put up with in order to get there, or to excuse the negative consequences of our own economic development.

He concludes, "One of the best things we can do for many 'undeveloped' peoples [from the perspective of Buddhism] is to leave them alone" (2002, 152). This is not based on indifference, but on the recognition that many of the things done in the name of economic development, especially by international financial organizations like the World Bank and the International Monetary Fund, actually worsen the problems of the poor rather than improve them (Belk 2000; Stiglitz 2003). Poverty is also relative and those who may look poor in comparison to the affluent West may be living happily in virtual self sufficiency, even though their incomes are meager.

WHERE ARE WE HEADED? BUDDHISM AND
VOLUNTARY SIMPLICITY IN A CHANGING WORLD

As already noted, the VS movement has had increasing competition from
the Green Movement, Anti-Globalization forces, Culture Jamming groups,
vegetarian and vegan movements and others. Because these tend to be movements that are sympathetic to VS ideas, the groups have tended to support
one another and rally together on occasions like Earth Day. In seeking to
align with these alternative movements, the premises of VS may have been
diluted. VS has also embraced Buddhism in many cases, albeit without a
religious emphasis and with some remaining differences noted earlier.

Buddhism has also changed in responses to conditions of the contemporary world, but in different ways. As Coleman (2002) documents, there
has been a steady growth of interest in Buddhism in the West, both as a
religion and as a set of secularised practices like chanting and meditation.
To be fair, Buddhism is not monolithic in Asia either and three different
versions of Buddhism—Zen, Theravada and Tibetan—have taken root in
the US where Coleman's work was carried out. The American practitioners of Buddhism have tended to be white, upper-middle-class liberals to
whom Buddhism's beliefs and practices have had an appeal, at least since
Jack Kerouac became fascinated with pop Buddhism in the 1950s when he
wrote *Dharma Bums* (Prothero 2002). Robert Pirsig's *Zen and the Art of
Motorcycle Maintenance* is another of the Buddhist best sellers in the West.
Prothero (2002, 163) suggests that "Boomer Buddhism" may be subverting
Buddhism itself, and continues:

> Instead of preserving the Dharma, Americans seem intent on co-opting
> and commercializing it, dissolving a religion deeply suspicious of the
> Self into an engine of self-identity and self-absorption.

There are other indictments of Buddhists beginning to embrace wealth
as a sign of spiritual blessing, not only in the West, but in Japan and Thailand as well (Watts and Loy 2002). Others worry about the trend toward
materialistic icons of Buddhism including "Buddha cell phone straps, Buddha car talismans, Buddha mouse pads, monk dolls, monk stationary, and
so on" (Loundon 2005).

Lest all this seem to be a Western perversion of Asian Buddhism, it is
worth noting that Buddhism in the East has also changed. Buddhist monks
in Asia take a vow affirming that they will "be prepared to robe themselves
in scraps of thrown-way cloth, to eat whatever food is given to them as
alms, to live at the root of a tree as their only shelter, and to use naturally
occurring remedies as medicine for sickness" (Amaro 2005, 183). Traditionally they are allowed only four possessions: a bowl, a robe, a needle
and a strainer to remove insects from their drinking water so that none are
harmed (Chappell 2005, 241). Where once Buddhists were not to handle

money and were to use a begging bowl to procure their one meal of the day, a recent trip to a number of Buddhist monasteries in Tibet reveals that monks handle money, eat junk food and sport cell phones, computers and iPods (although to be fair, some, but not all, of these are monks who lost their monasteries to the Chinese Cultural Revolution destruction of Buddhist institutions in Tibet). And in Thailand, Hutanuwatr and Rasbash (2005, 105) report that:

> The Thai Buddhist Sangha that is supposed to generate Buddhist values of simplicity, generosity, and compassion is now almost completely under the spell of goods such as mobile phones, BMWs, and portable computers.

Such materialistic behaviour does not negate the principles of Buddhism, but neither does it set a good example. And it raises the question of whether the "spiritual materialism" of much contemporary Buddhism threatens to render it less effective or ineffective in offering a philosophy for simpler consumption. There may, ironically, be hope in the transplantation of Buddhism from the "nonmaterialistic East" to the "materialistic West". Loundon (2005) reports that while many young Buddhists in the US adopt renunciation wholeheartedly and live quite simply, many of the young Buddhists in Penang have no problem pursuing MBAs and striving to be successful in business. Neither group sees any contradiction between their religious beliefs and their lifestyles.

Perhaps Loundon's example of young Buddhists in Penang should remind us that Buddhism preaches the middle way. Renunciation and conquering desires is not the same as living an austere monastic life. Furthermore, unlike voluntary simplicity, the Buddhist view of poverty means that one need not be comfortably rich (if that is not an oxymoron) in order to practice Buddhist simple living. The fact that most Western Buddhists come from upper-middle-class backgrounds (as is true of voluntary simplifiers), suggests that the real message of being part of a less consuming society is that it is a societal movement rather than an individual lifestyle choice. The support of a sharing caring community committed to living a life that does not champion the consumption of more and more may be the simplest and best philosophy for achieving moderation in consumption.

Major changes in consumption patterns nearly always require some momentous event—the rise of the eighteenth-century Dutch economy to sudden affluence, the Industrial Revolution, World War II, the Cold War or the destruction of the Berlin Wall, for example. Such cataclysms may provoke either rampant materialism and secularism or widespread material sacrifice and spirituality. More recent events that may trigger massive changes in consumer lifestyles include the terrorist attacks of 11 September 2001, the rapid economic rise of China, the relatively sudden recognition of global warming, dramatic volatility in energy prices and the widespread economic recession that began in 2006. Are such events, individually or in combination, likely to trigger a widespread embrace of Buddhist economics or VS? This remains to be seen, but there is some evidence that the world is beginning to slip back into its pattern of growing excessive consumption rather than adopting simpler material lifestyles. Returning to the earlier example of self-storage facilities in the US, Mooallem (2009) interviewed a number of self-storage owners, entrepreneurs and renters with the expectation that this bellwether of consumption excess would show a dramatic change in response to the domination of the flagging US economy, the dramatic increase in home foreclosures and the growing tide of unemployment, just as the 1990s economic and real estate bubble together with increased divorce by maturing baby boomers had led to a dramatic boom in storing our excess stuff. He did in fact find a number of people who were cleaning out their former storage spaces and relabeling the objects stored there as wasteful junk. They were stopping the expense of renting storage space in order to save money. But he also found a number of people who had lost their homes who were putting their possessions in what they hoped was temporary storage. Both Mooallem (2009) and Clayton (2003) report that many of those who had lost their homes clung to their possessions as a source of psychological security, but promptly got rid of most of these possessions once they were able to move into a new home. And, thus far, even those who suffered most from the bubble burst and recession still championed the strong belief that things would get better for them and that they and future generations would be able to look forward to increasing affluence, bigger homes and more stuff. If there is a coming cataclysm that will make us renounce our material appetites for a saner diet of spiritualism and simpler lives, it appears that even the economic shocks of the latter half of the first decade of the new millennium are not enough to have precipitated such changes.

REFERENCES

Adler, Margot. 2006. Behind the Ever-Expanding American Dream House. National Public Radio, 4 July. http://www.npr.org/templates/story/story.php?storyId=5525283.

Amaro, Ajahn. 2005. Three Robes Is Enough. In *Hooked! Buddhist Writings on Greed, Desire, and the Urge to Consume*, ed. Stephanie Kaza, 183–187. Boston: Shambhala.

Arnold, Jeanne E., and Ursula A. Lang. 2007. Changing American Home Life: Trends in Domestic Leisure and Storage among Middle-Class Families. *Journal of Family Economic Issues* 28:23–48.

Badiner, Allan Hunt, ed. 2002. *Mindfulness in the Marketplace: Compassionate Responses to Consumerism*. Berkeley, CA: Parallax Press.

Batchelor, Stephen. 2002. The Practice of Generosity. In *Mindfulness in the Marketplace: Compassionate Responses to Consumerism*, ed. Allan Hunt Badiner, 59–66. Berkeley, CA: Parallax Press.

Belk, Russell W. 1983. Worldly Possessions: Issues and Criticisms. In *Advances in Consumer Research*, ed. Richard P. Bagozzi and Alice M. Tybout, 514–519. Ann Arbor: Association for Consumer Research.

———. 1998. In the Arms of the Overcoat: On Luxury, Romanticism, and Consumer Desire. In *Romancing the Market*, ed. Stephen Brown, 41–45. London: Routledge.

———. 1999. Leaping Luxuries and Transitional Consumers. In *Marketing Issues in Transitional Economies*, ed. Rajiv Batra, 38–54. Norwell, MA: Kluwer.

———. 2000. Pimps for Paradise: Paradisal Versions Proffered by Missionaries, Monetary Funds, and Marketers. *Marketing Intelligence and Planning* 18 (6–7): 337–344.

———. 2006. Coola Skor, Cool Identitet [Cool Shoes, Cool Identity]. In *Skor Ger Mer: Makt Flärd Magi*, ed. Anne Marie Dahlberg, 77–90. Stockholm: Swedish Royal Armoury.

Belk, Russell W., Kenneth Bahn and Robert Mayer. 1982. Developmental Recognition of Consumption Symbolism. *Journal of Consumer Research* 9:4–17.

Belk, Russell W., Robert Mayer and Amy Driscoll. 1984. Children's Recognition of Consumption Symbolism in Children's Products. *Journal of Consumer Research* 10:386–397.

Boyd, Jonathan, and Richard Kirshenbaum. 1997. *Under the Radar: Talking to Today's Cynical Consumer*. New York: Wiley.

Chan, Kara, Hongxia Zhang and Iris Wang. 2006. Materialism among Adolescents in Urban China. *Young Consumers* 7 (2): 64–77.

Chappell, David W. 2005. Mutual Correction: Seeing the Pain of Others. In *Hooked! Buddhist Writings on Greed, Desire, and the Urge to Consume*, ed. Stephanie Kaza, 237–249. Boston: Shambhala.

Cherrier, Hélène, and Jeff B. Murray. 2005. Research Subcultures, Neotribes, Countercultures, or New Social Movements: The Case of Voluntary Simplicity. *European Advances in Consumer Research* 6.

———. 2007. Constructing Downshifting Identities: Toward an Understanding of Radical Changes in Consumption Lifestyles. *Consumption, Markets and Culture* 10 (1): 1–29.

Chödrön, Thubten. 2005. Marketing the Dharma. In *Hooked! Buddhist Writings on Greed, Desire, and the Urge to Consume*, ed. Stephanie Kaza, 63–75. Boston: Shambhala.

Chua, Amy. 2004. *World on Fire: How Exporting Free Market Democracy Breeds Ethnic Hatred and Global Instability*. New York: Anchor.

Clayton, Victoria. 2003. Psychology by the Square Foot: What the Ongoing Boom in Self-Storage Facilities Says About Human Nature, Uncertain Times and the Anxieties of American Culture. *Los Angeles Times*, 10 August.

Cohen, Lisabeth. 2003. *A Consumer's Republic: The Politics of Mass Consumption in Postwar America*. New York: Alfred A. Knopf.

Coleman, James W. 2002. *The New Buddhism: The Western Transformation of an Ancient Tradition*. Oxford: Oxford University Press.

Coleman, Simon. 2000. *The Globalization of Charismatic Christianity: Spreading the Gospel of Prosperity*. Cambridge: Cambridge University Press.

Craig-Lees, Margaret, and Constance Hill. 2002. Understanding Voluntary Simplifiers. *Psychology and Marketing* 19 (2): 187–210.

Croll, Elisabeth. 2006. *China's New Consumers: Social Development and Domestic Demand*. London: Routledge.

Cross, Gary. 2004. *The Cute and the Cool: Wondrous Innocence and Modern American Children's Culture*. Oxford: Oxford University Press.

Davis, Deborah, ed. 2000. *The Consumer Revolution in Urban China*. Berkeley: University of California Press.

De Graaf, John, David Wann and Thomas Naylor. 2001. *Affluenza: The All-Consuming Epidemic*. San Francisco: Berrett-Kohler.

Durning, Alan. 1992. *How Much Is Enough?* New York: W. W. Norton.

Elgin, Duane. 1977. Voluntary Simplicity. *Co-Evolution Quarterly* (Summer): 5–18.

———. 1981. *Voluntary Simplicity: Toward a Way of Life that Is Outwardly Simple, Inwardly Rich*. New York: William Morrow and Company.

Elgin, Duane, and Arnold Mitchell. 1977. Voluntary Simplicity: Lifestyle of the Future? *The Futurist* 11:200–209.

Ensley, Elizabeth. 1983. Voluntary Simplicity: A Segment of Concern to Marketers? In *American Marketing Association Educators' Proceedings*, ed. Patrick E. Murphy et al., 385–389. Chicago: American Marketing Association.

Etzioni, Amatai. 1998. Voluntary Simplicity: Characterization, Select Psychological Implications, and Societal Consequences. *Journal of Economic Psychology* 19 (5): 619–643.

Faber, Ronald J., and Thomas C. O'Guinn. 1988. Compulsive Consumption and Credit Abuse. *Journal of Consumer Policy* 11 (1): 97–109.

Frank, Thomas. 1997. *The Conquest of Cool: Business Culture, Counterculture, and the Rise of Hip Consumerism*. Chicago: University of Chicago Press.

Fromm, Erich. 1961. *Marx's Concept of Man*. New York: Fredrick Ungar Publishing.

Gandhi, Mahatma. 1930/1961. *Non-Violent Resistance (Satyagraha)*. New York: Schocken Books.

Ger, Güliz, and Russell Belk. 1996. I'd Like to Buy the World a Coke: Consumptionscapes of the "Less Affluent World". *Journal of Consumer Policy* 19 (3): 271–304.

Goldstein, Joseph. 2005. Desire, Delusion, and DVDs. In *Hooked! Buddhist Writings on Greed, Desire, and the Urge to Consume*, ed. Stephanie Kaza, 17–26. Boston: Shambhala.

Goodman, Barak. 2003. *The Merchants of Cool, 60-Minute Frontline Video*. Boston: WGBH/PBS.

Gore, Al, and Billy West II. 2006. *An Inconvenient Truth*. Hollywood, CA: Paramount Pictures.

Gorin, Zeey. 1980. Income Inequality in the Marxist Theory of Development: A Cross-National Test. *Comparative Social Research* 3:147–174.

Gould, Peter C. 1988. *Early Green Politics: Back to Nature, Back to the Land, and Socialism in Britain, 1880–1900*. London: Palgrave Macmillan.

Gregg, Richard. 1936. *The Value of Voluntary Simplicity*. Wallingford, PA: Pendle Hill.

Grønhaug, Kjell, and Torvald Ogaard Jr. 1982. Exploring Success and Failure in Intended Changes in Lifestyle. *Advances in Consumer Research* 9:302–305.

Halweil, Brian, and Lisa Mastney. 2004. *State of the World 2004*. New York: W. W. Norton.

Heath, Joseph, and Andrew Potter. 2004. *Nation of Rebels: Why Counterculture Became Consumer Culture*. New York: Harper Business.

Hirschman, Elizabeth C. 1979. The Relationship of Credit Card Acceptance to Retail Purchasing. *Journal of Consumer Research* 6:58–66.

Hutanuwatr, Pracha, and Jane Rasbash. 2005. No River Bigger than *Thanha*. In *Hooked! Buddhist Writings on Greed, Desire, and the Urge to Consume*. ed. Stephanie Kaza, 104–121. Boston: Shambhala.

Inoue, Shinichi. 2002. A New Economics to Save the Earth: A Buddhist Perspective. In *Mindfulness in the Marketplace: Compassionate Responses to Consumerism*, ed. Allan Hunt Badiner, 49–58. Berkeley, CA: Parallax Press.

Jing, Jun. 2000. *Feeding China's Little Emperors*. Stanford, CA: Stanford University Press.

Kaza, Stephanie. 2005. *Hooked! Buddhist Writings on Greed, Desire, and the Urge to Consume*. Boston: Shambhala.

Kolm, Serge-Christophe. 1985. The Buddhist of "No-Self". In *The Multiple Self*, ed. John Elster, 233–265. Cambridge: Cambridge University Press.

Lasn, Kalle. 1999. *Culture Jam: The Uncooling of America*. New York: William Morrow and Company.

Lee, Seung-Hee, Sharron J. Lennon and Nancy A. Rudd. 2000. Compulsive Consumption Tendencies among Television Shoppers. *Family and Consumer Sciences Research Journal* 28 (4): 463–488.

Leonard-Barton, Dorothy. 1981. Voluntary Simplicity and Energy Conservation. *Journal of Consumer Research* 8:243–252.

Leung, Kwok. 2008. Chinese Culture, Modernization and International Business. *International Business Review* 17 (2): 184–187.

Loundon, Sumi. 2005. In *Hooked! Buddhist Writings on Greed, Desire, and the Urge to Consume*, ed. Stephanie Kaza, 49–62. Boston: Shambhala.

Loy, David R. 2002. Buddhism and Poverty. In *Mindfulness in the Marketplace: Compassionate Responses to Consumerism*, ed. Allan Hunt Badiner, 144–160. Berkeley, CA: Parallax Press.

Lu, Pierre Xiao. 2008. *Elite China: Luxury Consumer Behavior in China*. Singapore: John Wiley and Sons.

Lyon, David. 2000. *Jesus in Disneyland: Religion in Postmodern Times*. Cambridge: Polity.

Maccarthy, Fiona. 1981. *The Simple Life: C. R. Ashbee in the Cotswolds*. Berkeley: University of California Press.

Manning, Robert D. 2000. *Credit Card Nation: The Consequences of America's Addiction to Credit*. New York: Basic Books.

Marx, Karl. 1844/1975. *Critique of Hegelian Philosophy of the Right (Introduction)*. New York: Vantage Books.

———. 1867/1978. *Capital: A Critique of Political Economy, Vol. 1*. Trans. Ben Forks. Harmondsworth: Penguin Books.

Mazzarella, William. 2003. *Shoveling Smoke: Advertising and Globalization in Contemporary India*. Durham, NC: Duke University Press.

Miller, Suzanne, and Jennifer Gregan-Paxton. 2006. Community and Connectivity: Examining the Motives Underlying the Adoption of a Lifestyle of Voluntary Simplicity. *Advances in Consumer Research* 33.

Miller, Vincent J. 2004. *Consuming Religion: Christian Faith and Practice in a Consumer Culture*. New York: Continuum International Publishing Group.

Mooallem, Jon. 2009. The Self-Storage Self. *New York Times*, online edition, 6 September.

Nearing, Scott. 1954. *Man's Search for the Good Life*. Harborside, MD: The Social Science Institute.

Norum, Pamela S. 2008. Student Internet Purchases. *Family and Consumer Sciences Research Journal* 36 (4): 373–388.

O'Guinn, Thomas C., and Russell W. Belk. 1989. Heaven on Earth: Consumption at Heritage Village, USA. *Journal of Consumer Research* 16 (September): 227–238.

Payutto, Ven. P. A. 2002. Buddhist Perspectives on Economic Concepts. In *Mindfulness in the Marketplace: Compassionate Responses to Consumerism*, ed. Allan Hunt Badiner, 77–92. Berkeley, CA: Parallax Press.

Prothero, Stephen. 2002. Boomer Buddhism. In *Mindfulness in the Marketplace: Compassionate Responses to Consumerism*, ed. Allan Hunt Badiner, 161–165. Berkeley, CA: Parallax Press.

Pryor, Frederic L. 1990. A Buddhist Economic System—In Principle. *American Journal of Economics and Sociology* 49 (July): 339–351.

———. 1991. A Buddhist Economic System—In Practice. *American Journal of Economics and Sociology* 50 (January): 17–33.

Quart, Alissa. 2003. *Branded: The Buying and Selling of Teenagers*. New York: Basic Books.

Ritson, Mark, and Richard Elliott. 1999. The Social Uses of Advertising: An Ethnographic Study of Adolescent Advertising Audiences. *Journal of Consumer Research* 26 (December): 260–277.

Rudmin, Floyd W., and William E. Kilbourne. 1996. The Meaning and Morality of Voluntary Simplicity: History and Hypotheses on Deliberately Denied Materialism. In *Marketing and Consumption: Macro Dimensions*, ed. Russell Belk, Nikolesh Dholakia and Alladi Venkatesh, 166–215. Cincinnati, OH: South Western Publishing.

Ryan, John C. 1998. Stuff: The Secret Life of Everyday Things. *The Futurist* 32 (2): 26–29.

Sahlins, Marshall. 1972. *Stone Age Economics*. Chicago: Aldine.

Sarkar, Sumit. 1973. *The Swadshi Movement in Bengal*. New Delhi: People's Publishing House.

Schor, Juliet, B. 1991. *The Overworked American: The Unexpected Decline of Leisure*. New York: Basic Books.

———. 1998. *The Overspent American: Upscaling, Downshifting, and the New Consumer*. New York: Harper Perennial.

Schor, Juliet B., and Betsy Taylor. 2003. *Sustainable Planet: Solutions for the Twenty-first Century*. Boston: Beacon Press.

Schudson, Michael. 1998. Delectable Materialism: Second Thoughts on Consumer Culture. In *The Ethics of Consumption*, ed. David Crocker and Toby Linden, 249–268. Lanham, MD: Rowman and Littlefield.

Schumacher, E. F. 1973. *Small is Beautiful: Economics as if People Mattered*. New York: Harper and Row.

Sharma, Avraham. 1981. Coping with Stagflation: Voluntary Simplicity. *Journal of Marketing* 45:120–124.

Shaw, Deirdre, and T. Newholm. 2002. Voluntary Simplicity and the Ethics of Consumption. *Psychology and Marketing* 19 (2): 167–185.

Shi, David. 2001. *The Simple Life: Plain Living and High Thinking in American Culture*. Athens: University of Georgia Press.

Shrum, L. J., ed. 2004. *The Psychology of Entertainment Media: Blurring the Lines between Entertainment and Persuasion*. Mahwah, NJ: Lawrence Erlbaum.

Sivaraksa, Sulak. 1992. *Seeds of Peace: A Buddhist Vision for Renewing Society*. Berkeley, CA: Parallax Press.

Stiglitz, Joseph E. 2003. *Globalization and its Discontents*. New York: W. W. Norton.

Thoreau, Henry David. 1854/1997. *Walden*. Boston: Beacon Press.

Updegrave, Walter. 2003. High-Debt Anxiety. *Money* 32 (4): 81.

Valaskakis, Kimon. 1979. *Conserver Society: A Workable Alternative for the Future*. New York: Harper and Row.

Van Hook, La Rue. 1923. *Greek Life and Thought: A Portrayal of Greek Civilization*. New York: Columbia University Press.

Varman, Rohit, and Russell Belk. 2009. Nationalism and Ideology in an Anti-Consumption Movement. *Journal of Consumer Research* 36 (December), 686–700.

Wang, Jing. 2008. *Brand New China: Advertising, Media, and Commercial Culture*. Cambridge, MA: Harvard University Press.

Wann, David. 2007. *Simple Prosperity: Finding Real Wealth in a Sustainable Lifestyle*. New York: St. Martin's Griffin.

Watts, Jonathan, and David R. Loy. 2002. The Religion of Consumption: A Buddhist Perspective. In *Mindfulness in the Marketplace: Compassionate*

Responses to Consumerism, ed. Allan Hunt Badiner, 93–103. Berkeley, CA: Parallax Press.

Watson, James, ed. 1997. *Golden Arches East: McDonald's in East Asia*. Stanford, CA: Stanford University Press.

Williams, Duncan. 2002. Right Livelihood, Spirituality, and Business. In *Mindfulness in the Marketplace: Compassionate Responses to Consumerism*, ed. Allan Hunt Badiner, 228–234. Berkeley, CA: Parallax Press.

Zavestoski, S. 2002. The Social-Psychological Bases of Anticonsumption Attitudes. *Psychology and Marketing* 19 (2): 149–165.

16 Well-Being the Path Out of the Consumption–Climate Dilemma?

John Holmberg and Jonas Nässén

RADICAL CHANGE REQUIRED FOR CLIMATE MITIGATION

The interrelated environmental, social and economic challenges imposed by global climate change will make it one of the most important political issues in the coming century. While there are still large uncertainties concerning the sensitivity of the climate system, the Intergovernmental Panel on Climate Change (IPCC) has concluded that most of the observed global warming since the mid-twentieth century is very likely due to human activities (IPCC 2007). This conclusion is well supported also in other parts of the scientific community. For example, all scientific bodies in the United States agree as well as the vast majority of papers published in refereed scientific journals (Oreskes 2004).

Decisions on what should be the long-term goal for climate policy can only partly be supported by science. Ultimately this judgement is an ethical and political issue. The United Nations Framework Convention on Climate Change (UNFCCC 1992), which is currently ratified by 191 countries, defines the goal as a stabilization of atmospheric greenhouse gases at a level that avoids "dangerous anthropogenic interference with the climate system" and that such a level should be achieved "within a time frame sufficient to allow ecosystems to adapt naturally to climate change, to ensure that food production is not threatened and to enable economic development to proceed in a sustainable manner".

The European Union expresses the long-term goal in terms of a temperature target, stating that the global average surface temperature should not exceed 2°C above the pre-industrial level (European Council 2005). Although studies based on cost-benefit analyses have argued for less stringent policy targets (see Tol 2007), a precautionary approach to climate change provides support for the 2°C target. For example, Azar and Rodhe (1997) argued that climate policies should work against temperature increases which substantially exceed the natural fluctuations of 1°C during the past millennium, until such levels have been proven to be safe. The 2°C target may also be sound in order to be on the safe side of "large-scale discontinuities" such as the collapse of the West Antarctic Ice Sheet (associated with four to six metre sea level rise) or major disruptions to ocean circulation (O'Neill and Oppenheimer 2002).

An exact translation of the long-term 2°C target into targets for carbon dioxide emissions reductions is not possible. It depends on several parameters such as the uncertainties in the climate sensitivity, and to less extent on uncertainties in the carbon cycle (Caldeira, Jain and Hoffert 2003), but also on the ascribed emission pathway (early or late action) and on the development of non-carbon-dioxide emissions (CH_4, N_2O, halocarbons, ozone precursors and particulate matter). In a study on multi-gas pathways to meet climate targets, Meinshausen et al. (2006) found that in order to meet the 2°C target with a certainty of 75 per cent, global fossil carbon dioxide emissions would have to be reduced to less than half the 1990 level by 2050 and to only a fraction by the end of the century.

STRATEGIES FOR CO_2 EMISSIONS REDUCTIONS

Scenarios and trends of carbon dioxide emissions can be described by changes in a series of factors or driving forces. The five factor equation given in Figure 16.1 is an extension of the four factor decomposition often referred to as the Kaya identity (Kaya 1990). This in turn is a special application of earlier decompositions such as the IPAT-equation, describing environmental impact (I) as the product of population (P), affluence (A), and technology (T) (Ehrlich and Holdren 1971; Commoner 1971).

Global trends in the parameters of this equation are shown in Figure 16.2. The development of energy service demand is omitted due to

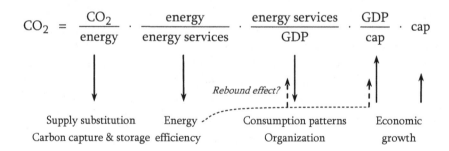

$$CO_2 = \frac{CO_2}{energy} \cdot \frac{energy}{energy\ services} \cdot \frac{energy\ services}{GDP} \cdot \frac{GDP}{cap} \cdot cap$$

Rebound effect?

Supply substitution
Carbon capture & storage

Energy
efficiency

Consumption patterns
Organization

Economic
growth

Figure 16.1 Decomposition of carbon dioxide emissions in five factors. Parameters that affect these factors are given under the equation. The arrows indicate the expected direction of change (e.g., in the IIASA-WEC scenarios; Nakićenović, Grübler and McDonald 1998). The arrows also indicate potential rebound effects, i.e., that parts of the improvements in technical energy-efficiency improvements may not be realized as actual energy savings.

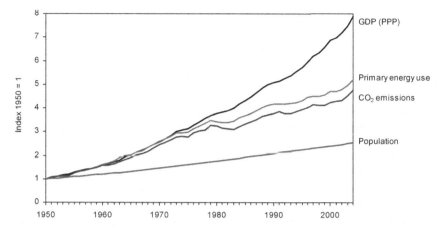

Figure 16.2   Global trends in population, GDP (purchasing power parities), primary energy use and carbon dioxide emissions from fossil fuels from 1950 to 2004 (Nässén 2007).

difficulties of both finding and aggregating such data (vehicle-km, indoor temperature, lighting, etc). The global economy grew by a factor of eight between 1950 and 2004. Primary energy use increased in proportion to economic growth until 1972, but since the oil crisis of 1973, a clear decoupling can be seen between these trends. Reduced energy intensity was also the most important factor behind the decoupling of carbon dioxide emissions from GDP.

A currently ongoing discussion is how these long term trends will be influenced by the global financial crisis. On this we can only speculate. Such a crisis can affect the global carbon dioxide emissions in many different ways. One direct effect is of course decreased demand and less investments (also in renewable and energy-efficient technologies). But there may also be indirect effects such as less political will for ambitious climate policy. The International Energy Agency tries to sum up this complex picture and claims in their recently released World Energy Outlook 2009 that although global energy use will fall in 2009 for the first time since 1981, the long-term upward trend will not be affected by the crisis.

In the following we briefly examine the principally different measures for carbon dioxide CO_2 abatement shown in the equation (Figure 16.1).

Much of the data used in this text, particularly on the demand-side of the economy originates from Swedish studies. Detailed studies necessary to understand the demand-side requires a significant amount of data which is difficult to acquire on the international scale. Even if the circumstances may differ between countries, we believe that much of the conclusions from the Swedish case can be generalised to other industrialised countries, but probably only to a very limited degree to non-industrialised countries. An ambition of our future research is to link our work to similar studies in non-industrialised countries.

DECARBONIZATION OF ENERGY SUPPLY

Measures to reduce the first factor of the equation (Figure 16.1) have often been the main focus of the discussion on abatement of carbon dioxide emissions. Decarbonization of energy supply can be achieved by substitution of carbon-neutral energy sources (renewable energy and nuclear) for fossil fuels, by substitution of low-carbon for high-carbon fossil fuels (e.g., natural gas instead of coal) or by utilizing carbon capture and storage technologies.

The sun presents an enormous opportunity, supplying more than the equivalent of ten thousand times the energy used in the global energy system. Using today's technology (solar cells made of silicon, the second most abundant element in the earth's crust), we can transform sunlight to electricity without any emissions at all—using an area the size of only 6 per cent of the Sahara—to supply the entire world with renewable energy. The problem is that these photovoltaic cells are still too expensive.

Historical trends in the carbon intensity of energy use are not very encouraging. Figure 16.2 shows a slight decoupling of carbon dioxide emissions from energy use between 1960 and 1990, but despite the increased focus on climate change and the establishment of the Kyoto Protocol, this trend has been reversed in recent years. Between 2000 and 2008, world coal consumption increased by 41 per cent (4.4 per cent per year), while total energy use increased by 22 per cent (2.5 per cent per year). Most of this dramatic increase in coal consumption occurred in developing countries, particularly in Asia (BP 2009).

Sweden is one of the few exceptions in this respect. The average carbon dioxide emission factor in Sweden decreased from 85 g/MJ in 1950 (higher than the emission factor of oil) to 30 g/MJ in 2000 (Kander 2002). This decarbonization can primarily be explained by governmental intervention, for example, through the support to the nuclear power program as a response to the oil crises in the 1970s and the gradual increase in carbon dioxide taxes from 1991, which has resulted in a fast expansion of bioenergy in the heat sector.

IMPROVED ENERGY EFFICIENCY

As shown by Figure 16.2 the global ratio of primary energy use to GDP has declined by one-third since the first oil crises in 1973. Technical improvements in energy efficiency account for a large part but not all of this change (the total energy intensity also depend on the structure of consumption and production). The scenario literature have also pointed to major contributions of reduced energy intensities and improved energy efficiency to the future abatement of carbon dioxide emissions. The IIA-SA-WEC "ecologically driven" scenarios presume global reductions of energy intensities (energy/GDP) by 1.4 per cent per year for the next fifty years, which results in more than twice as large emission reductions as the substitution of fuels in these scenarios (Nakićenović, Grübler and McDonald 1998). In the IEA "accelerated technology" scenario, end-use efficiency improvements (more fuel-efficient cars, better insulated houses, new lighting technologies, etc.) account for 45 per cent of the reduction in carbon dioxide emissions until 2050, compared to the baseline scenario (IEA 2006).

While the mentioned scenarios as well as studies of potentials for energy-efficiency improvements (e.g., Watson, Zinyowera and Moss 1996; Jochem 2000, 2004) are reasons for optimism regarding carbon dioxide abatement by means of energy efficiency, it is also important to recognise that the enormous potentials sometimes presented have historically failed to materialise. During the energy crises in the 1970s, several studies mapped how much energy could be saved by using more efficient technology.

In a detailed and internationally recognised study, Steen et al. (1981) demonstrated great potentials for saving energy in Swedish residences, transport and industry. The purpose of the study was to provide consistent scenarios to illustrate a variety of options. The researchers used two levels of technology: "best available technology", cost-effective at 1975 energy prices, and "advanced technology", estimated to become cost-effective within the study timeframe of twenty to thirty years.

The Steen study, using 1975 values, should now be compared with the actual course of events (Figure 16.3). The study actually overestimated the growth in energy service demand. Even so, energy use obviously did not decrease by as much as the study estimated was possible, particularly as far as energy consumption in buildings is concerned. The study demonstrated that it would be profitable to use more energy-efficient technologies; however, such technologies ended up being utilised only to a small extent.

The energy efficiency in Swedish buildings has improved very slowly since the mid-1980s (Nässén and Holmberg 2009). The same holds for our cars. Sure, cars have improved. The problem is that we have used this technology development to compensate for increased performance, rather than to save energy. In Sweden, cars sold in the past thirty years have increased dramatically in terms of engine strength, top speed, weight and acceleration, while fuel efficiency only has increased by a little. In fact, 65 per cent of the technology progress has been used to compensate for increases in performance, and only 35 per cent has been used to cut fuel

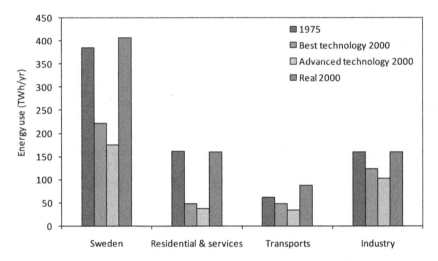

Figure 16.3   Actual energy use in Sweden for 1975 and 2000 compared to projections for 2000 made in Steen et al. (1981).

use (Sprei, Karlsson and Holmberg 2007). Why do we choose stronger, faster vehicles when the ones we already have are strong enough to pull a reluctant moose or two up a mountain and can go much, much faster than the legal limit? Today, the average top speed for cars sold in Sweden is 200 km/h.

In the equation (Figure 16.1) it was also indicated that improvements in energy efficiency may cause so-called rebound effects by increasing energy service demand as well as economic growth. This may result in that a part of the improvements in energy efficiency cannot be realised as reductions in energy demand. There are different mechanisms behind such rebound effects. First of all, energy-efficient technologies reduce the marginal cost of the energy services they provide (e.g., the cost of driving an extra kilometre is lower in a fuel-efficient car) and may therefore result in increasing energy service demand (e.g., driving longer distances). Secondly, energy-efficient technologies may in some cases save money which can be used for consumption of other goods and services (e.g., money saved on reduced consumption of fuel can be used for a ticket to Thailand). A third category of rebound effects are effects on the economy-wide level. Such effects may take place since reductions in energy demand by one actor may result in lower fuel prices which in turn cause increasing demand by other actors in the economy. See Nässén and Holmberg (2009) for an analysis and discussion about the quantification of rebound effects.

CHANGING CONSUMPTION PATTERNS

As mentioned in the previous section, society's energy intensity can be reduced not only by improvements in technical energy efficiency, but also by reduced energy service demand per unit of GDP. This is the third factor in the equation (Figure 16.1). These changes may come as a result of shifts in the composition of consumption and production.

A first analysis of the development of consumption patterns in Sweden can be made based on the Households Budget Surveys from Statistics Sweden. Combining these expenditure data with energy and emissions intensities from input–output analysis shows that there is a strong relationship between higher income, higher demand for energy services and more greenhouse gas emissions (Nässén, Larsson and Holmberg 2009) and that there is only a very weak decoupling at high income levels (see Figure 16.4a). However, it is also interesting to note that the spread in energy use within each income group is very large (approximately a factor four between the highest and lowest deciles as shown in Figure 16.4b). Similar findings have also been made in previous studies from the Netherlands (Vringer and Blok 1995; Vringer, Aalbers and Blok 2007).

Parts of the variation in the environmental load of consumption within the same income class may be explained by socio-economic parameters: people with high education spend more on culture than people with low education, families with small kids travel less than others, older people buy fewer clothes than young people, etcetera. However, consumption, particularly on transport, is also highly dependent on physical factors, such as urban form and where people live in relation to the functions they utilise. Comparisons of the energy use in different cities have shown that these parameters may be very important. Næss, Sandberg and Roe (1996) compared the sales of fuels in twenty-two Nordic towns and found that urban form parameters such as population density had a greater explanatory value than socio-economic parameters. Jaccard and Rivers (2007) compared the city regions of Vancouver and Seattle, which are very similar with respect to climate, age, size, economy, prices and living standard, but where the urban forms have developed in different ways. The more typical North American Seattle with highways to the city centre and growth of suburban sprawl had—although similar development in other aspects—30 per cent higher energy use per capita than Vancouver, where sprawl had been actively prevented.

Swedish consumption patterns are further described in Figure 16.5. The bars to the left show average and marginal expenditure shares. The latter is estimated from differences in consumption patterns between households with different income levels (regression analyses also including a set of other socio-economic variables; see Nässén, Larsson and

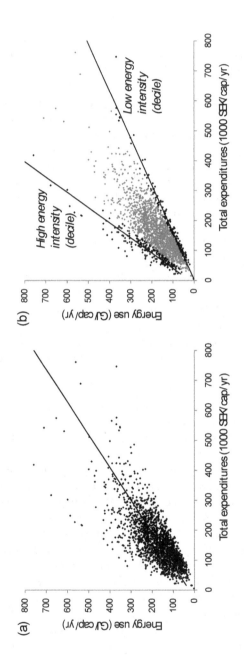

Figure 16.4   Energy use of Swedish households (direct and indirect energy use from consumption of products and services) plotted against total expenditures. (a) The average energy use increases sharply with higher income. (b) The difference between households with high and low energy intensities (J/SEK) is considerable (almost a factor of four between the highest and lowest deciles). Data: Statistics Sweden—Household budget survey (2006) and energy intensities from input–output analysis.

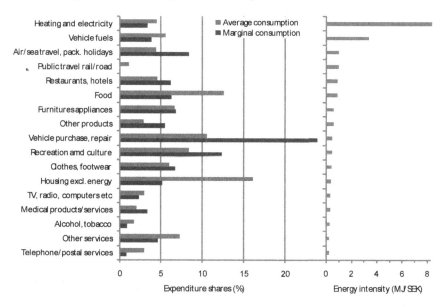

Figure 16.5 Average and marginal expenditure shares in Sweden together with energy intensities. Data: Statistics Sweden—Household budget survey (2006) and energy intensities from input–output analysis. More detailed data are presented in Nässén, Larsson and Holmberg (2009).

Holmberg 2009). The bars to the right show the energy intensities of the different expenditure categories.

Expenditure categories that are "large on the margin" (consumption that increases a lot with increasing income) include vehicle purchase, air travel, package holidays, recreation and culture, while expenditures on food and housing make up a relatively small share on the margin. Aggregating expenditures on consumption items results in what we presented in Figure 16.4a, that energy use grows by almost 0.9 per cent for an increase income by 1 per cent (a bit more at low income levels and a bit less at high income levels).

Swedes appear to choose to spend additional income on cars and holiday trips, but what if we grow even richer? Observing the very wealthiest Americans offers a clue (Figure 16.6). The very wealthiest Americans use a smaller share of their resources on vehicle purchases, which may be good from an energy perspective. On the other hand, they spend more of their income on extremely large residences. One possible explanation is that it is simply not possible to travel much more due to scarcity of time, and instead one builds climate-controlled mansions (to fill with all that stuff).

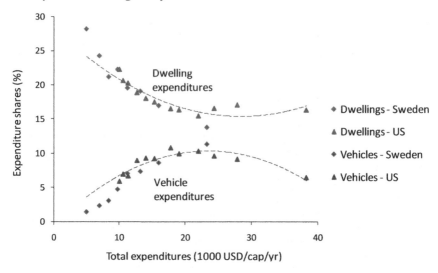

Figure 16.6   The shares of expenditure on dwelling (purchase and rents) and on vehicle purchase in Sweden and the United States (data from Swedish household budget survey, 2006, and US household budget survey, 2003).

LESS IS MORE?

The conclusion so far is that changed consumption is an important aspect of greenhouse gas abatement. This implies a shift in trends away both from energy-intensive marginal consumption patterns as well as from selection of energy-inefficient technologies. The hope lies in that we have fantastic opportunities to increase prosperity without steadily using more energy. Few of our basic needs—such as affection, understanding, inclusion and identity (see, e.g., Max-Neef 1986)—require large amounts of energy. More and more exciting studies are done discovering what really makes us happy (e.g., Kasser 2002; Lyubomirsky, Sheldon and Schkade 2005). The results indicate that if we take ourselves and our happiness seriously we can break the trends and emit less greenhouse gases while becoming happier!

In Table 16.1 are the results from a study of how 909 working women in the US spent their day and what they felt about the activities (positive affecting rate 0–6) (Kahneman et al. 2004). In the last column we have given a rough idea of the energy intensity associated with these activities, which indicates a promising reverse relationship between energy intensity and what we like to do.

As illustrated in Figure 16.4 the energy use increases with income, but there is a large variation within each income group. These trends can be related to the relationship between income and happiness. The *Easterlin Paradox* states that within a given country, people with higher incomes are more likely to report being happy. However, in international comparisons, the average reported level of happiness does not vary much with national income per person, at least for countries with high to very high income levels. Similarly, although income per person rose steadily in the United States between 1946 and 1970, average reported happiness showed no long-term trend, and declined between 1960 and 1970 (Easterlin 1974). Similar results have been reported in many studies since.

The fact that too much consumption can be both bad for the environment and hinder us from fulfilling basic needs has been discussed for a long time. Hirsch (1977) discussed it in relation to positional consumption. Some economists claim that positional consumption create externalities in the "arms race" for goods that might boost one's social status relative to others, but with little or no benefit for society as a whole. For example cars have been shown to be a highly positional good (Carlsson et al. 2007).

Another problematic aspect of consumption in rich countries is that some people fail to keep it under control. In a study by Koran et al. (2006), 6 per cent of women and 5.5 per cent of men in the United States have reported symptoms considered to be consistent with compulsive buying disorder

Table 16.1 The "Happiness" Ranking from 0 to 6 for Different Activities during a Working Day in the US (Kahneman et al. 2004) and a Rough Estimation of the Energy Intensity Associated with These Activities

Activity	Mean affect rating	Mean hours/ day	Energy intensity
Intimate relations	5.10	0.2	Low
Socializing	4.59	2.3	Low
Relaxing	4.42	2.2	Low
Pray/worship/meditate	4.35	0.4	Low
Eating	4.34	2.2	Low
Exercising	4.31	0.2	Low
Watching TV	4.19	2.2	Medium (use of appliances)
Shopping	3.95	0.4	Medium/High
Preparing food	3.93	1.1	Medium (use of appliances
On the phone	3.92	2.5	Medium (use of appliances)
Napping	3.87	0.9	Low
Taking care of myself children	3.86	1.1	Low
Computer/email/Internet	3.81	1.9	Medium (use of appliances)
Housework	3.73	1.1	Medium (use of appliances)
Working	3.62	6.9	Medium
Commuting	3.45	1.6	High

(CBD). The proposed diagnostic criteria for CBD include being frequently preoccupied with buying or subject to irresistible, intrusive and/or senseless impulses to buy; frequently buying unneeded items or more than can be afforded; shopping for periods longer than intended; and experiencing adverse consequences, such as marked distress, impaired social or occupational functioning and/or financial problems (McElroy et al. 1994). Koran et al. (2006) indicate that adverse consequences have included bankruptcy, family conflict, divorce, illegal activities and suicide attempts.

In the environmental movement some suggest that a reduction in work hours could be good for the environment (Hayden 1999; Axelsson 2005). They argue that the choice of path between a consumption-oriented future and a future with more spare time will have consequences for society's environmental impact. This thought has also been incorporated in some future scenarios for energy and environment (Azar and Lindgren 1998; Albertsen et al. 2007). The basic idea is that the development of energy use and greenhouse gas emissions is coupled to the volume of consumption, which in turn depends on to what extent society's increasing productivity is realized in terms of increasing income or in reduced work time (Schor 2005; Sanne 2007). This idea is especially forceful since shorter work hours have possible positive consequences, such as fewer problems with feelings of time pressure (Larsson 2007; Lippe 2007). Several studies have shown that shorter work hours are used for activities such as child care, sleep, meals, social contacts and volunteer work (Albertsen et al. 2007) and these types of activities have also been shown to be more important for subjective well-being than material consumption acquired by increasing income (Layard 2005). Layard (2005) also states that as people get used to higher income levels, their idea of a sufficient income grows with their income. If they fail to anticipate that effect, they will invest more time for work than is good for their happiness.

Even if many of the results from "happiness research" show promising opportunities to increase prosperity without steadily greater energy use and greenhouse gas emissions, it is a difficult area of research. It is even difficult to collect relevant data. It is, for example, contested whether measures such as subjective well-being really capture all dimensions of a good life (Ryan and Deci 2001). It is, for instance, questioned to what extent more fundamental aspects like sympathy, peace of mind and carefulness are measured. On the other hand—if these aspects could be captured, the picture might look even more promising!

ACKNOWLEDGEMENTS

We are thankful to Jörgen Larsson at the Department of Sociology who has contributed to the underlying research of this text. Financial support from the AES program of the Swedish Energy Agency and EON are gratefully acknowledged.

REFERENCES

Albertsen, Karen, et al. 2007. Working Time Arrangements and Social Consequences—What Do We Know? *TemaNord* 2007:607.

Axelsson, Svante. 2005. *Sveriges Natur. No 5.*

Azar, Christian, and Kristian Lindgren. 1998. *Energiläget år 2050. Rapport 1998:04., Naturvårdsverket.*

Azar, Christian, and Henning Rodhe. 1997. Targets for Stabilization of Atmospheric CO_2. *Science* 276 (5320): 1818–1819.

BP. 2009. *BP Statistical Review of World Energy 2009.* http://www.bp.com/statisticalreview.

Caldeira, Ken, Atul Jain and Martin Hoffert. 2003. Climate Sensitivity Uncertainty and the Need for Energy without CO_2 Emission. *Science* 299 (5615): 2052–2054.

Commoner, Barry. 1971. *The Closing Circle, Nature, Man, and Technology.* New York: A Borzoi Book.

Easterlin, Richard. 1974. Does Economic Growth Improve the Human Lot? In *Nations and Households in Economic Growth: Essays in Honor of Moses Abramovitz*, ed. Paul A. David and Melvin Reder. New York: Academic Press Inc.

Ehrlich, Paul, and John Holdren. 1971. Impact of Population Growth. *Science* 171 (3977): 1212–1217.

European Council. 2005. Presidency Conclusions, 7619/1//05 REV 1. Presented at the Council of the European Union, Brussels, 22 and 23 March.

Hayden, Anders. 1999. *Sharing the Work, Sparing the Planet: Work Time, Consumption and Ecology.* Toronto: Pluto Press.

Hirsch, Fred. 1977. *Social Limits to Growth.* Cambridge, MA: Harvard University Press.

IEA. 2006. *Energy Technology Perspectives 2006—Scenarios and Strategies to 2050.* Paris: OECD/IEA.

Intergovernmental Panel on Climate Change. 2007. *Climate Change 2007: The Physical Science Basis. Contribution of Working Group I to the Fourth Assessment Report of the Intergovernmental Panel on Climate Change.* Ed. Susan Solomon, Dahe Qin, Martin Manning, Zhenlin Chen, Melinda Marquis, Kristen Averyt, Melinda Tignor and Henry L. Miller. New York: Cambridge University Press.

Jaccard, Mark, and Nic Rivers. 2007. Heterogeneous Capital Stocks and the Optimal Timing for CO_2 Abatement. *Resource and Energy Economics* 29 (1): 1–16.

Jochem, Eberhard. 2000. Energy End-Use Efficiency. In *World Energy Assessment, 2000: Energy and the Challenge of Sustainability.* New York: UNDP.

———. 2004. *Steps towards a Sustainable Development—A White Book for R&D of Energy Efficient Technologies.* Zürich: Novatlantis, ETH.

Kahneman, Daniel, Alan Krueger, David Schkade, Norbert Schwarz and Arthur Stone. 2004. A Survey Method for Characterizing Daily Life Experience: The Day Reconstruction Method. *Science* 306:1776–1780.

Kander, Astrid. 2002. *Economic Growth, Energy Consumption and CO_2 Emissions in Sweden 1800–2000. Lund Studies in Economic History 19, Lund University, Almqvist & Wiksell.* Södertälje, Sweden: Lund University.

Kasser, Tim. 2002. *The High Price of Materialism.* Cambridge, MA: MIT Press.

Kaya, Yoichi. 1990. Impact of Carbon Dioxide Emission Control on GNP Growth: Interpretation of Proposed Scenarios. Paper presented at the IPCC Energy and Industry Subgroup, Response Strategies Working Group, Paris.

Koran, Lorrin M., Ronald J. Faber, Elias Aboujaoude et al. 2006. Estimated Prevalence of Compulsive Buying Behavior in the United States. *American Journal of Psychiatry* 163:1806–1812.

Larsson, Jörgen. 2007. Om föräldrarstidspress—orsaker och förändringsmöjligheter. En analys baserad på Statistiska centralbyråns tidsdata. PhD diss., Department of Sociology, University of Gothenburg.

Layard, Richard. 2005. *Happiness. Lessons from a New Science*. London: Penguin Books Ltd.

Lippe, Tanja. 2007. Dutch Workers and Time Pressure: Household and Workplace Characteristics. *Work, Employment and Society* 21 (4): 693–711.

Lyubomirsky, Sonja, Kennon M. Sheldon and David Schkade. 2005. Pursuing Happiness: The Architecture of Sustainable Change. *Review of General Psychology* 9:111–131.

Max-Neef, Manfred. 1986. Human-Scale Economics: The Challenges Ahead. In *The Living Economy*, ed. P. Ekins. London: Routledge and Kegan Paul.

McElroy, Susan L., Paul E. Keck, Harrison G. Pope, et al. 1994. Compulsive Buying: A Report of 20 Cases. *Journal of Clinical Psychiatry* 55:242–248.

Meinshausen, Malte, Bill Hare, Tom M. L. Wigley, Detlef Van Vuuren, Michel G. J. Den Elzen and Rob Swart. 2006. Multi-Gas Emissions Pathways to Meet Climate Targets. *Climatic Change* 75 (1–2): 151–194.

Næss, Petter, Synnøve L. Sandberg and Per G. Roe. 1996. Energy Use for Transportation in 22 Nordic Towns. *Scandinavian Housing and Planning Research* 13 (2): 79–97.

Nakićenović, Nebosja, Arnulf Grübler and Alan McDonald, eds. 1998. *Global Energy Perspectives*. Cambridge: Cambridge University Press.

Nässén, Jonas. 2007. Energy Efficiency—Trends, Determinants, Trade-Offs and Rebound Effects with Examples from Swedish Housing. PhD diss., Chalmers University of Technology.

Nässén, Jonas, and John Holmberg. 2009. Quantifying the Rebound Effects of Energy Efficiency Improvements and Energy Conserving Behaviour in Sweden. In *Energy Efficiency*, ed. Springer.

Nässén, Jonas, John Holmberg and Jörgen Larsson. 2009. The Effect of Work Hours on Energy Use: A Micro-Analysis of Time and Income Effects. Presented at ECEEE Summer Study, La Colle sur Loup, France, 1–6 June.

O'Neill, Brian C., and Michael Oppenheimer. 2002. Climate Change—Dangerous Climate Impacts and the Kyoto Protocol. *Science* 296 (5575): 1971–1972.

Oreskes, Naomi 2004. Beyond the Ivory Tower—The Scientific Consensus on Climate Change. *Science* 306 (5702): 1686–1686.

Ryan, Richard M., and Edward L. Deci. 2001. On Happiness and Human Potentials: A Review of Research on Hedonic and Eudaimonic Well-Being. *Annual Review of Psychology* 52:141–166.

Schor, Juliet. 2005. Sustainable Consumption and Worktime Reduction. *Journal of Industrial Ecology* 9 (1–2): 3750.

Sprei, Frances, Sten Karlsson and John Holmberg. 2007. Better Performance or Lower Fuel Consumption? Technological Development in the Swedish New-Car Fleet 1975–2002. *Transportation Research Part D*.

Steen, Peter, Thomas B. Johansson, Roger Fredriksson and Erik Bogren. 1981. *Energi—till vad och hur mycket?* Stockholm: Framtidsbilder, Liber.

Tol, Richard S. J. 2007. Europe's Long-Term Climate Target: A Critical Evaluation. *Energy Policy* 35 (1): 424–432.

United Nations Framework Convention on Climate Change. 1992. *United Nations Framework Convention on Climate Change*. http://www.unfccc.int.

———. 1997. *Kyoto Protocol to the United Nations Framework Convention on Climate Change.* http://www.unfccc.int.

Vringer, Kees, Theo Aalbers and Kornelis Blok. 2007. Household Energy Requirement and Value Patterns. *Energy Policy* 35 (1): 553–566.

Vringer, Kees, and Kornelis Blok. 1995. The Direct and Indirect Energy-Requirements of Households in the Netherlands. *Energy Policy* 23 (10): 893–902.

Watson, Robert T., Marufu C. Zinyowera and Richard H. Moss, eds. 1996. *Technologies, Policies and Measures for Mitigating Climate Change.* Geneva: Intergovernmental Panel on Climate Change.

17 What Is to Be Undone
The Making of the Middle Class in China

Patricia M. Thornton

Deng Xiaoping's introduction of market reforms in 1978–1979 unquestionably represents a watershed moment in the history of the modern Chinese state and society. The vast economic transformation that ensued, described by some as a consumer revolution (Davis 2000; Chao and Myers 1998), has lifted an estimated 635 million people out of poverty, altered social structures and practices after decades of egalitarian redistributive policies and introduced new patterns of household spending for the first time in China since 1949. Even with memories of the Mao era "shortage economy" (Kornai 1980) and strict rationing that characterized centralized economic planning still fresh in the minds of many, PRC citizens have taken avidly to window-shopping in enormous indoor shopping malls, perusing a ready selection of luxury brand items and frequenting the upscale department stores that now dot the new central business districts sprouting up in China's major cities.

As remarkable and revolutionary as these achievements appear, there is rising concern about the growing inequalities between urban and rural standards of living, the ecological and environmental impact of encouraging mass consumerism and personal automobile ownership in the world's most populous nation and worrying trends toward "extreme marketization" manifest in the rise of markets for items generally not regarded as commodities (like babies, blood plasma and human body parts) that have surfaced during the reform era (Gerth, 2010). Clearly, part of what is now being consumed—and reinvented, reconfigured and reproduced—is China's revolutionary tradition, in part through the medium of "red tourism", and recurrent waves of "Mao fever" (Barme 1996). Indeed, the still emerging but vibrant consumer economy has happily repackaged the social revolutionary transformations following 1949 into myriad forms of consumable leisure culture, and Mao's own image as kitsch hawked to domestic consumers and international tourists alike. With the Party now warmly welcoming successful capitalists into its ranks (Dickson 2003), early predictions that market liberalism would spell the demise of the Party are now open to question. Indeed, insofar as the initial stage of reform during the 1980s entailed a "liberation of productive forces", the more recent shift away from "heavy production and light consumption" (*zhong shengchan qing xiaofei*) has been christened a "liberation of consumption forces" by Party theoreticians who aim to "build a moderately well-off society in an all-round way" (*quanmian jianshe xiaokang shehui*). The apparent success of these efforts appear to have shored up, at least for the foreseeable future, the tottering legitimacy of a party crippled following the disastrous 1989 crackdown against the student demonstrators in Tiananmen Square, a scant two decades ago.

Yet whereas the rise of the middle class in the historiography of the West depicts a largely gradual process of class formation outside of—and increasingly in opposition to—the authority of feudal absolutist states, what is perhaps most remarkable about the Chinese transformation has been the extent to which is has been not only supported, but even deliberately engineered from above as part of the state-building process. As Pieke (2009) recently observed, the latest iteration in the historic process of Party-led social transformation fuses elements of marketization, centralization and globalization beneath the rubric of *market Leninism*, relying on governing practices consonant with the Party's revolutionary roots. Yet what the smooth elision between Leninist party control and robust capitalist markets in reform era China heralds may not the end of history, as Fukuyama announced famously two decades ago, but, rather, the steady unmaking of Mao era political projects that sought to contain the ruthless expansion of the market.

In *What Is to Be Done?*, Lenin famously argued that the obligation and the duty of the revolutionary party "consists in a *struggle against spontaneity*", because the spontaneous impulses of the masses had resulted only in the "enslavement of the workers by the bourgeoisie". Lenin proposed that his "party of a new type" would "*drag* the labor movement *away*" from its spontaneous tendencies, and train society continuously in the direction of revolution, creating self-conscious and self-aware classes that would struggle against the retrenchment of capitalism. In the wake of Mao's death, the Leninist project was deliberately unmade, and the revolutionary classes that once served as the vanguard of the Maoist vision have been refashioned, in part from above, as consumers. The apparent success with which the Party has effected this 180-degree reversal not only questions the dictum that democratization follows inevitably in the wake of market liberalization, it further suggests that there may well be an ideological and institutional congruence between market capitalism and certain forms of authoritarian rule (Gat 2007).

The regime's response to the current global economic downturn may well prove a case in point: although the current administration's quick and decisive response by way of stimulus appears to have spared the booming Chinese economy from the doldrums that continue to dog most Western countries, over the long-term, the implementation of the November 2008 program under the leadership of Hu Jintao and Wen Jiabao has reinforced—perhaps dangerously—the Party-state's already overloaded hand in driving and shaping consumption.

THE MIDDLE CLASS THE PARTY MADE

A recent survey conducted by the Chinese Academy of Social Sciences (CASS) estimated that the new middle class in the PRC has grown 1 per cent every year since 1999 and, by 2003, included up to 19 per cent of the population (Xinhua News Agency 2004a). The post-Mao Party's ambitious blueprint for constructing a "moderately well-off society" (*xiaokang shehui*) predicts that China's new middle class could expand to include as much 35 per cent of the population by 2020, if current growth rates continue (*China Daily* 2002). This upwardly mobile and high-consuming sector of the urban population has been linked to the emergence of independent entrepreneurs and "cadre capitalists", and identified by Chinese sociologists as the "the fourth generation of those who got rich first" (*xian fu qunti*) as result of market liberalization. The first such generation was comprised of peasant entrepreneurs in the late 1970s; the second were entrepreneurs in rural township and village enterprises in the early 1980s, followed by real estate speculators and construction magnates of the 1990s. This fourth generation, by contrast, is predominantly comprised of urban professionals and skilled employees in the public and private sectors, and defines itself largely through its patterns of consumption (Tomba 2004, 4–5).

Fearing that the country's traditionally low consumption rate may hinder economic development, the Chinese leadership identified stimulating consumption and triggering consumer desire as core goals in its "10th Five Year Plan", primarily in order to sustain the country's remarkable economic growth (*People's Daily Online* 2001). In 2002, the National Bureau of Statistics suggested raising the overall private consumption rate from 60 per cent to 65 per cent of the gross domestic product, bringing Chinese consumption in line with that of other East Asian countries (National Bureau of Statistics Research Group 2002). The following year, then premier Zhu Rongji reflected that the four generous raises granted to largely urban public service employees between 1999 and 2003 had been carried out precisely in order to "boost consumption demand" (Zhu 2003) from this new and still emerging class. These efforts came on the heels of earlier macroeconomic tinkering to devise a material basis for consumerism: in 1996, the interest rate was lowered twice, and four more times in 1998, inducing the emerging urban middle class to save less and to consume more (Wang 2001, 75).

In addition to such measures, Chinese leaders have attempted to instill and cultivate a new leisure culture aimed at this new upwardly mobile social stratum, particularly with the adoption of the forty-four-hour workweek and double leisure day (*shuangxiu ri*), otherwise known as the weekend. In 1995, the year that the compulsory five-day workweek was originally introduced, *Beijing Youth Daily* began publishing weekly special editions of periodicals devoted solely to leisure culture. As part of this broader effort to inculcate leisure consumption, in 1996 the Beijing Municipal Commission's Department of Propaganda published a "Civilization Contract with Residents", mobilizing twelve subcommittees to implement a nine-month campaign under the rubric of a "double leisure day action package". Featured leisure activities were promoted, including sightseeing, visiting museums and learning how to drive; leisure activities linked to specific commodities (i.e., automobiles, computers and sports gear and clothing) were singled out for special attention, ostensibly with the hope that increased consumer demand would soak up inventory and accelerate mass production (Wang 2001, 77–80). Likewise, enormous energy has been focused on the development of the "holiday economy" (*jieri jingi*): in 1999 in Shanghai alone, retail sales of consumer goods amounted to 159 billion yuan, of which holidays consumption accounted for 50 per cent (Li 1995, 64). Other national holidays have also been given over to stimulating consumption: for example, in recent years, some newspapers have begun urging their readers to commemorate National Humiliation Day, a holiday officially recognized in 2001 to note the razing of Beijing by British and French troops during the second Opium War, by purchasing "national products" like patriotic cigarettes, straw hats and face towels (Callahan 2006, 202).

The top-down nature of this effort also clearly seen in the creation of new consumers' associations that blend a nominal level of interest articulation and protection with overt attempts through tried and true propaganda efforts aimed at encouraging desirable consumer behaviours, beginning in the early 1980s at the local and provincial levels and, with the establishment of the China Consumers' Association (*Zhongguo Xiaofeizhe Xiehui*, or CCA) in 1984, at the national level. According to the *Beijing Review*, the CCA is a "semi-official [organization with] positions of responsibility . . . held by government officials" that seeks "to protect consumers' interests, to guide the broad masses in consumption, and to promote the development of the socialist commodity economy". Two of its presidents have concurrently served as vice presidents of the State Administration for Industry and Commerce; CCA office-holders are usually officials of provincial or municipal Bureaus of Industry and Commerce. Each year since 1995, the CCA launches a major media campaign on International Consumer's Day (15 March) featuring the ten worst cases of consumer abuse of the preceding year under the rubric of consumer education. More commonly, on a day-to-day basis, there are radio and television programs that offer advice on how viewers might become discriminating consumers. Special interest periodicals like *Shopping Guide* (*Jingpin gouwu zhinan*) and *Commodities Review* (*Shangpin pinjie*) published by CCA-affiliated enterprises document the latest consumer trends (Hooper 2005, 8).

PRODUCING AND CONSUMING CHINESE NATIONALISM

As Gerth (2003) has documented, a prominent feature of Chinese consumerism since the first half of the twentieth century has been the fusion of nationalist or patriotic sentiments with particular commercial products or services. In the new consumerism fostered by the post-Mao Party-state, this trend remains salient, with state-affiliated companies or enterprises bolstering appetites for goods and services with Party-friendly themes. For example, in the wake of the crackdown against the Tiananmen Square demonstrations of 1989, the former paramount Party leader, Chairman Mao Zedong, re-emerged not only as a revolutionary icon, but as a commodity brand. Possibly dating back to a 1989 car wreck in which the passengers claimed they had survived because of the supernatural protection afforded them by a Mao medallion hanging from the rearview mirror (Zhou and Yao 2003), the Party leadership quickly discovered that the fad not only proved lucrative for state publishing houses, but it also served to quell recent social tensions. In early 1990, a front-page story in the *People's Daily* reported a rush on posters of figures from the communist pantheon in certain parts of western Hunan. From August 1989 through the end of the year, state-controlled Xinhua bookstores in ten counties and municipalities in west Hunan sold an unprecedented sixty thousand posters of Chairman Mao. In Yuanling County alone, over thirty-five thousand posters were sold (Chen 2006, 27). Other entrepreneurial state-run enterprises quickly joined the fray. Government-owned publishing houses reprinted millions of volumes of Mao's works; one newspaper reported that seven hundred thousand copies of Mao's *Selected Works* sold out in only four months. The astonishing success of such volumes prompted new compilations, including a *Mao Zedong Dictionary*, another detailing his military theories (Kyodo News Service 1991). In early 1993, the Central Archives and Central Document Research Office quickly entered into a cooperative agreement with Shenzhen's Xianke Recreational and Communications Corporation to produce a set of compact discs of seven of Mao's recorded speeches, including his October 1, 1949 speech marking the founding of the PRC, sold under the title "Voice of the Giant—Mao Zedong". State-run Central Literature Publishing House rushed into production of 130 photo albums of the former chairman, edited by his daughter (Xinhua News Agency 1993; Driver 1993).

These sentimental celebrations of the Maoist past bolstered not only China's new consumer culture, but proved a formidable stimulus for its nascent tourist industry. Beginning in 1990, Shaoshan, the place of Mao's birth, recorded nearly twenty-five hundred visitors per day, and nearly three thousand per day by 1993 (Dutton 2005, 159). A decade later, Party leaders have turned to marketing "red tourism" both as a means of patriotic education and as vehicle for stimulating development in the resource-poor rural areas in which the early communist leaders founded the first soviets or to which they retreated in the face of attack. During his 2003 inspection tour of "patriotic education bases", Li Changchun paused briefly at the former headquarters of the Eighth Route Army in the foothills of the Taihang mountains to make the case that developing "red tourism" "is a political project of solidifying the party's ruling-party position, a cultural project of advocating the national spirit . . . and an economic project of advancing economic and social development of old revolutionary areas and improving the living standards of the masses" (Xinhua News Agency 2004b). Accordingly, at the behest of the Central Committee and State Council, the National Tourism Administration declared 2005 the "Year of 'Red Tourism'" and issued lists of "30 choice red tourism routes" and "100 classic red tourism sites". Referring to this effort not as a "campaign" but instead as a "program", an official serving on the national coordination group organizing the effort projected that the three-phase plan would bring an estimated twenty billion yuan, or US$2.41 billion in benefits each year to the 150 designated sites, stimulating new construction, commerce and investment in infrastructure (Xinhua News Agency 2005).

Cashing in on the overwhelming success of these largely state-engineered trends, in April 2004, a group of private entrepreneurs in Sichuan's Dayi County broke ground on the country's first Cultural Revolution museum complex. The blueprint currently includes a restaurant, a hotel and a tea-house; when completed, the complex is planned as one part of a broader theme park designed to celebrate a commercialized version of China's revolutionary past without evidence of either the convulsive violence it spawned or the ideological critique of capital that drove it. Promoting revolutionary nostalgia at a hefty price, the complex is designed to appeal to well-heeled middle-class tourists in need of a break from the stresses of the Chinese capitalist rat race. The restaurant is designed to be a perfect replica of the "worker-peasant-soldier canteen" (*gong-nong-bing dashitang*) of the 1960s; the hotel will be a perfect simulacrum of a Red Guard "reception centre" (*Hongweibing jiedaizhan*); and the teahouse is to be named Spring Cometh (*Chunlai*), after a teahouse that appeared in one of Jiang Qing's revolutionary model operas (Dutton 2005, 163–164). Ironically, the literal transformation of Mao's revolution into a dinner party, served by waiters parading as Red Guards at Shenzhen's popular eatery, the "Number One Production Brigade" (Ruwitch 2007), effectively shifts any serious recon-sideration of the interests and passions that inspired it outside the mar-gins of reasoned public discourse. The institutionalized "dictatorship over needs" (Feher, Heller and Marcus 1983) that characterized "actually exist-ing socialism" in Mao's China and elsewhere has refashioned itself into a totalitarian regime of endless consumer desire.

MARKET DEVELOPMENT AND THE STIMULATION OF DESIRE

Under what Wang Hui (2004) has referred to as China's neoliberal gov-ernance during the era of reform, first comradeship and then citizenship have become increasingly defined by acts of self-disciplined selective con-sumption shaped by a discourse of discernment and quality. Unlike classi-cal liberalism, which promotes participation in the free market economy and democratic government as modes of individual empowerment, the depoliticized forms of engagement under Chinese neoliberalism construes rights as a function of cultural development, and in particular links it to the processes of raising the cultural level (*wenhua shuiping*) and improving the "quality" (*suzhi*) of the national population. The revolutionary potential of ordinary peasants and workers, celebrated and even revered in Mao's day, has been reframed as an expression of backwardness as reform era discourses focus instead on "turning peasants into modern Chinese citizens", pushing parents to have fewer children but invest more in their education (Murphy 2004). The same elite-engineered discourse took pains to link the quality (*zhiliang*) of commodities to the quality (*suzhi*) of the Chinese citizenry, and exhorted the consumption of luxury items by a better educated, and more discerning, public. Reform era university administrators and faculty now openly apply the terms *chanpin* (product) and *zhiliang* (quality) to describe recent graduates, proposing, for example, that "students are now more like products (*chanpin*)" and "they need to be packaged a bit" in order to be competitive in today's labour market (Hoffman 2001, 59).

The new reform era obsession with quality, both of commodities as well as of people, effectively *unmakes* the Chinese proletariat—the very vanguard of Mao's revolution—as a "class-for-itself". As Pun Ngai observes, the ongoing "subsumption of production . . ." a "process whereby the extraction of the surplus value of labor is hidden and suppressed by the overvaluation of consumption and its neoliberal ideologies of self-transformation . . . allows consumption to appear as if it were a 'democratic show'—a consumer 'revolution' in which all could participate" (2003, 469). Mirroring patterns seen elsewhere in the world, in a large-scale survey undertaken in 2004, nearly 70 per cent of Chinese respondents identified themselves as either "upper middle" (7.1), "middle" (38.4) or "lower middle" (23.2) class (as cited by He 2006, 69), whereas 2003 government statisticians estimated that only 19 per cent of the population could rightly be classified as "middle-income". According to a new report by Global Demographics, there are currently 212 million households in China earning between US\$2,500 and US\$10,000 per year, a number that Global Demographics predicts should rise to 390 million in 2028, with 60 per cent of those households earning between US\$5,000 and US\$10,000 per year (China Economic Report 2008, 46). A report commissioned by China Merchants Bank found that by 2008, approximately 2.3 per cent of China's population controlled private assets worth 29 per cent of the nation's GDP (Zhaoxing he Jian'en Gongsi 2009: 3).[1] Management consultancy firm McKinsey classifies a mere two million Chinese households as "wealthy", with annual earnings of US\$30,000 or more a year. This stratum of the population, popularly known as "suddenly wealthy households" (*baofahu*), tends to engage in consumption that is extravagantly conspicuous, preferring, for example, four-door luxury sedans with ample leg room for owners that ride in the backseat and can afford to leave the driving to a chauffeur. Their upscale appetites favour fine cognacs and an increasing array of dairy products—which play a very small role in the traditional Chinese diet—ivory chopsticks and 24-carat gold jewelry

(*Financial Times* 2009). Gerth (2010) notes that when one Shanghai-based magazine that focuses its coverage on the lives of the wealthy recently interviewed six hundred Chinese millionaires to identify their preferred brands, the expensive tastes of China's new elite inclined toward high-end Western names. Christie's was voted the best auctioneer; Vacheron Constantin the best watch; Davidoff the best cigar; Giorgio Armani the best designer; Hennessy, Chivas Regal and Dom Perignon the best liquors; Princess the best yacht; and Ferrari the best sports car.

However, such indulgences are enjoyed only by a small handful; in the light of the recent economic slowdown, the vast majority of Chinese consumers remain, in the view of the director of one well-known advertising agency, "penny pinching, ruthless, suspicious shoppers" (*Financial Times* 2009). Fan recently found that lower-income and older consumers experience considerable financial pressure as they attempt to emulate the lifestyles of those farther up the "ladder of consumption" (2000, 82–87). In a study of a toy fad that swept the Chinese mainland in 1989, Zhao and Murdock found that the mostly young families who sought to accommodate the increasingly desperate desires of their children to possess Hasbro Transformers frequently feared that the toys they had purchased might in fact be second-hand models "dumped" on the Chinese market by US distributors, or, even worse, cheap imitations made in Taiwan or Guangdong (1996, 212). As the penetration of the forces and artifacts of global capitalism both widens and deepens, Chinese consumers as well as officials are justifiably experiencing rising levels of counterfeit anxiety over both foreign and domestic products (Pang 2006), as the recent Sanlu milk powder tragedy, and ensuing scandal, demonstrate. Li Chunling, a researcher at the highly respected CASS, argues that China's much celebrated new middle class is itself a fake: "The so-called Chinese middle class is nothing but a myth and a bubble conjured up by some media organizations and researchers" (Xin 2004). The recently published McKinsey report, despite its overall optimistic tone, likewise examined Chinese private consumption in comparative, and more sobering, terms: weighing in at nearly US$1.2 trillion in 2008, total Chinese private consumption only slightly tops that of France (around US$1.0 trillion) and remains considerably lower that of Germany (about US$1.3 trillion). It still falls far short of the UK's US$1.4 trillion and Japan's US$3.2 trillion, to say nothing of the juggernaut of US private consumption, which topped US$9.4 trillion last year—nearly eight times the size of China's meager rate. Despite impressive economic growth, Chinese consumption remains astonishingly low. Consumption across Europe tends to remain within 55 to 65 per cent of GDP range. In developing countries, like those in Latin America, it can easily rise to 65 to 70 per cent. US consumption has hovered in the 70 to 72 per cent range in recent years. By comparison, China's current rate of 35 per cent is astonishingly low, even by Asian standards. South Korean and Malaysian consumption is around 50 per cent of GDP, while in other major Asian economies, like India,

Japan, Taiwan and Thailand, consumption hovers in 55 to 60 per cent of GDP range (Pettis 2009).

The Chinese were not always such reluctant consumers: McKinsey and the National Bureau of Statistics data demonstrate that in 1990, consumption represented just a little over 50 per cent of GDP. During the inflationary crisis of 1993–1994, it dropped to around 45 per cent of GDP and remained at that level until shortly after the 1997–1998 Asian financial crisis, when it began to drop markedly, first to 40 per cent in 2003–2004 before sinking to its current level of about 35 per cent. What these statistics suggest is that, over time, crises pull the household consumption rate down, while fast-paced bull markets during ostensible periods of recovery fail to pull it back up. Meanwhile, while the Chinese household savings equaled 12–15 per cent of disposable income at the end of the 1980s, in 1992 it began rising steadily until 1998, when it stabilized at around 24–25 per cent. It currently stands at approximately 26 per cent of disposable income. The report correctly notes that the real increase in national savings in recent years was caused by the sharp increase in corporate savings, although, as Pettis (2009) has argued, corporate savings growth in China is often caused by transfers from household savings at low interest rates. This strongly suggests that China's recent strategy of economic growth has basically forced households to subsidize investment and production, generating rapid economic and employment growth at the expense of household income growth, thereby constraining private consumption.

As Aziz and Cui (2007) have demonstrated, recent declines in the share of household consumption in China's GNP cannot be explained solely by its persistent "culture of savings", the much-publicized reverse mirror image of the American "culture of debt", because the rise in household savings rate during the 1990s accounts for only a small percentage of the decline in consumption. While it is certainly true that increased uncertainty over the future reliability of pensions, health care and education costs—benefits previously guaranteed by the state—has prompted Chinese consumers to save more and spend less, aggregate data strongly suggests that it was the simultaneous decline in household income, and particularly the decline in wage income, that played the more significant role in the rise in the saving rate. Enterprise-level data suggest that small and medium-sized firms in China tend to rely on bank financing for working capital to pay current expenditures, including wages. Beginning in the 1990s, pressures forced Chinese banks to become more conservative in their lending operations, tightening the borrowing constraints of privately owned firms and prompting a marked decline in the overall wage share. Domestic consumption has not kept pace with China's impressive GDP growth because real wage growth has likewise lagged behind; as China's large and risk-averse state-run banks continue to favour the state-owned sector of the economy.

The effective unmaking of the proletariat masses alongside the concomitantly spectacular displays of the privileged few has resulted in an unbalanced market economy, the weaknesses of which are likely to grow more apparent as a result of the global economic recession. The nature of the aggressive stimulus package implemented by the current regime in the face of the global economic slowdown has arguably extended these consumption trends by vastly increasing government investment to state-approved projects at the expense of boosting small-scale private and household lending. The Hu Jintao and Wen Jiabao administration's initial economic stimulus program, announced in November 2008, involved an increase in official investment for four trillion RMB, an amount equal to 13 per cent of China's GDP in 2008, and urgent directives to local governments to speed up construction spending and to state-run banks to increase their lending for government-approved projects. The Chinese banking industry sprang into action, lending more than 7.4 trillion RMB—a whopping 24 per cent of GDP—in the first half of 2009 alone. However, as Naughton (2009) aptly noted, in order to move that level of credit in short order, the state-run banks immediately turned neither to small and medium-sized private firms nor to household creditors, but instead to the very large and mostly state-run companies that could quickly absorb such liquidity. Household loans, by contrast, made up a mere 15 per cent of this increased lending, a significant decline from a peak of one-third of all bank lending in 2007. Huang Yasheng at MIT recently estimated that since the onset of the economic recession, the Chinese state may have increased its own consumption as much as 40 per cent, while household consumption has likely fallen to a world-record low of 30 per cent of GDP (Garnaut 2009). Thus, while the current regime earned well-deserved kudos for its rapid-fire and largely successful response to the economic crisis, the longer-term prospects for distributing capital in a manner conducive to more equitable and self-sustaining growth are justifiably open to question.

THE BRAVE NEW WORLD OF THE POST-PROLETARIAT

The Dengist market reforms, initiated in 1978, were predicated on the assumption that, as higher levels of productivity would boost standards of living, the nation as a whole would prosper, even as individuals were increasingly compelled to shoulder more responsibility for their welfare as the retreating state abdicated its social commitments. The new vision of society offered by the post–Cultural Revolution Party was of a depoliticized egalitarian consumer public unsullied by divisions of socio-economic class, a democratic leisure and consumption culture safeguarded by the creation of a secure (*anquan*) and stable (*anding*) society. Central to this reformist agenda is the cultivation of a new, upwardly mobile middle-income class whose desire to consume will continue to fuel economic growth and at the same time bolster the existing order. As a recent State Development and Planning Commission report observed, "only if a large number of people will enter the middle income strata will it be possible to protect the existing stability of the social structure" (Zhou 2001, 2; see also Li 2001, 91).

Yet if the emergence of capitalism in the West heralded the rise of a new class that pushed back against the demands of the *ancient regimes*, and ultimately forged constitutional republics and liberal democracies, China's new middle class seems prepared to tread a rather different path. David Goodman notes that "as long as the CCP maintained its commitment to economic growth, there were few if any grounds for structural conflicts between the new middle classes and the party-state" (1999, 261). Sociologist Xiao Gongqin goes even farther, noting that the imbrication of the emerging middle-income stratum with the booming mainland economy:

> hardly made them adventurous political reformists. On the contrary, they worried that too much political change too last would cause social upheavals and endanger their material interests. So far there is scant evidence that the middle class is seeking anything more than political security. Wanting neither a return to socialism nor a leap into the uncertain future of radical political change, they gravitated to the pragmatic utilitarianism of the new technocrats, perhaps comforting themselves with the belief that economic development would eventually lead to democracy and the rule of law. (2003, 62)

Ordinary Chinese workers, once valorized by the Maoist state for their boundless energy and productive capacity, are now imagined by the central leadership as a vast untapped reservoir of potential desire, and a tireless motor of consumption that, properly mobilized, may drive the Chinese economy to new heights. Yet consumer-driven and self-sustaining market growth remains an unrealized goal by a leadership that appears, if recent measures of China's Gini coefficient are indeed accurate, increasingly sheltered from the pressing needs and day-to-day concerns of the majority of its citizens.

Yet this phenomenon, too, is hardly new to China. As Wu (2005) perceptively noted, in the final analysis Maoism likewise succeeded in "cannibalizing its own rebellious children", even as it failed to "fundamentally alter the relationships between the political elite and the subordinated popular classes" before mutating into a new/old form of bureaucratic state capitalism. Recent characterizations (i.e., Lee 2009) of the vast underclass of the post-proletariat as part the "bottom billion" newly left behind in the state-orchestrated Chinese "economic miracle" wrongly disregard the considerable gains that have been made in alleviating real poverty in China. Recently released national economic data collected in 2005 based upon an updated Purchasing Power Parity rate have revealed that while its estimated level of poverty is significantly higher than previously imagined, China has also made more progress against poverty than any country in the world since the 1980s (Chen and Ravallion 2008, 3). Nonetheless, continued economic growth in China, as well as economic and political stability, depend largely upon the effectiveness of the regime's ability to meet these challenges in a global environment that has only grown more uncertain and volatile over time.

NOTES

1. I am grateful to Daniel Koldyk for bringing this report to my attention.

REFERENCES

Aziz, Jahangir, and Li Cui. 2007. Explaining China's Low Consumption: The Neglected Role of Household Income. IMF Working Paper WP/07/181. http://papers.ssrn.com/sol3/papers.cfm?abstract_id=1007930.

Barme, Geremie. 1996. *Shades of Mao: The Posthumous Cult of the Great Leader.* Armonk, NY: M. E. Sharpe.

Callahan, William A. 2006. History, Identity and Security: Producing and Consuming Nationalism in China. *Critical Asian Studies* 38:2.

Chao, Linda, and Ramon H. Myers. 1998. China's Consumer Revolution: The 1990s and Beyond. *Journal of Contemporary China* 7 (18): 351–368.

Chen, Shaohua, and Martin Ravallion. 2008. China is Poorer than We Thought, But no Less Successful in the Fight against Poverty. The World Bank Development Research Group Policy Research Working Paper 4621 (May).

Chen, Xiaoya. 2006. Lishishangde zhenjia "Mao Zedong chongbai"—Mao Zedong pinpaihua, shenhua jiqi tuihua [True and False "Mao Zedong Worship" in History—The Brandifcation, Deification and Degeneration of Mao Zedong]. *Beijing zhi chun [Beijing Spring]* 162 (November): 27.

China Daily. 2002. Blueprint for an Overall Xiaokang Society in China, 3 December.

China Economic Report. 2008. Shopping Spree. (October): 44–51.

Davis, Deborah, ed. 2000. *The Consumer Revolution in Urban China.* Berkeley: University of California Press.

Dutton, Michael. 2005. From Culture Industry to Mao Industry: A Greek Tragedy. *boundary2* 32:2.

Fan, Chengze Simon. 2000. Economic Development and the Changing Patterns of Consumption in Urban China. In *Consumption in Asia*, ed. Beng-Huat Chua, 82–97. London: Routledge.

Feher, Ferenc, Agnes Heller and Gyorgy Marcus. 1983. *Dictatorship over Needs.* New York: Palgrave Macmillan.

Financial Times. 2009. Shopping Habits of China's "Suddenly Wealthy", 21 August.

Garnaut, John. 2009. China's Rivers of Cash Flowing Wrong Way. *Sydney Morning Herald*, 26 October. http://www.smh.com.au/business/chinas-rivers-of-cash-flowing-wrong-way-20091025-henx.html.

Gat, Azar. 2007. The Return of Authoritarian Great Powers. *Foreign Affairs* 86 (4): 59–70.

Gerth, Karl. 2003. *China Made: Consumer Culture and the Creation of the Nation.* Cambridge, MA: Harvard University Asia Center.

———. 2010. As Goes China, So Goes the World: How Chinese Consumers Are Transforming Everything. New York: Hill and Wang.

Goodman, David S. 1999. The New Middle Class. In *The Paradox of China's Post-Mao Reforms*, ed. Merle Goldman and Roderick MacFarquhar, 241–261. Cambridge, MA: Harvard University Press.

He, Li. 2006. Emergence of the Chinese Middle Class and Its Implications. *Asian Affairs* 33 (2): 67–83.

Hoffman, Lisa. 2001. Guiding College Graduates to Work: Social Constructions of Labor Markets in Dalian. In *China Urban: Ethnographies of Contemporary Culture*, ed. Suzanne Gottschang and Lyn Jeffery. Durham, NC: Duke University Press.

Hooper, Beverley. 2005. The Consumer Citizen in Contemporary China. Lund University Centre for East and South-East Asian Studies Working Paper No. 12.

Kornai, Janos. 1980. *The Economics of Shortage*. Stockholm: Institute for International Economic Studies, University of Stockholm.

Kyodo News Service. 1991. China to Upgrade Mao's Birthplace, Hong Kong Papers Say, 24 June.

Li, Guoren. 1995. Jiari jingji mianmian guan [A Comprehensive Analysis of the Holiday Economy]. *Beijing Di'er Waiyuxue Xuebao* 95 (May): 63–64.

Li, Qiang. 2001. *Shehui fenceng yu pinfu chabie* [*Social Stratification and Inequality*]. Xiamen: Lujiang chubanshe.

Murphy, Rachel. 2004. Turning Peasants into Modern Chinese Citizens: "Population Quality" Discourse, Demographic Transition and Primary Education. *China Quarterly* 177:1.

National Bureau of Statistics Research Group. 2002. Tigao chengxiang goumaili shuiping shi kuoda neixu de guanjian [Improving Urban and Rural Consumption Levels is Crucial to Expanding Domestic Demand]. *Jingji yanjiu cankao* [*Economic Research Documents*] 5.

Naughton, Barry. 2009. In China's Economy, the State's Hand Grows Heavier. *Current History* (September): 277–283.

Ngai, Pun. 2003. Subsumption or Consumption? The Phantom of Consumer Revolution in "Globalizing" China. *Cultural Anthropology* 18 (4): 469–449.

Pang, Laikwan. 2008. "China Who Makes and Fakes": A Semiotics of the Counterfeit. *Theory, Culture and Society* 25:117–140.

People's Daily Online. 2001. Premier Reports on Outline of Five-year Plan, 6 March.

Pettis, Michael. 2009. The Difficult Arithmetic of Chinese Consumption. 5 December. http://mpettis.com/2009/12/the-difficult-arithmetic-of-chinese-consumption/#comments.

Pieke Frank. 2009. *The Good Communist: Elite Training and State Building in Today's China*. Cambridge: Cambridge University Press.

Ruwitch, John. 2007. Eateries Capitalize on the Revolution: Restaurants Modeled on Mess Halls From the Mao Era Appeal to Chinese Nostalgia for a Simpler Time. *Vancouver Sun*, 20 October, A21.

Tomba, Luigi. 2004. Creating an Urban Middle Class: Social Engineering in Beijing. *China Journal* 51 (January): 1–26.

Wang, Hui. 2003. *China's New Order: Society, Politics, and Economy in Transition*. Ed. Theodore Huters. Cambridge, MA: Harvard University Press.

———. 2004. The Year 1989 and the Historical Roots of Neoliberalism in China. *positions* 12 (1): 7–69.

Wang, Jing. 2001. Culture as Leisure and Culture as Capital. *positions* 9 (1): 69–104.

Wu, Yiching. 2005. Rethinking "Capitalist Restoration" in China. *Monthly Review* 57:6. http://www.monthlyreview.org/1105wu.htm.

Xiao, Gongqin. 2003. The Rise of the Technocrats. *Journal of Democracy* 14 (1).

Xin, Zhigang. 2004. Dissecting China's "Middle Class". *China Daily*, 27 October. http://www.chinadaily.com.cn/english/doc/2004–10/27/content_386060.htm.

Xinhua News Agency. 1993. Firms Cash in on Rising Mao Fever. BBC Summary of World Broadcasts, 15 September.

———. 2004a. Chinese Middle Class Covers 19 Percent by 2003, Up One Percent Per Year, 29 March.

———. 2004b. Chinese Official Urges "Red Tourism" to Boost Ideological Train-ing. BBC Worldwide Monitoring, 13 November.

———. 2005. China Boosts "Red Tourism" in Revolutionary Bases. BBC World-wide Monitoring, 22 February.

Zhao, Bin, and Graham Murdock. 1996. Young Pioneers: Children and the Mak-ing of Chinese Consumerism. *Cultural Studies* 10 (2): 201–217.

Zhaoxing he Jian'en Gongsi. 2009. 2009 Zhongguo siren caifu baogao [2009 Report on Private Wealth in China]. http://live.cmbchina.com/webpages/pfr2009/index.html.

Zhou, Changcheng, ed. 2001. *Shehui fazhan yu shenghuo zhiliang* [*Social Devel-opment and the Quality of Life*]. Beijing: Shehui kexue wenxian chubanshe.

Zhou, Qun, and Xinrong Yao. 2003. Xinjiu Mao Zedong chongbai,. *Ershiyi shiji* [*Twenty-First Century*] 21 (December).

Zhu, Rongji. 2003. *Government Work Report to the 10th National People's Congress.*

Contributors

Zygmunt Bauman is Emeritus Professor of Sociology at the University of Leeds and the University of Warsaw. He was born in Poznan in 1925 but left Poland in 1971, because of the anti-Semitic campaign unleashed by the communist regime, and settled in the UK. He has published almost sixty books in Polish and in English, covering topics such as globalization, modernity and postmodernity, consumerism and morality. Among them are *Modernity and the Holocaust* (1989); *Liquid Modernity* (2000); *Liquid Times: Living in an Age of Uncertainty* (2006); *Consuming Life* (2007); *Does Ethics Have a Chance in a World of Consumers?* (2008); and *The Art of Life* (2008). His books are translated into many languages. Bauman was awarded the European Amalfi Prize for Sociology and Social Sciences in 1992 and the Theodor W. Adorno Award of the city of Frankfurt in 1998.

Russell Belk is past president of the International Association of Marketing and Development and is a fellow and past president of the Association for Consumer Research. He initiated the Consumer Behavior Odyssey, the Association for Consumer Research Film Festival and the Consumer Culture Theory Conference. His awards include the Paul D. Converse Award and the Sheth Foundation/*Journal of Consumer Research* Award for Long-Term Contribution to Consumer Research. His research involves the meanings of possessions, collecting, gift-giving, materialism and global consumer culture. His current research projects include Envy and Social Comparison, Sharing, Naming, The Enigmatic Smile, Clean and Dirty Consumption, Making Shangri-La in China, Global Consumer Ethics and Skin Color and Beauty in Asia. He is currently the Professor of Marketing and Kraft Foods Canada Chair in Marketing at the Schulich School of Business, York University in Toronto, Canada, and holds honorary professorships in North America, Europe, Asia and Australia.

Franck Cochoy is Professor of Sociology at the University of Toulouse, and member of the CERTOP-CNRS, France; he is a visiting professor at the University of Gothenburg, Sweden. He works in the field of economic sociology. His research is focused on the sociology of organizations and markets, and more precisely on the different mediations that frame the relation between supply and demand. In this respect, he conducted several projects and case studies on the role of marketing, packaging, self-service, standardization, corporate social responsibility, trade press, etcetera. He is the author of *Une histoire du marketing* (La Découverte, 1999) and *Une sociologie du packaging ou l'âne de Buridan face au marché* (Presses Universitaires de France, 2002). His most recent publications in English appeared in *Theory, Culture and Society, Marketing Theory*, the *Journal of Cultural Economy* and *Organization*.

Maurie J. Cohen is Director and Associate Professor with the Graduate Program in Environmental Policy Studies at the New Jersey Institute of Technology. He has held prior academic positions at the University of Leeds (UK), Binghamton University (State University of New York), Mansfield College of Oxford University (UK) and Indiana University. His current work is at the intersection of environmental social science, sustainability science and innovation studies and centres on socio-technical transitions toward more sustainable forms of household consumption. Dr. Cohen is the editor of *Sustainability: Science, Practice, and Policy* and co-founder of the Sustainable Consumption Research and Action Initiative (SCORAI). His books include *Exploring Sustainable Consumption: Environmental Policy and the Social Sciences* (with Joseph Murphy), *Risk in the Modern Age: Social Theory, Science, and Environmental Decision Making, and The Exxon Valdez Disaster: Readings on a Social Problem* (with J. Steven Picou and Duane Gill).

Karin M. Ekström is Professor in Marketing at University of Borås, Sweden. She is initiator and former director of the Centre for Consumer Science (CFK), an interdisciplinary consumer research centre. Her research area in marketing is consumer behaviour, specically consumer culture. Her research concerns family consumption, consumer socialization, collecting, design and the meaning(s) of consumption. She has edited several books and published in journals such as *Academy of Marketing Science Review, Journal of Consumer Behaviour, Journal of Macro Marketing, Journal of Marketing Management and Research in Consumer Behaviour*. She is a member of the Royal Society of Sciences and Letters in Gothenburg, the Swedish Meal Academy, the Council for Research Issues at the Swedish Competitive Authority and chair of the Scientific Council for Research at the Swedish Consumer Agency. A new research project concerns recycling of clothes.

Robert H. Frank is the Henrietta Johnson Louis Professor of Management and Professor of Economics at Cornell's Johnson Graduate School of Management and the co-director of the Paduano Seminar in business ethics at NYU's Stern School of Business. His "Economic View" column appears monthly in the *New York Times*. His books, which include *Choosing the Right Pond, Passions within Reason, Microeconomics and Behavior, Principles of Economics* (with Ben Bernanke), *Luxury Fever, What Price the Moral High Ground?, Falling Behind* and *The Economic Naturalist,* have been translated into twenty-two languages. *The Winner-Take-All Society,* co-authored with Philip Cook, received a Critic's Choice Award, was named a Notable Book of the Year by the *New York Times* and was included in *BusinessWeek*'s list of the ten best books of 1995.

Kay Glans started his career as a freelance writer for the Swedish daily newspaper *Svenska Dagbladet* in 1979. Recurrent themes in his essays are psychoanalysis and its relation to literature, and German and Austrian history and culture in the twentieth century. He published his first book of poetry in 1980 and a second collection in 1986. He has written the manuscript for a documentary about Vienna for Swedish Television, worked for Swedish Radio and was vice president of the Swedish PEN-club from 1987 to 1990. In 1995 he became editor of the essay section in *Svenska Dagbladet* and in 2001 he started the magazine *Axess,* published by the Ax:son Johnson Foundation. He was editor in chief for the magazine until August 2006 and simultaneously member of the advisory board of the foundation. He has been the editor of several books, among them *The Swedish Success Story?* (2001). He is editorial coordinator at Glasshouse Forum.

Dr. Neva Goodwin is Co-Director of the Global Development And Environment Institute at Tufts University (www.gdae.org). She is the lead author of two introductory college-level textbooks: *Microeconomics in Context* and *Macroeconomics in Context,* published by M. E. Sharpe. These are the starting points for her effort to develop an economic theory—"contextual economics"—that will have more relevance to real-world concerns than does the dominant economic paradigm. Goodwin is also director of a project that has developed a Social Science Library: *Frontier Thinking in Sustainable Development and Human Well-Being.* Containing a bibliography of ninety-three hundred titles, including full-text PDFs of about a third of these, this will be sent on USB drives or CDs to all university libraries in 136 developing countries. As a member of the board of Ceres, and in other activities outside of her academic work, Goodwin is involved with efforts to motivate business to recognize social and ecological health as significant, long-term corporate goals.

John Holmberg is Professor at Chalmers University of Technology, where he holds the position of vice president. He also holds an UNESCO-chair in Education in Sustainable Development. He is member of the editorial board of the international *Journal of Industrial Ecology*; member on the board of Swentec, Swedish Environmental Technology Council; member of the steering committee of the Balaton Group; member of the board of The Centre of Environment and Sustainability; member of UNESCO expert panel for the UN decade for ESD; and member of an expert panel for eco-innovations in EU. He gives many external lectures each year to other universities, corporations, authorities, organizations and to the general public. He also has a broad experience in publishing in non-scientific journals and of contributing in television and radio programs. His present research focus is in the field between well-being and sustainable development. He also has present research interest in eco-innovations, energy efficiency and education for sustainable development.

Jan Owen Jansson got his doctorate in 1980 at the Stockholm School of Economics. His doctor's thesis, *Transport System Optimization and Pricing*, was published by John Wiley in 1984. He worked as a research leader at the National Road and Transport Research Institute in Linköping from 1980 to 1993, and was appointed Professor of Transport Economics at Linköping University in 1994. Besides Transport Economics a main field of his research in recent time has been the service sector. In 2006 a book entitled *The Economics of Services—Development and Policy* was published by Edward Elgar, which summarizes his recent research in this area. In the book it is argued that conventional economic theory is too focused on material goods markets. By making the special character of services (immaterial goods) as market objects the starting point for the economic analysis, a new view of the big problems of a mixed economy is offered.

Gilles Lipovetsky, born in France in 1944, is married with two children and lives at Grenoble in France. He is Professor agrégé in philosophy. He is Docteur Honoris Causa de l'Université de Sherbrooke (Canada), Docteur Honoris Causa de la Nouvelle Université Bulgare (Sofia), Chevalier de la Légion d'Honneur, and member of Conseil d'Analyse de la Société auprès du Premier Ministre. His published works are: *L'Ere du Vide* (1983); *L'Empire de l'Ephémere* (1987, translated into English as *The Empire of Fashion*, 1994); *Le Crépuscule du Devoir* (1992); *La Troisième Femme* (1997); *Métamorphoses de la culture libérale* (2002); *Le Luxe éternel* (2003); *Les Temps hypermodernes* (2004, translated into English as *Hypermodern Times*, 2005); *Le bonheur paradoxal. Essai sur la société d'hyperconsommation* (2006); *La société de déception* (2006); *L'écran global* (2007); and *La Culture-monde. Réponse à une société désorientée* (2008). His books are translated or are being translated in eighteen countries.

Diane M. Martin is an associate professor of marketing at the University of Portland, a marketing consultant, a consumer ethnographer and a lead researcher for the firm Ethos Market Research LLC. Martin's life reflects passion for dance, mountains, deep forests and sustainability. She earned a PhD in organizational communication from the University of Utah, and for a decade prior to that, she owned and ran the consulting firm, Oregon Attractions Marketing. Martin's research has appeared in *Journal of Qualitative Marketing Research, Consumption, Markets and Culture, Journal of Applied Communication Research, Journal of Business Ethics, Communication Research Reports* and the *Southern Communication Journal*. She is the lead author of the textbook, *Sustainable Marketing*, upcoming from Pearson Prentice Hall.

Deirdre Nansen McCloskey teaches economics, history, English literature and communications at the University of Illinois at Chicago. An internationally known economic historian and rhetorician of science, she has written fifteen books and several hundred articles on topics ranging from mathematical models of medieval agriculture to the poetics and economics of magical beliefs. Her recent books include *Bourgeois Virtues: Ethics for an Age of Commerce* (2006), *The Cult of Statistical Significance: How the Standard Error Costs Jobs, Justice, and Lives* (with Stephen Ziliak, 2008) and *Bourgeois Dignity: Why Economics Can't Explain the Modern World* (2010). Educated at Harvard, she taught for twelve years at the University of Chicago in its best years of scientific creativity, and then for nineteen years at the University of Iowa. She holds doctorate degrees *honoris causa* from the National University of Ireland at Galway and from the University of Gothenburg.

Daniel Miller is Professor of Material Culture at the department of anthropology, University College London. His recent books include *Stuff* (2010), which is an introduction to his approach to the study of material culture and *The Comfort of Things* (2008), which looks at the material culture of a street in South London. Both are published by Polity Cambridge. Another book forthcoming with *Polity is Tales from Facebook*. Recent books published with Berg include the Edited volume *Anthropology and the Individual*, and *Global Denim* edited jointly with Sophie Woodward. He is currently completing a study of denim in North London with Woodward and a book on polymedia and the impact of new media on transnational mothering by Filipina domestic workers, together with Mirca Madianou. He recently established a new programme on Digital Anthropology at UCL.

Jonas Nässén is a researcher and teacher at the division of Physical Resource Theory at Chalmers University of Technology. His principal research interest is in the field of interdisciplinary energy systems studies, in particular on the role of demand-side changes for climate change mitigation. He has previously been involved in research projects on energy efficiency trends, rebound effects of energy efficiency improvements, trade-offs between energy efficiency improvements at different levels in the energy system and on the link between time use and energy use in households. His current research activities include a project which seeks to explain the variance in consumption patterns and greenhouse gas emissions between households and a related interdisciplinary project on the relationship between well-being and sustainable development.

John W. Schouten is an associate professor of marketing at the University of Portland, a consumer ethnographer, a co-owner of Ethos Market Research LLC, a poet and a novelist. His academic research has appeared in *Journal of Consumer Research, Journal of Marketing, Consumption Markets and Culture* and *Journal of the Academy of Marketing Science*, among others. He is a co-author of *Sustainable Marketing* with Diane M. Martin. Schouten has published dozens of poems in literary journals and in marketing journals, including *Consumption Markets and Culture, Journal of Advertising, International Journal of Research in Marketing* and *Journal of Consumer Research*. His first novel, *Notes from the Lightning God*, is available from BeWrite Books of the UK. He resides in Portland, Oregon, where he is currently working on his second novel and his first screenplay.

Jonathan E. Schroeder is is the William A. Kern Professor of Communication at Rochester Institute of Technology in New York, and Honorary Professor of Marketing at University of Exeter. He has held visiting appointments at Wesleyan University (Center for the Humanities), Göteborg University (Centre for Consumer Science), University of Auckland (Centre for Digital Enterprise), Indian School of Business and Bocconi University in Milan (Program in Fashion, Experience and Design). Schroeder has published widely on branding, communication, consumer research and marketing aesthetics. He is the author of *Visual Consumption* (Routledge, 2002) and co-editor of *Brand Culture* (Routledge, 2006). He is editor of *Consumption Markets and Culture* and serves on the editorial boards of *Advertising and Society Review, Critical Studies in Fashion and Beauty, European Journal of Marketing, Innovative Marketing, International Journal of Indian Culture and Business Management, Journal of Business Research, Journal of Historical Research in Marketing, Journal of Macromarketing* and *Marketing Theory*.

Patricia M. Thornton is a University Lecturer in the Department of Politics and International Relations at the University of Oxford and a Tutorial Fellow at Merton College. She is the author of *Disciplining the State: Virtue, Violence and State-making in Modern China* (Harvard University Press, 2007) and *Identity Matters: Ethnic and Sectarian Conflict* (Berghahn, 2007), as well as numerous articles and chapters. Her current research interests include developments in

Chinese cyberspace, social mobilization and protest, the impact of marketization and the rise of consumerism in the post-Mao era. She is currently writing a book on the Chinese state's attempts to manage market forces over time.

Frank Trentmann is Professor of History at Birkbeck College, University of London, and was director of the £5 million Cultures of Consumption research program. Recent publications include *Free Trade Nation* (Oxford University Press, 2008); Food and Globalization, edited with Alexander Nützenadel (Berg, 2008); *Citizenship and Consumption*, edited with Kate Soper (Palgrave Macmillan, 2007); and *Consuming Cultures, Global Perspectives*, edited with John Brewer (Berg, 2006). He is completing a book for Penguin—*The Consuming Passion: How* Things *Came to Seduce, Enrich, and Define our Lives.*

Richard Wilk is Professor of Anthropology and Gender Studies at Indiana University. He has also taught at the University of California, New Mexico State University and University College London, and has held fellowships at Gothenburg University and the University of London. His research in Belize, the United States and West Africa has been supported by three Fulbright fellowships, the National Science Foundation and many other organizations. He has also worked as an applied anthropologist with UNICEF, USAID, Cultural Survival and a variety of other development organizations. With his spouse and colleague, archaeologist Anne Pyburn, he has lived and worked in Belize for more than thirty-five years. His initial research on farming and family organization was followed by work on sustainability and consumer culture, globalization, television, beauty pageants and food. Much of his recent work has turned towards the history of food and the origin of modern masculinity. His most recent edited books are *Time, Consumption and Everyday Life: Practice, Materiality and Culture* (with Frank Trentmann and Elizabeth Shove, Berg Publishers), *Off the Edge: Experiments in Cultural Analysis* (with Orvar Lofgren, Museum Tusculanum Press) and *Fast Food/Slow Food* (Altamira Press).

Index